THE WASTE MAKERS

THE WASTE MAKERS

VANCE PACKARD

PUBLISHING

BROOKLYN, NEW YORK

Printed in the United States of America
10 9 8 7 6 5 4 3 2 1

No part of this book may be used or reproduced in any manner without written permission of the publisher. Please direct inquires to:

Ig Publishing
392 Clinton Avenue
Brooklyn, NY 11238
www.igpub.com

Library of Congress Cataloging-in-Publication Data

Packard, Vance, 1914-1996.
The waste makers / Vance Packard ; introduction by Bill McKibben.
    p. cm.
Includes bibliographical references and index.
ISBN 978-1-935439-37-0
1. Waste (Economics)--United States. 2. Industries--United States.
I. Title.
HC110.W3P3 2011
363.72'80973--dc23
                              2011030465

To my Mother and Father who have never confused the possession of goods with the good life.

CONTENTS

INTRODUCTION

There's a long tradition in American letters of decrying the advance of advertising, the false desires it creates, and the trouble that causes for planet and society. Henry David Thoreau, for instance, took the back streets of Concord to avoid the small signs hanging at the blacksmith's shop or the general store (placards that would now be preserved in museums as emblems of a gentler age). The signs, he wrote, were "hung out on all sides to allure him; some to catch him by the appetite, as the tavern and victualler's cellar; some by the fancy, as the dry goods store and the jeweller's; and others by the hair or the feet or the skirts, as the barber, the shoemaker, or the tailor." A hundred years later, when Vance Packard took up the same theme in *The Waste Makers*, things had advanced—in fact, in 1960, when this book was originally published, we were right on the cusp of the great change, moving out of the old American mores and straight into the high-consumer world we now inhabit. It still seemed a little strange; we hadn't entirely made the leap just yet. For instance: there were still repair shops for household appliances, but "the trend was to encourage customers to replace *parts* rather than bother repairing them." (italics mine). "A television announcer extolling the wonders of the sponsor's cigarette lighter stated that if the lighter became defective it could be fixed in a jiffy just by replacing the entire lighter mechanism." The fact that cigarette lighters were not entirely disposable is what will shock the modern reader.

Likewise, credit cards had recently appeared on the scene—Diners Club is the only name given—it "regularly had men handing out application cards to passers-by on both floors of Grand Central Station." *Both floors!*

But in fact, if Packard seems a little shrill to our jaded sensibilities, he was smart enough to recognize that something very new was going on in America—that we were making the transition into the world we now live in, which is chiefly about buying, not the making or growing which had marked the previous 100 years. He quotes a banking industry official urging his colleagues to change their attitudes towards credit: "The lending man should 'get up from his desk, and smile and shake hands with the prospective borrower, no matter how poor a credit risk he appeared to be.'" From there it is only a matter of time to the great housing bust that marks our day.

And perhaps he sounds a little old-fashioned when he decries the fact that television viewers "have to sit and watch ladies shaving their legs to 'protect their loveliness,' watch pictures of toes throbbing for lack of Outgro for their ingrown toenails, and hear that the sponsor's girdle is never 'clammy or sticky.'" But given that the decline in standards has now reached the point where Congressmen don't think twice about tweeting pictures of their sexual organs, you take his point.

In fact, though this book was marketed as being about "planned obsolescence," the scheme by which manufacturers built shoddy wares so that their customers would soon have to replace them, he quickly discards this notion as relatively unimportant. Yes, there are some light bulb makers who have shortened the lives of their filaments, but he seems to have realized pretty quickly that this was small potatoes, for after a single chapter he drops the topic and continues on to the much more potent idea of "the planned obsolescence of desirability," the continuous flow of fashion designed to get people to buy new things even when their old ones work just fine. These were the tail-fin days, and the hemline era—both come under discussion. But it was more than that—it was the sense of newness.

Car buyers held their vehicles for an average of two and a quarter years, and "The Ford Motor Company in one of its advertisements said this showed how smart and shrewd the average motorcar owner was becoming. At that age, it pointed out, the car starts showing minor ailments and dents. Further, it stated, 'The car is two years old in style. Its fine edge is gone.'" Substitute Apple for Ford and Ipod for motorcar, and it's a sentence that could be written this afternoon—indeed, it could be written on a blog, where the sentiment would be obsolete by dinner.

Packard also strikes on ideas that very few were thinking about in 1960, but which now loom very large in our debates. I was amazed by the prescience he showed in understanding that even though the U.S. was then the world's biggest producer of oil, "the United States is clearly approaching depletion. The rate of discovery of new fields has been declining in recent years. Those discovered ten to be at the bottom of deeper and deeper holes." In the future, he predicted, "the United States will be drawing more and more upon foreign oil fields, and this is putting the United States deep into the hands of Arabian and Latin American politicians." Sometimes the predictions enter the range of the uncanny: "suppose that ten or twenty years from now an opposition leader on the order of Peron or Trujillo or Castro comes into power in Venezuela with a highly nationalistic and perhaps anti-United States orientation?" Hello, Mr. Chavez—currently the nation's biggest supplier of petroleum. Though there was no way Packard could have known about climate change—the biggest threat produced by our way of life—he was nonetheless hinting ominously about the 'strain on resources' and the loss of topsoil. There is, he writes, an 'impending water crisis,' and 'millions of acres of farmland' are being 'covered with homes, shopping centers, and factories.' Nuclear power won't save us because it's too expensive, and "disposal of the mounting radioactive wastes will become a monstrous problem." All of this before the publication of Silent Spring, usually regarded as the first real environmental book.

Still and all, it's not primarily the details that Packard got right, but the broad strokes. He understood what kind of country we were building. He understood, fundamentally, that growth had become its own religion. Even ten years before economists had doubted that the size of the U.S. economy would grow much larger—FDR had said we had more factories than we'd ever need. But in the wake of World War II, the boom to end all booms (at least until China's) was leaving us with a new theology: "Out of all the anxieties created by the desire to make the economy hum at ever higher levels has come a clamor for 'growth.' Economic thinkers of many strips have joined in the call. Certainly this is the first time in history that the felt need for growth has been so self-consciously vocalized." A brief recession in the late 1950s had made it clear that we had a new master. "At a press conference, President Eisenhower was asked what the people should do to make the recession recede. Here is the dialogue that followed:

A-Buy

Q-Buy what?

A-Anything

There's not much distance between that moment and President Bush informing all of us in the wake of 9/11 that our job was to go shopping. Packard quotes another leader—marketing consultant Victor Lebow, writing in the *Journal of Retailing*: "Our enormously productive economy...demands that we make consumption our way of life, that we convert the buying and use of goods into rituals, that we seek our spiritual satisfactions, our ego satisfactions, in consumption. We need things consumed, burned up, worn out, replaced and discarded at an ever increasing rate."

If there's a moral to this book, fifty years later, it's that No One Can Saw We Weren't Warned. If we didn't get it from Thoreau, we should have gotten it from Packard. That we didn't get it is indisputable, and now—as the Arctic melts and the oceans acidify—we'll pay the price in ways even he couldn't have imagined. But he did imagine pretty much all the rest.

A Society in which consumption has to be artificially stimulated in order to keep production going is a society founded on trash and waste, and such a society is a house built upon sand. —Dorothy L. Sayers in *Creed or Chaos*

PART I

THE DEVELOPING DILEMMA

1. CITY OF THE FUTURE?

What will the world of tomorrow be like? In the course of this book we shall examine a number of probabilities based on projections of current trends. Spokesmen for industry like to speculate about tomorrow even more than the rest of us. They invite us to peer out onto the horizon and see the wondrous products their marketing experts are conceiving for us. We are encouraged to share their dreams and to tingle at the possibility of using voice writers, wall-sized television screens, and motorcars that glide along highways under remote control.

Most of these marketing experts, despite their air of chronic excited optimism, are grappling with a problem that would frighten the wits out of less resolute people. That problem is the specter of glut for the products they are already endeavoring to sell. If we could probe the real dreams of these marketing people as they slumber restlessly at night, we would find—when a smile finally settles on their faces—that they are not dreaming merely of more bewitching products to sell to us. More likely, they are dreaming that they are in their private world of the future, where selling has again become easy because the haunting problem of saturation has been vanquished. This Utopia might be called Cornucopia City, and its setting is out on the misty horizon of time.

In Cornucopia City, as I understand it, all the buildings will be made of a special papier-mâché. These houses can be torn down and rebuilt every spring and fall at housecleaning time. The motorcars of Cornucopia will be made of a lightweight plastic that develops fatigue and begins to melt if driven more than four thousand miles. Owners who turn in their old motorcars at the regular turn-in dates—New Year's, Easter, Independence Day, and Labor Day—will be rewarded with a one-hundred-dollar United States Prosperity-Through-Growth Bond for each motorcar turned in. And a special additional bond will be awarded to those families able to turn in four or more motorcars at each disposal date.

One fourth of the factories of Cornucopia City will be located on the edge of a cliff, and the ends of their assembly lines can be swung to the front or rear doors depending upon the public demand for the product being produced. When demand is slack, the end of the assembly line will be swung to the rear door and the output of refrigerators or other products will drop out of sight and go directly to their graveyard without first overwhelming the consumer market.

Every Monday, the people of Cornucopia City will stage a gala launching of a rocket into outer space at the local Air Force base. This is another of their contributions to national prosperity. Components for the rockets will have been made by eighteen subcontractors and prime contractors in the area. One officially stated objective of the space probing will be to report to the earth people what the back side of Neptune's moon looks like.

Wednesday will be Navy Day. The Navy will send a surplus warship to the city dock. It will be filled with surplus play-suits, cake mix, vacuum cleaners, and trampolines that have been stockpiled at the local United States Department of Commerce complex of warehouses for surplus products. The ship will go thirty miles out to sea, where the crew will sink it from a safe distance.

As we peek in on this Cornucopia City of the future, we learn that the big, heartening news of the week is that the Guild of Appliance Repair Artists has passed a resolution declaring it unpatriotic for any member even to look inside an ailing appliance that is more than two years old.

The heart of Cornucopia City will be occupied by a titanic pushbutton super mart built to simulate a fairyland. This is where all the people spend many happy hours a week strolling and buying to their heart's content. In this paradise of high-velocity selling, there are no jangling cash registers to disrupt the holiday mood. Instead, the shopping couples—with their five children trailing behind, each pushing his own shopping cart—gaily wave their lifetime electronic credit cards in front of a recording eye. Each child has his own card, which was issued to him at birth.

Conveniently located throughout the mart are receptacles where the people can dispose of the old-fashioned products they bought on a previous shopping trip. In the jewelry section, for example, a playfully designed sign by a receptacle reads: "Throw your old watches here!" Cornucopia City's marvelous mart is open around the clock, Sundays included. For the Sunday shoppers who had developed a churchgoing habit in earlier years, there is a little chapel available for meditation in one of the side alcoves.

Is Cornucopia City to become not a feverish dream, but, instead, an extreme prototype for the City of Tomorrow? Certainly in the next twenty years the broad outlines of Cornucopia City will come to seem less and less fanciful, if current trends continue. Already a chapel has been built in a shopping center outside Miami. Already the General Dynamics Corporation has under development a lifetime electronic credit card. Already watches are being sold as fashion accessory items. Already paper houses are being marketed. Already the life expectancy of motorcars has been showing a notable drop. Already supermarkets are staying open around the clock in many areas, with push-button markets under development. Already the stockpiling and disposing of subsidized but unwanted agricultural products have become a world-wide scandal. Already some home furnishings are being built to break down within a few years, and product makers have been showing a disconcerting fascination with the idea of setting "death dates" for products.

And, finally, already the pressures to expand production and consumption have forced Americans to create a hyperthyroid economy that can be sustained only by constant stimulation of the people and their leaders to be more prodigal with the nation's resources.

This presents us with another specter, one so disconcerting that Americans have thus far chosen to suppress awareness of it. That is the dangerous decline in the United States of its supply of essential resources. Once fabulously rich in these, the United States is now a have-not nation and is becoming more so every month. United States industrial firms are grinding up more than half of the natural resources processed each year on this planet for the benefit of 6 per cent of the planet's people. In the lifetime of many, if not most, of us, Americans will be trying to "mine" old forgotten garbage dumps for their rusted tin cans.

The people of the United States are in a sense becoming a nation on a tiger. They must learn to consume more and more or, they are warned, their magnificent economic machine may turn and devour them. They must be induced to step up their individual consumption higher and higher, whether they have any pressing need for the goods or not. Their ever-expanding economy demands it.

If modifications are forced upon the private-enterprise system of the United States in the future, it will be because that system did too good a job of filling many of the needs of the people. Defeat on such terms, we should all agree, would be saddening.

Man throughout recorded history has struggled—often against appalling odds—to cope with material scarcity. Today, there has been a massive break-through. The great challenge in the United States—and soon in Western Europe—is to cope with a threatened over-abundance of the staples and amenities and frills of life. Conceivably, even the longimpoverished and slower-starting Soviet Union may someday find itself trying to deal with an overflowing of goods. The United States, however, already is finding that the challenge of coping with its fabulous productivity is becoming a major national problem and is inspiring some ingenious responses and some disquieting changes. This book will deal with the systematic efforts being made to encourage citizens to be more careless and extravagant with their nation's resources, and what these efforts imply.

When I refer to the waste makers at large in the land, I refer primarily to those who are seeking to make their fellow citizens more prodigal in their daily lives. In a broader sense, however, it could be asserted that most Americans are becoming waste makers. If I can help it, there will be no villains in this book. A charge of rape cannot be sustained by any adult when consent or co-operation has been given. Prodigality is the spirit of the era. Historians, I suspect, may allude to this as the Throwaway Age.

Further—and let's face it—a good many Americans and Europeans have a pretty direct stake in the failure or success of businessmen in inducing us all to be more wasteful. The wife of a supermarket operator, the engineer working for an appliance company, the schoolteacher who owns a few shares of stock in a motorcar company—all these kindly people may feel uneasy about the wastefulness they see, and yet they have a vested interest in its accelerated perpetuation. And the professional marketer whose efforts to induce prodigality they may deplore is simply the trained expert employed to work on behalf of the firms that contribute to their own support.

While our focus will be on the wastefulness being promoted by United States industry in order to sell its ever-mounting stockpiles of products, we should recognize that wastefulness has become a part of the American way of life. The landscape of the globe is becoming strewn with armaments and other materiel abandoned by employees of the United States government. A spokesman for the United States Army Ordnance Corps acknowledged in 1960 that the Army had goofed in losing track of a million dollars' worth of motorcycle parts squirreled away in a Georgia warehouse. When they were found after fifteen years, the parts had become worthless except for scrap. And it wasdisclosed that the Navy had been paying $21 for lamp sockets selling for 25 cents in retail stores.

Many labor practices, too, have become a part of this pattern of wallowing in waste. Many workingmen today show more concern for feather-bedding, gold-bricking, getting onto their boats, or collecting their "rocking chair" compensations, than they do for developing a standard of workmanship for themselves that is worthy of pride. They want their tri-level house in the suburbs but often aren't willing to put in a decent performance to earn it.

In a restaurant in Eau Claire, Wisconsin, I overheard a businessman, with tears in his eyes, tell his wife he had decided to abandon his business because his employees were goofing off so badly that he could not get a decent day's work out of them.

But all these forms of wastefulness in American life seem to stem in large part from the fantastic productivity of the nation's mechanized, often automated offices, factories, and farms. That productivity is the central fact. And its impact is seen most conspicuously in the efforts of United States business to cope with it by promoting ever-higher levels of private consumption and a philosophy of waste. Where are we drifting under the pressures to make us more wasteful, imprudent, and carefree in our consuming habits? What is the impact of all this pressure toward wastefulness on the United States and on the behavior and character of its people? These, I think, are momentous questions. Let us explore them with all the compassion and forbearance we can muster.

2. THE NAGGING PROSPECTS OF SATURATION

"Marketing men across America are facing a fact that is hard for them to swallow. America's capacity to produce may have outstripped its capacity to consume."—Ernest Dale, Graduate School of Business and Public Administration, Cornell University

Today, the average citizen of the United States is consuming twice as much in the way of goods as the average citizen consumed in the years just before World War II. Nearly two fifths of the things he owns are things that are not essential to his physical wellbeing. They are optional or luxury items. And there are signs that physical possessions are becoming too plentiful to accommodate comfortably. Visiting foreigners comment that the abundance of America seems to spill over into the aisles of stores, spread along the highways, and bulge out the doors, windows, and attics of houses. There is this general evidence of profusion of material wealth even though there is a substantial residue, numbering millions of families, that remains unquestionably ill-fed, ill-clothed, ill-housed. And the television set may be substituting for adequate food in the family budget.

In a good-humored forecast of things to come, the senior editor of *Sales Management* asserted on May 6, 1960: "If we Americans are to buy and consume everything that automated manufacture, sock-o selling and all-out advertising can thrust upon us, each of our mounting millions must have extra ears and eyes and other senses—as well as extra income. Indeed, the only sure way to meet all the demands may be to create a brand new breed of super customers."

Consumption must rise, and keep rising. Some marketing experts have been announcing that the average citizen will have to step up his buying by nearly 50 per cent in the next dozen years, or the economy will sicken. In a mere decade, advertising men assert, United States citizens will have to improve their level of consumption as much as their forebears had managed to do in the two hundred years from Colonial times to 1939.

The recent exhortations for greater consumption have been inspired by bulging inventories of goods, which in turn are caused primarily by two factors. One is the ever-growing efficiency of the United States productive force, thanks in large part to the introduction of automated equipment in the offices and factories of nearly a hundred thousand United States companies. During the postwar years, the amount of goods and services that one man can turn out in an hour has increased about 3 per cent every year. This increased output can be absorbed if each citizen consumes more, or if there are, each year, more citizens. Otherwise, there will be less work.

The other factor is the great expansion of United States productive facilities based on the conviction in executive suites that the public can be induced to consume more each year. In 1959, the advertising and marketing journal, *Printers' Ink,* asserted: "Our automobile plants could turn out eight million cars this year if they dared." But it said the industry would be lucky to sell about half that number. And it added that several other major industries were facing the same "dilemma." Labor leader Walter Reuther complained that in four years the United States had "lost" nearly one hundred billion dollars' worth of potential output because of "under-utilization" of its productive capacity.

Much of the postwar boom in sales has come from supplying products that were badly wanted, if not badly needed. But after a dozen years the specter of satiation is rising to challenge the sellers of many products. A true salesman rejects the concept that a market can ever be satiated; but even the salesmen are beginning to admit that much of the urgency is going out of the demand for their products. *Sales Management* conceded: "The American consumer has been surfeited with all kinds of wonderful products since the end of the war. He's probably tired, a little jaded, eager for something different."

Today, about nine out of ten American homes contain at least one refrigerator, one television set, and one electric or gas stove. And seven out of ten have a vacuum cleaner, an electric toaster, and an electric food mixer. There are more passenger cars in the land than there are families.

If you are a producer and most families already own your product, you are left with three possibilities for making further sales. You sell replacements; you sell more than one item to each family; or you dream up a new or improved product—or one that at least seems new or improved—that will enchant families that already own an "old" model of your product. (A fourth possibility is to move into a different line.)

The challenge of finding significant improvements that can be made in existing products, however, is becoming more difficult each year. How much more can a toaster or sofa or carpet sweeper or sewing machine be improved, really?

When the Appliance Technical Conference was held in Chicago in 1958, the vice-president of engineering for Whirlpool Corporation made a notably candid statement. He said: "The industry has wrung the last possible ounce of research out of the present appliance products. We can only offer prettier equipment." He urged the industry to start basic research in the properties of clothing and meats in order to come up with radically new products.

All this is not to suggest that genuine technological improvements are not being made—or in prospect of being made—in some products. The push-button and long-distance dialing telephone and the jet passenger airplane are improvements that have produced considerable enchantment among consumers. There is the probability that Americans soon will be offered improvements in home products that will produce a degree of enchantment in some circles:

refrigerators with no moving parts, ultrasonic dishwashers that reportedly will remove fried egg from plates, remote-control stoves, lighting based on electroluminescent phosphors for ceiling or wall panels.

But how much should we rejoice when a company introduces a toaster with nine buttons, which make it possible to obtain a piece of toast in any of nine shades? How much should we rejoice when another company introduces a mechanical martini-stirring spoon, which relieves the person stirring from the labor of twisting his wrist? And what American housewife is dreaming of the day when she can prepare breakfast by simply flicking a bedside switch, which will turn on an electronic recipe maker coded on punch cards?

A columnist for *Advertising Age*, the forthright E. B. Weiss, took note of the general drying up of spectacular product improvements when he wrote: "Certainly when one compares the 1959 models of autos and major appliances and TV sets with the 1956 models, one must be compelled to wonder whatever happened to the great scientific improvements that must have been the result of hundreds of millions spent by these manufacturers over this period in research work of every kind." A year earlier, Mr. Weiss complained that much of the product improvement "has tended increasingly toward small details of trim, as in the case of the upswept rear fins on cars of late vintage, and toward gimmicky gadgets of little true importance." The changes that were being wrought in the laboratories frequently were simply superficial changes and improvements that could be used as selling points by copy writers.

Whenever engineers in the appliance industry assembled at conferences in the late fifties, they frequently voiced the lament that they had become little more than push buttons for the sales department.

It should also be noted that much of the straining to bring out new products was inspired to a very large extent by a desire on the part of producers to gain more shelf space in the supermarket jungle.

Consumer Reports, which is issued by Consumers Union, explained the strategy in this way: "A good deal of what is called product research today actually is a sales promotion expenditure undertaken to provide what the trade calls a profitable 'product mix.' A judicious product mix is, among other things, a combination of brands designed to commandeer for the advertiser the greatest possible shelf space in the supermarket." The result was often a multiplication of brands. A single soap company thus might have three liquid detergents competing with one another. Frequently the so-called new product was simply a new packaging concept. A professor of pharmacology at the University of California charged that much of the publicized money going into the research of new drugs was actually being spent in a quest for patentable variations on things that were already selling well.

During this same period, Americans were seeing a similar slowdown in the unveiling of brand-new kinds of products. At a time when appliance dealers were pleading for something new and exciting to stir public interest, *Home Furnishings Daily* reported: "Major advances in existing appliances and introduction of completely new appliances cannot be expected for at least several years."

When *Fortune* magazine reviewed the fifties for its readers from business management, it stated that in consumer goods "the fifties held few surprises." Among the few significant new products it could think of were tranquilizing pills. And it could point to such notable improvements on existing products as power steering, power brakes in motorcars, and stereophonic sound in phonographs. But these, it conceded, "were relatively modest accomplishments, from a technical point of view." It stated that during the fifties the makers of consumer products had not brought forth "a single innovation comparable to the automobile (which became commercially important at about 1910), the radio (early twenties), the mechanical refrigerator (mid-twenties), the automatic washing machine (late thirties), home air conditioning and television (late forties)."

Furthermore, it said that no product of impact comparable with the automobile, radio, television, etc., was in sight for the sixties. *Fortune* professed to find it somehow comforting that business had learned how to increase sales year after year when it had little significantly new to offer the public. Writer Roger Burlingame also previewed the sixties and reported he could see nothing at the moment that was basically new in products for the use of the common man. The exciting advances were being made in such fields as preparation for space travel.

The growing dependence of the United States economy upon programs financed by the federal government that might in a more sane day be abolished also has created apprehension among those concerned about the future of the economy. Several billion dollars are being spent each year to encourage fanners to raise crops the country does not want or need. Farmers happily pour fertilizer in record-breaking carloads into soil that should be resting. Billions of bushels of the resulting crops are moved into government-built storage bins, costing billions of dollars, made from millions of tons of metal that is scarce in the United States. Some have called the program plain corruption. And Max Moxley, farm editor in Sterling, Kansas, complained, "Our farm prosperity is entirely artificial. There's surplus grain piled everywhere you look. It rather takes away the joy of a good harvest for me. I'm sure the whole folly will come falling down around our ears—and soon, perhaps."

Even more massive and crucial in terms of its stimulus to the United States economy has been the defense spending, which has reached nearly fifty billion dollars a year—or a tenth of the nation's entire output of goods and services. Many United States senators find themselves under strong pressure to protect big aircraft and missile contracts, Naval installations, and Army bases in their states. Any cutbacks would throw some constituents out of jobs, and hit some of their local industries. In 1959, when stock-market prices dipped briefly after President Eisenhower announced that he was meeting with Russian Premier Khrushchev, some financial analysts reported the dip was caused by "peace jitters" among the traders. Financial columnist Sylvia Porter noted that every time there has been a suggestion of a major cut in Pentagon spending "the stock market has gone into a tail spin." On the other hand, in May, 1960, when the Russian capture of the U-2 plane was followed by the collapse of the summit meeting, Wall Street stockmarket prices advanced during seven successive days. The Russians, too, apparently had been having internal trouble because of the "peace scare." Various accounts of the turn to greater belligerence on the part of the Soviet Union cited as influential the lobbying of two hundred and fifty thousand Soviet officers who were scheduled, under disarmament plans, to be demobilized. They reportedly did not relish the prospects of going into civilian jobs as rank-and-file comrades.

The recession in the late fifties served as a sharp reminder to many of the developing dilemma posed by the need for ever-greater production. Recessions were nothing new. But this one was the most severe of the three postwar recessions. In many industries, companies found themselves with heavy inventories of goods and began cutting back production. The public was still buying, but not fast enough. A bewildered advertising executive was reported complaining that up until the last few months Americans had been the most desiring people in the world. As unemployment became a worrisome problem, a marketing journal warned that the unemployed worker produces nothing that can be advertised and sold, and he consumes little beyond necessities.

Marketers reacted to the challenge of coping with mounting glut during the recession by shifting to the really hard sell. In Flint, Michigan, sales executives began firing a cannon every time a motorcar was sold. Citizens across the land were admonished by industrialists and government leaders of all stripes to begin buying for their own good. At a press conference, President Eisenhower was asked what the people should do to make the recession recede. Here is the dialogue that followed:

"A.—Buy."
"Q—Buy what?"
"A.—Anything."

The President was advised that this was possibly an oversimplified response in view of the fact that his own Secretary of the Treasury was then urging people to put their money into government bonds. The President then said the public should buy only what it needs and "wants." An appliance store in Killingsley, Connecticut, immediately responded by putting this sign in its window: "OKAY IKE, WE'RE DOING OUR PART!"

The countryside rang with slogans that drummed home the patriotic or selfish reasons why everyone should pitch in and consume more. In Detroit, a forty-five-voice chorus cried out five hundred times a week over television and radio: "Buy days mean paydays . . . and paydays mean better days. . . . So buy, buy! . . . something that you need today." Other slogans beamed at the American public were:

"You auto buy now."

"Buy now—the job you save may be your own."

"Buy and be happy."

"Buy, buy, buy; it's your patriotic duty."

"Buy your way to prosperity."

The Advertising Council unleashed a campaign to create "Confidence in a Growing America." And the State Commerce Commissioner of New York conferred with business and labor leaders and then launched a campaign to persuade the public to "Buy it now!" The onus was on the consumer to save the day.

Whether dutiful consumers licked the recession is not clear. The federal government, while it acted quietly, certainly played a major role. It poured several billion extra dollars into the economy for such things as pay raises, farm subsidies, missiles, and highways, thus unquestionably helping to quicken the enfeebled national economic pulse. But consumer spending was probably decisive, because there never was any serious over-all decline in buying by consumers. In fact, four billion dollars more was spent for goods and services in 1958 than in 1957. Consumers spent less for big-ticket items such as appliances and motorcars, but their spending for services such as amusement and for "soft goods" such as food, clothing, tobacco, and drugs rose all during the recession.

By 1959, prosperity had returned even to the automobile and appliance industries. Cash registers were ringing merrily. Finally, too, but with plaguing slowness, the massive clot of unemployment began to dissolve into manageable proportions. Automation in three years had wiped out nearly a million jobs in industrial production, forcing many people to find jobs in the service industries. Meanwhile, increases in output per man seem likely to rise by about 40 per cent by 1970, and at least a million additional workers will be coming onto the labor market each year. The problem of absorbing them comfortably is likely to be most challenging.

The United States economy is depending on the willingness of consumers and the government to spend more each year than they have the preceding year. Some economists suggest that whenever United States citizens fail to step up their over-all consumption by at least 4 per cent in any given year they are inviting a "failure-to-grow recession." How to live with mounting productivity is each year becoming a more urgent problem for Americans, and soon it will be plaguing Western Europeans. In the United States, unused productive capacity is edging up almost every year. It has quadrupled in a decade.

In the early months of 1960, *U.S. News & World Report* indicated that the cornucopia of the United States was perhaps working too well when it said: "Goods are superabundant. Unsold cars in the hands of dealers are at a near record level. So are inventories of many kinds of household equipment. Steel output is having to be cut back." This was when consumers were breaking an all-time record in their spending.

At about the same time, President Eisenhower in his annual economic message said that prosperity could be sustained only if consumers—as well as management and labor—"perform their economic functions." Seymour Harris, Harvard University economist, aptly summed up the challenge facing the United States by stating: "Our private economy is faced with the tough problem of selling what it can produce."

3. "GROWTHMANSHIP"

"Men's appetite for goods must be quickened and increased."—Paul Mazur

Out of all the anxieties created by the desire to escape the developing dilemma and to make the economy hum at ever-higher levels has come a clamor for "growth." Economic thinkers of many stripes have joined in the call. Certainly this is the first time in history that the felt need for growth has been so self-consciously vocalized. Marketers talk of the need to increase sales of consumer goods and services by a hundred and fifty to two hundred billion dollars within a decade. Labor spokesmen have called for "rapid expansion." Political candidates for the Presidency in both parties have called for more growth. Conservatives who became uneasy about some of the novel ideas their rivals were offering to promote growth sneered that the rivals were making a high-level game of "growthmanship." In 1960, both party platforms called for more growth and differed only on how it should be achieved.

Some people have pointed to the Russian claims of rapid growth as a justification for the United States to embark on a crusade to increase its total output. With many of these, any output is considered to add to the military potential of the nation whether it involves more deodorants, more hula hoops, more electric rotisseries, or more pinball machines. The fact that the United States is already outproducing Russia in consumer durables by at least twenty to one is generally ignored. Also ignored is the fact that Russia has managed to startle the world by sending a giant satellite around the moon with a total national output that has been less than half of that of the United States. Russia simply has a different set of national priorities.

Furthermore, the Soviet example being held up as a challenge to the United States becomes less impressive on close inspection. Its rate of economic growth, for example, is less remarkable than that of Mexico, Japan, or West Germany. Compared with that of the United States, its percentage of annual growth of output seems impressive simply because it is starting from a lower base and because it is an underdeveloped country trying to catch up with an overdeveloped one. Economist W. Allen Wallis, special assistant to the President, observed in 1960: "Even if Russian growth rates continue higher than ours, the absolute gap between us will continue to increase for some time to come.... There is no possibility that the Russian economy will overtake ours at any time in the visible future—certainly not in this century."

Still, the Russian growth rate is widely held up as a minimum challenge for Americans if they are to hold up their heads in the world. Whether the growth is particularly needed to promote the well-being of the American people is rarely even considered. No one has considered that you can make a country overgrow just as the Pentagon has concluded that you can "over-kill" any possible enemy if you keep on producing hydrogen bombs beyond any rational need. And few have considered that while some selective kinds of growth may well be needed in the United States, other kinds are undesirable or would produce only surfeit. It is just assumed that any growth is good. Growth is fast becoming a hallowed word alongside Democracy and Motherhood.

Some—but not all—planners in the federal government have also been preoccupied with the idea that any growth is good for the country. As novelist John Keats pointed out, "Washington's planners exult whenever a contractor vomits up five thousand new houses on a rural tract that might better have remained in hay." In mid-1960, reports from Washington revealed that there was a strong feeling within the Administration that more liberal allowances should be made for the obsolescence of business equipment in order to "foster economic growth," by permitting faster tax write-offs of existing equipment.

How will all the sought-after growth be achieved? That has been the chief point of contention. Businessmen have been wary of some of the ideas tossed around by politicians and liberals as smacking of boondoggling. They are passionately convinced that the great challenge facing the nation is to make sure the citizenry will be induced to enjoy more and more of the good things of life—which they, of course, will be more than happy to produce.

To a pre-1950 economic thinker this would seem like no challenge at all. Historically, economists have assumed that people will automatically consume eagerly everything that their nation's economy can turn out for them. This concept is often referred to as Say's Law. A French economist of the past century, Jean Baptiste Say, concluded that production is bound to equal distribution. Say's Law was conceived in an era of scarcity. There was so much poverty of even the necessities of life that a ready and eager market was assumed.

In the mid-twentieth century's era of abundance, however, his law became less and less relevant. Desire did not necessarily keep pace with productive capacity. More pertinent for the new era were the concepts of Paul Mazur, partner of a Wall Street investment house, who has become widely accepted as a leading apostle of "consumerism." Early in the fifties, he pointed out that every recent United States recession had been caused by the failure of business to gear its production down to what could clearly be consumed, or a failure to see that consumption kept pace with production. The result was jammed warehouses and a depressed market. In his *The Standards We Raise*, widely admired at least by the marketers of industry, he asserted:

"The giant of mass production can be maintained at the peak of its strength only when its voracious appetite can be fully and continuously satisfied. . . . It is absolutely necessary that the products that roll from the assembly lines of mass production be consumed at an equally rapid rate and not be accumulated in inventories."

Thus the challenge was to develop a public that would always have an appetite as voracious as its machines. The chief economist of the world's largest advertising agency, J. Walter Thompson, asserted in 1960 that Americans would need to learn to expand their personal consumption by sixteen billion dollars per year if they were to keep pace with this production ability. All this backlog of what he called consumer need was awaiting "activation by advertising." This, he said, represented the "real opportunity" of the day.

The central problem was to stimulate greater desire and to create new wants. And this was becoming a little more difficult each year. Inthe late fifties, Advertising Age carried this headline: "CREATING DESIRE FOR GOODS GETS HARDER." It quoted the chief of research of a Los Angeles newspaper who stated: "Productive capacity has outstripped our efficiency in creating desire for goods." He added that it was becoming increasingly hard to create a burning desire for things.

People should be persuaded to expand their wants and needs, and quickly. The head of J. Walter Thompson made that point and explained: "We must cut down the time lag in expanding consumption to absorb this production." This agency's various pronouncements on the state of the nation indicated that it had become infatuated with the phrase "time lag." Everything could be blamed on the time lag. This implied that Americans had great unrecognized wants which they would inevitably discover eventually. They just had to be educated and activated. The agency's research director, however, warned that "the velocity of change in living standards needed to match the most conservative estimates of future productive ability nearly staggers the imagination."

The emerging philosophy was most fervently and bluntly stated perhaps in two long articles in *The Journal of Retailing* during the midfifties. The author was Marketing Consultant Victor Lebow. He made a forthright plea for "forced consumption."[1]

"Our enormously productive economy . . . demands that we

make consumption our way of life, that we convert the buying and use of goods into rituals, that we seek our spiritual satisfactions, our ego satisfactions, in consumption. . . . We need things consumed, burned up, worn out, replaced, and discarded at an ever increasing rate."

At other points he spoke of the "consumption requirements of our productive capacity" and of the "obligation" of retailers "to push more goods across their counters."

As businessmen caught a glimpse of the potentialities inherent in endlessly expanding the wants of people under consumerism, forced draft or otherwise, many began to see blue skies. In fact, Sales Management featured a blue sky on the cover of one of its issues as the sixties approached with this exhortation from management to marketers: "Go GET US A TRILLION-DOLLAR ECONOMY."

At the time this order was given, the United States economy was still approaching the *half* trillion mark.

Such heady resolutions could be implemented if the public could somehow be induced to feel the need to buy more and more products and services. Men's appetite for goods needed indeed to be quickened and increased.

Old-fashioned selling methods based on offering goods to fill an obvious need in a straightforward manner were no longer enough. Even the use of status appeals and sly appeals to the subconscious needs and anxieties of the public—which I have examined in earlier works[2]—would not move goods in the mountainous dimensions desired.

What was needed was strategies that would make Americans in large numbers into voracious, wasteful, compulsive consumers—and strategies that would provide products assuring such wastefulness. Even where wastefulness was not involved, additional strategies were needed that would induce the public to consume at ever-higher levels.

Happily for the marketers, such strategies were emerging or were at hand. They had been forged in the fires of the fifties and were being perfected for use in the sixties.

It is nine such strategies and their implementation that we shall explore in detail in the next thirteen chapters. They need to be understood because, for better or worse, they are influencing profoundly the climate in which the people of the United States—and, to a growing extent, the people of the rest of the Western world—live.

PART II

IN RESPONSE, NINE STRATEGIES

4. THERE'S ALWAYS ROOM FOR MORE

"Every family needs two homes."—The Douglas Fir Plywood Association.

As the marketing experts groped for ways to keep sales soaring in the face of mounting saturation, one of the first thoughts that struck them was that each consumer should be induced to buy more of each product than he had been buying. The way to end glut was to produce gluttons. But, of course, it would not be put that baldly. Consumers should be provided with plausible excuses for buying more of each product than might in earlier years have seemed rational or prudent.

Thus it was that carpet makers announced, through their Carpet Institute, that each family should buy more rugs because "HOME MEANS MORE WITH CARPET ON THE FLOOR." Rug retailers were advised in *Home Furnishings Daily* that they could expand their sales in three ways: sell more rug per room (the ideal was wall-to-wall); sell more rooms in the house as rooms that deserve coverage by rugs; and "trade up"—selling prospects higher-priced material than they had planned to buy.

The makers of one deodorant introduced a he-she kit for husbands and wives, so that they could get two applicators rather than one in each master bathroom. Men previously had tended to use their wives' applicator rather than buy their own.

Hosiery manufacturers began trying to sell more pairs of stockings to each American woman by introducing colored stockings. Women were told that their stockings should match whatever costume or accessories they would be wearing. This concept of more-sales-through-matching took hold in a number of fields. A spokesman for Revlon, Inc., the cosmetics firm, explained that one of the secrets of the company's fabulous success during the late fifties was that it "taught women to match their nail enamel to their moods and occasions, so that they bought more."

The major makers of women's swimming suits not only managed to double the average price of suits in a decade, but managed to put more swim suits into each woman's wardrobe. Women who once possessed only one suit were owning several. One of the Big Four swim-suit producers, Catalina, began promoting the idea of having one suit for the morning sun, one for the noonday sun, and a third for the evening sun. And another of the Big Four, Rose Marie Reid, began urging that women use one suit for swimming, one for sunning, and one for "psychology."

Makers of eyeglasses set their sights on the goal of selling more spectacles per head. The Optical Wholesalers National Association began promoting the notion that every person wearing glasses needs more than one pair. A spokesman explained: "We want glass wearers toown several pairs now—not only for safety but for style as well." He explained that glasses had definitely become a fashion accessory. "There are plenty of women today," he added triumphantly, "who buy a new pair of glasses to match every new outfit. Style-conscious men own several pairs, too. They buy them for business and sports wear—just like a suit."

The concept of color "matching" in order to broaden sales was also used in promoting home accessories. A spokesman for Kleenex tissue announced over a television network that "there's a color for every room in your home." And the Bell System sought to get more telephone extensions in each home by the same there's-a-different-color-for-everyroom approach. American Telegraph and Telephone urged, in fact, that families install a second, entirely new line into the house for extra convenience. A Midwestern telephone company official told me of a study made in motels that showed that telephoning could be increased about 20 per cent by the use of phones in a color other than the conventional black. Apparently bright colors promote an impulse to call someone just for the heck of it.

A campaign by the world's largest manufacturer of wedding rings to popularize the "double ring" ceremony greatly increased the sale of gold wedding rings. Several hundred radio commentators and society editors began making special note of the fact if the groom, as well as the bride, wore a nuptial ring.

The makers of a number of products for the home concluded that no home was really a home if it did not have doubles in the products they were promoting. The president of Servel, Inc., announced that the American standard of living now called for "two refrigerators in every home." The chief of the washer division of the American Home Laundry Manufacturers Association declared that a well-equipped home should have two washers and two driers. Meanwhile, the Plumbing Fixture Manufacturers Association began promoting the "privazone" home. In a privazone home, each member of the family has his own private water closet. Radio manufacturers disclosed with pride that they had succeeded in selling an average of three radios to every family in the land.

Perhaps the ultimate of this two-or-more-of-a-kind concept—which began so humbly in the twenties with the political promise of two chickens in every pot—was the promotion of the idea of two homes for every family. Home builders began pressing the idea. Others joined in. Building suppliers, appliance manufacturers, and advertising agencies excitedly grasped the potentialities inherent in spreading the idea that every family needed a town house and a country house, or a work house and a play house. The marketing possibilities were spelled out by an official of the plywood association in these terms: "The second home is going to . . . provide tremendous markets for everybody in the building materials field, for appliance manufacturers, builders, and developers, lending agencies, etc. We in the plywood industry are leading the parade."

Another leader of the two-house parade was the J. Walter

Thompson advertising agency, which began pointing out in business journals the inviting potentialities of the two-house family. "With the two-house family," it said, "America has clearly entered a new age of consumption for household equipment." It pointed out that the two-house family is likely to have: three or four bathrooms, two to four television sets, two fully equipped kitchens, four to twelve beds, multiples of furniture, linens, rugs, china, etc.

And, of course, a two-house family would have to have more than one car. J. Walter Thompson called for an "aggressive advertising and selling" campaign to overcome the public's "habit lag" in sticking with one car when two cars were obviously desired for modern living. One attempt at aggressive re-education was conducted by the Chevrolet company. Its announcer on the Dinah Shore program began talking of those deprived citizens who were victims of "one-car captivity." The essence of the message, as television critic John Crosby assimilated it, was that, "You peasants who own only one car . . . are chained to the land like serfs in the Middle Ages." The way to liberation, of course, was to buy a second car. And business writers reported that the idea was rapidly taking hold. By 1960, one family in six had become a multiple car owner. In the Los Angeles area, the ratio was far higher. A largescale Eastern farmer tells me that every single one of his farm hands now owns two cars.

Some car owners might complain that the streets and highways in many sections of the United States were already agonizingly overcrowded, but marketers felt a great increase in motorcar ownership was needed. J. Walter Thompson found that there was a "latent potential demand" for thirty million additional cars on the road. That would bring the total number of motorcars on the roads up to about ninety million. (Other estimates indicated that at the present rate of economic and population growth there should be four times as many motorcars on United States highways by A.D. 2000!)

Another tack that the marketers took was to try to induce Americans to demand more with each product bought. It should be either bigger or more complex, or both, in order to be appropriate for modern living. The goal was to justify a higher price tag. Victor Lebow in his blueprint for "forced consumption" put this imperative of a higher price tag in these words: "The second essential is what we might call 'expensive consumption. ' " Even dolls became bigger and more expensive.

The lawn mower offers an excellent illustration of the strategy of upgrading the nation's concept of what is appropriate. A simple-minded, intensely rational person might assume that hand mowers would be increasingly popular today and that power mowers would be almost impossible to sell. After all, lawns are getting smaller all the time. And adult males are feeling more and more the need for physical exercise as they spend more time in sedentary, short-week jobs. They come home from the office beating their chests and growling for exercise. The situation that has developed, however, shows how dangerous it has become to try to anticipate consumer behavior by the application of humorless logic, and ignoring the role marketing strategies may play.

The lawn-mower industry was able to convince American males that it was somehow shameful to be seen pushing a hand mower. And power mowers were promoted as a wonderful new gadget. Powermower sales rose seventeenfold in fifteen years! By 1960, more than nine out of every ten lawn mowers sold were powered. Such powered mowers cost from three to five times as much as hand mowers. Furthermore, having a mere motor on your mower was not enough in some neighborhoods. You also needed a seat on it. Hundred of thousands of American males began buying power mowers with seats. These, of course cost ten times as much as a hand mower. A Midwestern auto-accessory chain began using a "save your heart" theme to promote sales of self-propelled power mowers. One trade journal reported that this merchandiser "makes it a practice to trade customers up into higher-priced units." And so the mower industry was able to keep its dollar volume rising in a most satisfying manner. Apparently more advances were still to come. *Newsweek* carried a prediction that by 1970 electronic lawn mowers would be sweeping over lawns on preprogramed patterns without human attendants.

A few months ago, I was present when a technical expert from the British Standards Institution inspected a display of American refrigerators and stoves. He kept shaking his head in amazement. Some of the stoves had twenty-eight dials and push buttons. He smiled. But it was the gargantuan size of the United States products that most puzzled him. "Why so big?" he kept asking. One stove had eighteen inches of empty surface space between burners. "We wouldn't ordinarily want so much space," he said. It was explained to him that Americans had been conditioned to demand a big-looking stove—and to excuse it on the ground of needing work space. We turned to the giant "fridges," as he called the refrigerators. He observed: "We keep in an ordinary pantry many of the things you put in the 'fridge.'"

As with most marketing techniques, the strategy of loading more and more of the product onto each consumer was brought to fullest flower in the motorcar industry. Each year during most of the fifties, Detroit doggedly and energetically added "more car per car." The now familiar additions—all costly— took the form of greater bulk, greater power, more power accessories, and more chrome.

Chevrolet offered a good case in point. During the thirty-year period ending in 1958, the Chevrolet car grew four feet in length and underwent a fivefold increase in horsepower. Its passenger car had more horses under its hood than many large trucks. Originally few buyers had shown much interest in its most dressed-up, most expensive model, the Bel Air. But over the years the Chevrolet selling staff succeeded in trading up so many prospects to the Bel Air that it became the company's most popular model, and in 1959 the Impala was introduced to top the Chevrolet line.

The result of all this customer loading in the motorcar industry was that, by the late fifties, a United States workingman had to work fifty-three hours longer in order to buy its cheaper models than he did a decade earlier. (And this figure does not make any allowance for the greater burden of installment charges in the late fifties; nor does it take into account the far greater cost of upkeep.) As motorcars became heavier and more powerful, the many power accessories quickly sucked the life out of batteries and required expensive replacements. Laurence Crooks, automotive consultant to Consumers Union, summed up the greater wear and tear of the big motorcars that were developed in these words: "Nearly every factor which increases engine output has a price in wear or durability. . . . Multiple carburetors, high-lift valves, stiffer valve springs, bigger manifolds, all take their toll in one way or another."

And then there were the once lowly mufflers. The rate at which they collapsed underneath the large, highly powered motorcars became the basis for one of the nation's fastest-growing industries. Mufflers were burning out substantially faster than they had a decade earlier. A half-billion-dollar industry emerged to replace mufflers. Partly the ravaging of mufflers was due to the higher acidity of high-octane gasoline that was recommended for the high-powered motorcars.

Partly it was due to the greatly increased use of dual exhaust systems supposedly required to cope with all those extra horses under the hood. Dual exhausts began protruding from a third of all motorcars sold, and were esteemed as symbols of prestige since they first appeared on very high-priced motorcars. The trouble with the duals was not only that they added to the cost of the vehicle and cost twice as much to replace but also that they corroded faster, especially in stop-and-start city driving. With the duals, mufflers often did not become hot enough to clear out the eroding condensation.

But perhaps most important, the boom in mufflers was greatly stimulated by shrewd merchandising. Until the fifties, mufflers had been sold matter-of-factly. Marketers hadn't seen the possibility of promoting them as profitable impulse items for uneasy motorists. Now muffler makers were finding they could often double muffler sales at a service station within a few weeks merely by putting up a curbside sign reminding motorists that their mufflers might need replacing. In two years, Midas, Inc., built up a network of muffler-installation dealers. Aside from the quality of its product, in order to help attract customers on further grounds, it beamed much of its multimillion-dollar advertising campaign at housewives. Midas painted its mufflers a golden color. And it hired psychologists to instruct its installation personnel how to behave in a refined manner around the ladies who would be waiting for their mufflers to be replaced.

The greatest toll of the large and complex motorcar, however, was in the way that the land yacht guzzled gasoline and oil. Despite vague open-end claims in the motorcar ads about fuel economy ("up to 15% savings"), gas mileage dropped relentlessly. *Tide*, the advertising journal, reported that mileage dropped from close to twenty miles per gallon to fifteen miles per gallon in the first eight years of the fifties. The motorcar industry's annual ritual of the Economy Run became an embarrassment. This run had been conceived to prove that the new cars were better than ever. The decline in miles per gallon was obscured for a number of years by the fact that the winners were judged on a tonmile basis. This is the amount of work done by a gallon of gasoline, as in moving a ton of motorcar through one mile. On this basis, the winners usually were multi-tonned monsters. *Popular Science* made a long-range analysis of actual miles-per-gallon figures of the races and concluded that by 1958 mileage had "sagged down" to almost 14 per cent below the twenty-year average. And this occurred despite the great advances in the ingenuity of drivers in nursing their motorcars along the course.

For the average motorist the mileage decline meant he had to buy approximately one hundred more gallons of gasoline per year. A number of New York City garage managers concluded that in four years their parking capacity had shrunk 15 per cent because of the growth in the size of motorcars. They began applying a surcharge on the biggest of the big motorcars.

It was in this setting that the makers of small foreign cars first began making noticeable inroads on the United States market. The Detroit planners had not counted on this factor to upset their controlled market. Until the foreign cars appeared, they had succeeded in frightening Americans away from the idea of a compact car by referring to it in derogatory terms such as "stripped down." As Eric Larrabee put it, in Detroit "the equations are fixed: small equals cheap equals bad, and large equals expensive equals good. Detroit has no way of appealing to the small-car customer without insulting him; it offers him the tail end of the procession, and never lets him forget it."

As pressure grew upon Detroit to offer the public the option of buying less ponderous motorcars, one automobile executive reflected the general lack of stomach for meeting such a need when he said: "If the public wants to lower its standard of living by driving a cheap, crowded car, we'll make it."[1]

And so it was that compact motorcars started emerging from the plants of Detroit's Big Three. Furthermore, they emerged with every contrivable manifestation of exultation. Now citizens were able to read stirring accounts which revealed how the chiefs of some of the major companies had really, in secret, been dreaming of and planning for this great day of offering a compact car for nearly a decade.

At first Detroit expected—and undoubtedly hoped—that the compact market would be confined to a modest percentage of the whole market. Any such hopes were dashed as millions of Americans— delighted to be rid of their oversized gas guzzlers without suffering serious social stigma—sought to buy the modest-sized American and foreign-made motorcars. In a sense, the Detroit-built dam broke. There were clearly limits to the power to manipulate public taste. United States compacts and small foreign motorcars began accounting for a third of all sales. Some dealers begged Detroit not to feature the smaller cars so much in advertising because their profit per unit was smaller on the small cars (even though business journals reported that very generous profit allowances had been arranged in the pricing structure).

Many marketers of motorcars began taking an exceedingly dim

view of the rush to compacts. *Printers' Ink* reported: "Companies and dealers are both glum about the trend. It means shaved profits per unit on the smaller cars, increased sales effort to move more cars." Some economists expressed concern, too, about what the trend implied for the steel industry. The compacts required a half-ton less steel per car. And they wonder how a drop in gas consumption will influence roadbuilding plans that were based on assumed revenues from taxes.

Gradually, however, the motorcar marketers began seeing that the situation was not without promise. They discovered that it might be possible to return to a situation in which the American family would again be spending more dollars each year for its transportation. If the public had the choice of motorcars of all sizes, it should be easier to lure more families into the ranks of the two-car families. It was now perfectly safe and appropriate socially to park a compact car in front of one's house provided one also had a regular-sized car parked there. A Ford engineering executive told a convention of ad-men that in the days ahead the size and kind of car one owned might not be as important as the *number* of cars one owned.

The marketers also began seeing another basis for optimism. They decided that the prospects were good for gradually raising the price they received by adding size, accessories, and luxury touches to the compacts. *Fortune* magazine rhetorically asked its executive-type readers in late 1959: "Can the [motorcar] industry still go on increasing its take per unit?" The magazine's answer was a resounding yes. It explained: "There are good reasons why it can. To begin with, the compact versions of the expensive cars doubtless will not be low-priced compacts—any more than the Jaguar sedan, though it is a compact auto, is a low-priced one . . . the industry doubtless will apply the more-car-per-car formula to smaller cars as well as to larger autos. . . . many devices may make compact cars more expensive than the 1960 models—such as air conditioning, automatic transmissions, and stationwagon versions of the compacts. . . . Other accessories may well be loaded on even the most austere cars."

Some of the other journals with a wide readership among marketers also rang out the hopeful news of trends to come. *Business Week* reported, "Detroit has started a new lap of the horsepower race, this time with the new compact cars." The Chrysler Valiant, for example, could now be had with 148 horsepower instead of 101 horsepower. *Advertising Age* quoted a cheerful Buick dealer in Houston as stating: "Having little cars won't make any difference to us. We'll build customers up to a little better car." And *U.S. News & World Report* predicted that "newcomers in the field will be substantially larger and more luxurious than those now on the market. The present compacts are already adding extra features."

And so happy days would come again. But more about strategies to induce us to step up our consumption of motorcars later, when we take up planned obsolescence.

Another general tack the marketers took was to try to induce people to get rid of the products they already owned. In its broadest form this took the form of encouraging people to throw things away.

5. PROGRESS THROUGH THE THROWAWAY SPIRIT

"I do love having new clothes . . . but old clothes are beastly. . . . We always throw away old clothes. Ending is better than mending . . . ending is better than mending . . . ending is better. . . ." —Soft voice of sleep teacher indoctrinating the young while they sleep in Aldous Huxley's *Brave New World*.

In the hair-raising utopia that Mr. Huxley projected for six centuries hence, babies come in bottles and the zombie-like citizens move about in doped-up bliss. To keep the industrial machines humming, each citizen is "compelled to consume so much a year." To that end, newness as a trait is cherished. And sleep teachers stress love of newness because they have the responsibility of "adapting future demand to future industrial supply." The dictator of the Utopia, Mustapha Mond, at one point explains: "We don't want people to be attracted by old things. We want them to like the new ones."

When Huxley wrote his book in 1932, he was visualizing what might come about in the distant future. But within a quarter century the people of the United States, without any help from dictators or out-andout sleep teachers, were exhibiting a throwaway mood that would tickle even Mustapha Mond. Much of this was deliberately encouraged. The voice of the television announcer—in 1960—chanted, "You use it once and throw it away. . . . You use it once and throw it away." This specific chant was used to promote the sale of a deodorant pad. And a steel company, in a television commercial, showed a pleased housewife dropping a metal can that had contained soft drinks into the wastebasket. No fussing with returns!

Residents of the United States were discarding, using up, destroying, and wasting products at a rate that offered considerable encouragement to those charged with achieving ever-higher levels of consumption for their products. A business writer for *Time* magazine related, as the sixties were about to begin: "The force that gives the U.S. economy its pep is being generated more and more in the teeming aisles of the nation's stores. . . . U.S. consumers no longer hold on to suits, coats, and dresses as if they were heirlooms. . . . Furniture, refrigerators, rugs—all once bought to last for years or life—are now replaced with register-tingling regularity."

The new mood of the disposable era was reflected in the pages of the *Engineering News Record*, which observed: "Nowhere in the world except in the U.S. would a skyscraper office building in sound condition be torn down merely to be replaced by another one."

Dennis Brogan has characterized modern Americans as a people "who go away and leave things." The voluptuous wastefulness of modern Americans could be seen not only in their littered parks but in market surveys. The industrial-design firm, Harley Earl Associates of Detroit, reported. "In most households we found there were two to five rolls of Scotch tape—but no one could locate any of them."

Americans have developed their own democratic version of sleep indoctrination of the young. There are the soft, insistent commercials the youngsters hear during their weekly twenty-odd hours of television watching. And there are the breakable plastic toys, which teach them at an early age that everything in this world is replaceable.

An American sales executive told me of the shock his Dutch mother exhibited at the wastefulness of Americans when she visited his Connecticut home town for the first time. Apparently she could not endure what she saw. On the last day of her visit she took the son triumphantly to the closet of her room. The closet was stacked high with neatly folded metal foil, plastic containers, paper wrappings, and cord.

Americans like to think that in the earlier days, if not today, frugality was the rule. The maxim, "Waste not, want not," was often repeated. The pioneers of the United States did cherish and guard their bread pans and iron pots. When they moved on and had to leave furniture behind, they did not drive to the dump as modern Americans do. Instead, they held an auction. Each fabricated item was cherished, perhaps because it was hard to come by. It had what economists call high marginal utility.

On the other hand, all through the last half of their history, since A.D. 1800, Americans have been careless with their nation's natural resources such as buffalo and timberlands, perhaps because they once seemed to have so much of them. Louis Jones, director of the New York State Historical Association, told me: "I think prodigality has been a bright-colored thread running through all of our history from the Revolution on." Mr. Jones made the point, however, that in earlier days much greater care was taken to produce "a product that would satisfy a customer for a long time." Durability was esteemed. And the national ideal was to make the most of what one had.

Against this background let us take note of some of the efforts that have been made to promote the throwaway spirit in North America recently.

Steaks and other meats have appeared in disposable aluminum frying pans. When the steak is done, just throw away the pan along with the nasty old grease. Muffins come in throwaway baking tins. Hungarian goulash began being offered in throwaway plastic boil-in bags. Charles Mortimer, the chairman of General Foods, exulted that Mrs. Consumer was learning to expect "dinners which can be popped into the oven, heated, served in the pan, and the pan tossed into the trash can after dinner!"

Even the bother of popping the dinner into the oven apparently was soon to be ended. A sales executive of the Aluminum Company of America announced that the day was at hand when packages would replace pots and pans. Electric food packages were being planned with their own plugs, and single-use cooking containers were being prepared for pre-packaged meats.

Pre-prepared, no-fuss, no-mess meals bought at extra cost may make sense for the minority of families where the wife holds a job. But for the great majority of families there was little such justification. Yet all were coaxed to indulge.

A number of companies began perfecting new push-button foods that would squirt up out of metal aerosol cans. Under development were such squirtables as omelettes, angel-food cake mix, fruit whips, catchup, barbecue sauce, and spreads for cocktail crackers. More than a hundred million cans of squirtable whipped cream were being sold a year. Just throw away the dead squirt can.

One aspect of the aerosol cans of special interest to those anxious to promote higher levels of consumption was that the dead cans often were still not empty of food. The compressed gases inside that have been widely used tend to lose pressure before the containers are empty of food. Packagers speculated on "what the consumer will accept as a reasonably economic amount of the product."[1] In short, how much food could remain inside the dead can without causing resentment or suspicion? My eighteen-year-old son first demonstrated to me the food loss when an aerosol can of chocolate sauce for Sunday-night sundaes seemed to be empty. Disregarding warnings not to "puncture" the can, he hammered a hole in the bottom of the can and retrieved several spoonfuls. In two other instances he retrieved enough whipped cream from apparently empty cans to cover two and three strawberry shortcakes lavishly. Now we whip our own.

Fortunes were made as the craving for convenience which Mr. Mortimer referred to swept the nation. A company called Standard Packaging, which specializes in making "disposables," tripled its sales in four years to become a hundred-million-dollar corporation. This company makes trays that can be cooked, bags that can be boiled, bowls and other eating utensils that can be discarded to eliminate dishwashing. Its hard-running young boss, R. Carl ("Hap") Chandler, explained happily: "Everything that we make is thrown away."[2] *Sales Management* sought to analyze the secrets of Stan-Pak's phenomenal success. One of its headlines offered this clue: "STAN-PAK'S RESEARCH EXPLOITS LAZINESS." It went on to explain that as the company conceived the future, "Tomorrow, more than ever, our life will be 'disposable.'"

All this packaging and disposing were not a free dividend to the consumer. In some instances the package was costing ten times as much as the product inside. Salt coming in small throwaway containers costs seventeen times as much as salt bought by the pound. The metal aerosol can with squirt mechanism and chemical propellant adds at least a third to the cost of getting a topping for a sundae.

By the time Americans finish paying for all the inviting packaging they are induced to buy, the annual bill is twenty-five billion dollars. That is just the cost of the packaging, the wrapping. It is a figure worth pondering for a moment. Divide it by the number of families in the United States, and you come up with a staggering statistic, one almost beyond belief. The average United States family today spends five hundred dollars of its income each year just for the package!

And this apparently is only the beginning. As Mr. Chandler pointed out in referring to the vistas opening for packagers in the food field: "The growth in convenience foods is going to be terrific. We're just at the beginning of the era." Industrial designers were solemnly explaining in trade journals that often the package called for more careful research and planning than the product it contains.

The throwaway mood was meanwhile invading many fields far removed from food. Here are some random examples:

A throwaway mousetrap housed inside an aluminum shield was being marketed. No messing around with the mouse. Just throw away the whole unit. You don't even have to look at the victim.

Rochester Razor, Inc., began selling, in vending machines, a throwaway plastic razor with built-in blade. The complete unit goes into the wastebasket after use.

Corporate Research, Inc., placed on the market disposable paper camping equipment, including tents and sleeping bags, for modern campers.

One large New York department store advertised paper coveralls— the main point being to throw them out.

Millions of Americans, instead of seeking an old-fashioned "lifetime" watch, began buying inexpensive but serviceable watches and then threw them away when they needed repairs, or when a more up-to-date model hit the market. A men's clothing chain in New York announced, "Watches have become carefully styled items in a man's wardrobe." It was offering them as accessories.

Bud Berma Sportswear, Inc., made an unusual offer to tempt men who already owned a sports jacket. It promised a five-dollar prize to any man buying one of its jackets, provided he mailed in his old jacket for disposal. The firm promised to give it "to some needy person overseas." And it added: "For your generosity to someone in need, you get this luxurious Bud Berma sports shirt in a choice of seven handsome colors" as a bonus.

Your author recently lost a dental inlay after accepting a piece of taffy from his daughter. In the emergency I sought the services of a strange dentist in the New England town where I happened to be at the moment. Only two weeks before I had received a thorough checkup from my regular dentist, a man outstanding in his field. The new dentist packed my mouth with gauze and a suction tube to drain saliva. While waiting for his preparation to harden, he began tapping and picking at my other teeth. I could not protest because of all the packings. He announced worriedly that two of my existing fillings were in "bad shape" and needed replacing. He probed around some more among my thirty-odd fillings and then finally declared: "As a matter of fact, it would be a good idea to replace all your fillings. They're getting pretty old. It would save you money in the long run." I made strangled sounds and shook my head violently. He changed the subject.

Each year American housewives were throwing away hundreds of pounds of food scraps that used to be fed to dogs. Meanwhile, they were spending a third of a billion dollars for prepared dog food. The most popular, by 1960, was pressure-blown puffed meal chunks.

A color consultant from Toronto explained to the Inter-Society Colour Council meeting in New York an ingenious scheme which a client company had conceived for increasing the sale of potato peelers. He began by pointing up a puzzling fact. Although potato peelers "never wear out," enough are sold in two years in his country to put one in every home. What happens to them? He gave this answer. "Investigation reveals that they get thrown away with the potato peelings." One of his colleagues, he added, had then come up with a dazzling plan for helping along this throwaway process. He proposed that their company paint its peelers a color "as much like a potato peeling as possible." However, a potato-colored peeler wouldn't have much eye appeal on the sales counter. They decided to solve that by displaying the peeler on a colorful card. Once the housewife got the peeler home and removed the bright card, the chances that she would lose the peeler were excellent. He explained how this would work to the benefit of the company in these terms:

"As most people wrap their peelings in newspaper . . . we figure that if they once lay the knife down, it will disappear and be thrown out. Next year we expect to double our sales."

A friend who ordered new kitchen cabinets from a national cabinet-producing company found that the factory had sent wrong-sized doors. A representative immediately ordered new doors. But what about the wrong-sized doors? The representative replied: "Oh, shucks, throw them away! That is cheaper than taking them back."

In some cases the consumers have no choice but to be waste makers because of the way products are sold to them. Many paste pots come with brushes built into the cover, and the brushes fail by a half inch to reach the bottom. No amount of wiggling or maneuvering will reach the remaining paste. Thus millions of "empty" paste jars are thrown away with a few spoonfuls of paste still in them. Likewise, millions of "used" tubes of lipstick are thrown away with a half inch of lipstick remaining in the tube because the mechanism will not bring up all the lipstick.

And then there are the billions of pills that are thrown away because the druggist's label does not indicate what ailment they were intended to relieve. The label will say "2 pills, 3 times a day" but usually it will not say "For chest congestion," etc. Even the brand names—which are occasionally listed—are not much help. Because of the proliferation of brand-name drugs, there are many thousands of names. I find in my own medicine chest eight bottles of nearly full pills whose labels have no meaning to me or to my wife Virginia. One says "Polaramine," another says "Emprazil," a third says "Niamid—3 each day." Still another merely states, "One, three times a day." And one reads, "2 at start, 2 this evening, then one three times a day."

In a less wasteful society it would seem reasonable to expect that the bottles would note the ailment they were prescribed to relieve, and the expected life potency of the pills or fluid contained in the bottles.

The throwaway strategy was especially tempting to the makers and sellers of automotive supplies such as spark plugs, since billions of dollars' worth of materials was involved. Sometimes, however, the marketing forces found themselves pulling in opposite directions. For a number of years the American Petroleum Institute urged motorists to throw away their dirty old sludge and install bright-new oil every thousand miles. Motorcar manufacturers, in contrast, have stressed that their gentle cars could nurse oil for a long, long time. In 1959, Ford was promising prospective buyers that they would need to change oil only once every four thousand miles. Later that year, the Petroleum Institute grudgingly made a gesture toward bringing its advice within shouting distance of that being offered by the motorcar manufacturers (some of whom were promoting oil filters). It proposed that motorists change their oil according to a formula that ran like this. In winter change every two thousand miles or every thirty days, whichever comes first. And in summer change every two thousand miles or every sixty days, whichever comes first. Under this formula, the majority of drivers usually would be changing their oil long before the two-thousand mark was reached.

Runzheimer & Company reports that with well-managed company fleets oil is likely to be changed somewhere between two thousand and three thousand miles, depending on a number of factors including the grade of oil used. Where sixty-cent oil is used, for example, the change is likely to occur at three thousand miles.

The makers and sellers of "permanent" antifreeze—a quarter-billion-dollar market—had got themselves into a particularly awkward spot in their sales claims. In fact, businessmen might find their dilemma poignant. As *Sales Management* explained it, they were being forced to "un-merchandise their earlier advertising."[3] They were now protesting with quivers of anguish in their voices that the public had taken their "permanent" claim too seriously.

It seems that motorists took their claim that antifreeze was "permanent" so seriously that almost half were using their antifreeze for more than one winter. More shocking to the marketers was the discovery in a du Pont survey that almost half of the dealers believed antifreeze was really "permanent." Another 12 per cent wouldn't be pinned down on the subject. The result of all this faith in the permanence of antifreeze was that the sale of antifreeze was slipping. As *Sales Management* put it: "A large segment of the motoring public *swears* on last year's antifreeze and the marketers are boiling over. . . . When the marketers unwittingly labeled glycol 'permanent' they oversold the product—and undermined future sales. Many brands are labeled permanent, including some of the top-selling private labels and two of the four manufacturers' makes. Olin Mathieson and DuPont huff and puff about re-use—but Olin calls its glycol product 'Permanent Pyro' and DuPont calls its Zerex 'Permanent Type Anti-Freeze.'"

A massive re-education campaign was launched by many antifreeze makers. Some began talking about their "all-winter antifreeze." The gist of the new theme widely sounded was that antifreeze—even "permanent" antifreeze—was good for one winter only. One company made a dealer movie in which bad guy John Carradine rumbled ominously, "Why torture your motor?" However, another company was offering a "full year's" protection at double the cost of glycol. And one brave, company—Du Pont—revealed it hoped to promote a really permanent antifreeze for about $7.50 per car. Or at least it is permanent if it doesn't give a warning by changing color—from red to yellow— because of contamination due to cooling-system failure.

The most flagrant attempt to promote a throwaway mood was that of the Holland Furnace Company of Holland, Michigan. This company is the largest seller of replacement furnaces in the nation, with five hundred retail branches. In 1958, the Federal Trade Commission ordered Holland to stop the strategy that had been used by some of its salesmen to frighten furnace owners into replacing existing furnaces with new Holland equipment. What follows in the next two paragraphs is taken from reports of the commission.

The salesmen involved, according to the Federal Trade Commission, sometimes posed as government or utility inspectors in order to get into the homes. And some misrepresented themselves as "heating engineers." A householder in the St. Louis area testified that two young men came to her house and said, "We are from the government inspecting furnaces," and asked for admission to the house. She refused them permission and called the police. When the men were picked up by the police and questioned, they identified themselves as Holland salesmen. They denied telling her they were government officers but admitted they had told her they were working with the "government fuel-conservation program."

Once the Holland canvassers gained access to a home—either by pretext or in response to invitations resulting from company advertisements offering cleaning service or free inspections—"in many instances" they dismantled furnaces without the owners' permission. In some cases, the Federal Trade Commission asserted, "they then refuse to reassemble them when requested, misrepresenting that this would involve grave danger of fire, gas, and explosion." In other cases, it said, they declared that the existing furnaces were beyond economical repair or that companies making them were out of business. "Some of the furnaces condemned by these agents," the Federal Trade Commission order 4 asserted, "were proved to be either in safe condition or safely repairable."

The Federal Trade Commission order upheld its examiner's ruling that Holland's "false claims and improper business methods had caused many owners to discard competitive furnaces prematurely in fear of grave danger from continued use of this 'condemned' equipment." The company denied or minimized the various accusations and turned to the federal courts for relief. At this writing—two years and three court decisions later—the matter is still under litigation.

6. PROGRESS THROUGH PLANNED OBSOLESCENCE

"Once in my life I would like to own something outright before it's broken! I'm always in a race with the junkyard! I just finish paying for the car and it's on its last legs. The refrigerator consumes belts like a goddam maniac. They time those things. They time them so when you've finally paid for them, they're used up."—Lament of Willy Loman in Arthur Miller's *Death of a Salesman*.

Willy's lament, of course, was just the intuitive outburst of a badly exasperated man. But businessmen themselves, when in a joking mood, sometimes ask the definition of the phrase "durable goods." Their playful answer: any products that will outlast the final installment payment.

What are the facts about the alleged short life of American consumer goods? And if their life sometimes seems unreasonably short, is it so by design?

The recent fascination of many businessmen with "planned obsolescence" has been one of the major developments of the postwar period. Its use as a strategy to influence either the shape of the product or the mental attitude of the consumer represents the quintessence of the throwaway spirit. Financial columnist Sylvia Porter reported in the late fifties that "behind closed doors in the executive suites of giant corporations from coast to coast" the wisdom of pursuing policies of planned obsolescence was being argued. She added: "Never has a debate of this sort—which touches the foundation of the American standard of living—erupted so openly." Even on the floor of the United States Congress a representative from Missouri offered his sympathy to the millions of people "who find their new gadgets of all kinds falling apart in use."

The phrase "planned obsolescence" has different meanings to different people. Thus many people are not necessarily defending deliberately shoddy construction when they utter strong defenses of obsolescence in business. *The Management Review* of the American Management Association, for example, reprinted an article with the headline: "Obsolescence Can Spell Progress." This article referred to the kind of obsolescence that is "a healthy dissatisfaction with doing things less well than they can be done."

A somewhat different meaning apparently was involved when *Retailing Daily* printed the assertion that "it is not only our privilege to obsolete the minimum home and many home furnishings. It is our obligation. We are obligated to work on obsolescence as our contribution to a healthy, growing society."

And Brooks Stevens, a leading industrial designer, explained obsolescence planning in these terms: "Our whole economy is based on planned obsolescence, and everybody who can read without moving his lips should know it by now. We make good products, we induce people to buy them, and then next year we deliberately introduce something that will make those products old fashioned, out of date, obsolete. . . . It isn't organized waste. It's a sound contribution to the American economy." Other designers, I should add, disagreed with Stevens' viewpoint.

The American people themselves have been conditioned over the years to respond favorably to some kinds of obsolescence. Many might be appalled at the idea of owning a motorcar that would splendidly meet their transportation needs for twenty or thirty years.

Webster's dictionary defines obsolescent as meaning going out of use. For our purposes in examining modern marketing practices, we should refine the situation by distinguishing three different ways that products can be made obsolescent. There can be:

Obsolescence of function. In this situation an existing product becomes outmoded when a product is introduced that performs the function better.

Obsolescence of quality. Here, when it is planned, a product breaks down or wears out at a given time, usually not too distant.

Obsolescence of desirability. In this situation a product that is still sound in terms of quality or performance becomes "worn out" in our minds because a styling or other change makes it seem less desirable.

The first type of obsolescence—the functional type—is certainly laudable when planned. We all applaud when piston-driven passenger planes are outmoded by swifter, quieter jet planes. We all applaud when the hard-to-see twelve-inch television screen gives way to the twentyone-inch screen. We all applaud when we can dial a number hundreds of miles away rather than work through operators. Many of us applaud when high-fidelity recordings start to give way to stereophonic sound, even though it means doubling much of the equipment.

In this last instance, however, it should be noted that there has been—and increasingly will be—overtones of manipulation. Stereo was held back in its development for many years because there was felt to be no urgent need for it. The original patent for stereo was taken out by a Briton in 1931, and soon thereafter some American companies acquired the rights. By the late fifties, however, tens of millions of Americans owned comparatively new phonographs, and the demand for additional new-model hi-fi sets was slowing. In fact, a glut in the pipelines of distribution threatened. A dramatically new product was felt to be needed to force dealers to clear the channels and to induce owners of existing hi-fi sets to feel their product was now inadequate. Stereo was rushed into production to ease the impasse. And stereo, it should be noted, offered the possibility of continuing to create obsolescence for a long time to come. After the market for two-channel stereo is saturated, the producers can switch to three-channel stereo. At these higher levels, however, the obsolescence created is apt to be more of desirability than of function. As a matter of fact, by 1960 several major producers had introduced three-channel stereo equipment. On tape, four-track, five-track, and even eight-track stereo are projected. A trade journal, however, reported it was unable to find any manufacturer who was willing to claim that three-channel stereo was a true technical improvement. But most of them felt the public could easily be influenced by numbers.

Let us grant that we are all heartily in favor of the functional type of obsolescence that is created by introducing a genuinely improved product. In this book we shall confine our scrutiny to the two morecontroversial types of obsolescence creation—of quality and desirability. We shall first take an over-all look at the evidence of the use of obsolescence of quality as a strategy to promote sales. This type of obsolescence—when deliberately planned—is certainly the most dubious of all the types.

What is the state of the quality of consumer products in America today? Obviously, in many fields, the quality is good. The makers of men's socks should be applauded for greatly prolonging the life of their product, often by combining nylon and wool. For most men, the exasperation or embarrassment of finding a hole at the heel is becoming a more and more infrequent occurrence. But in many other products significant deterioration appears to have set in, and often by intent. At this point two comments by experts might be noted. The first witness is Gordon Lippincott, one of the nation's leading industrial designers. Mr. Lippincott, co-chief of the firm of Lippincott & Margulies, stated in 1958: "Manufacturers have downgraded quality and upgraded complexity. The poor consumer is going crazy."

The other witness is Colston E. Warne, president of Consumers Union, the world's foremost nonprofit product-testing organization. At approximately the same time that Mr. Lippincott spoke out, Mr. Warne expressed his concern about the emphasis developing in recent years on "hidden quality debasement," "built-in obsolescence," and a "growing disregard" for maintaining quality levels.

In addition to having obsolescence deliberately built into it to shorten its life, a product may be shoddy for a number of reasons.

The shoddiness may be due to haste caused by the strain of bringing out a new model every year. It may be caused by skimping on the product itself in order to feed advertising and sales costs. Or it can be caused by just plain corner-cutting. The point to remember, however, is that all these forms of shoddiness aid in producing obsolescence in the product, and the obsolescence puts the owner into the market for a replacement. If the debasement of the product is not obvious to the owner, or if he has low expectations, there is no serious complication in selling him a replacement. On the other hand, if the debasement becomes conspicuous, the seller is in trouble.

Businessmen over the years have developed a variety of phrases to describe that critical point when their product will, or is likely to, collapse. They speak of "the point of required utility," of "time to failure," or "product death date." Establishing the probable lifetime of a product is not too difficult. Often you can do it by determining the life span of its weakest link. The life of a product tends to be as long as that link, especially if that link is difficult to replace. Oliver Wendell Holmes anticipated the work of modern design engineers when he wrote of that wonderful one-hoss shay which was built in such a logical way that on a given day "it went to pieces all at once."

Even the best of products, of course, wears out sometime. Therefore a company cannot be legitimately criticized for estimating the death date of its product. It is vulnerable to criticism, however, if it sells a product with a short life expectancy when it knows that for the same cost, or only a little more, it could give the customer a product with a much longer useful life. In such situations one may properly wonder about the company's motives.

I should stress that all which follows here does not change the fact that many hundreds of American companies still do their very best to give their buyers a long-lasting product, especially in fields not heavily dependent upon replacement sales.

The idea of creating obsolescence of quality through material failure is not a new concept. In the late twenties, *Advertising & Selling* carried a statement by J. George Frederick on the problem of increasing consumption. He dismissed as a "mere minor stopgap" the proposals of political liberals that more money be put into consumers' hands. A far more powerful lever, he said, was the "principle" for which he had dreamed up the name "progressive obsolescence." This simply meant indoctrinating the people who do have spending money with the habit of "buying more goods on the basis of obsolescence in efficiency, economy, style, or taste."

Obsolescence planning was spelled out much more bluntly—and specifically in terms of quality—a few years later in a speculative article entitled "Outmoded Durability" in *Printers' Ink* (January 9, 1936). Its author was Leon Kelley, identified as an executive of Fishier, Zealand & Co. The article's subtitle was: "If Merchandise Does Not Wear Out Faster, Factories Will Be Idle, People Unemployed."

Mr. Kelley explained that man traditionally has cherished the notion that durability is a prime feature of merit in products and that the longer a thing lasts the more completely you realize a return on the money you paid for it. He cited the grandfather's clock that had been in his family for two hundred years and still worked fine. Advertisers, he said, have tended to stress durability of their product as a major feature.

This harping on durability, he said, was out of date and should stop. It didn't meet the needs of the times. To illustrate those new needs, he cited a radio repairman who berated him because he still had the same radio after six years, even though "it functions better than ever." The radio man complained, "The trouble with this country is we expect things to last too long. If you're a good 100 per cent American, you ought to buy a new radio!" Kelley also cited a department-store executive who told him that if everyone insisted on long wear there would be few repeat sales.

Next, Mr. Kelley mentioned a survey that had been made of the attitudes of men in the home-furnishing field toward durability in collapsible portable chairs. It was found that nine out of ten experts preferred a chair selling at $1.00, capable of serving the customer approximately one year, to a chair that would cost $1.25, which might well last for about five years.

He concluded that United States marketers faced the task of selling the public away from the deep-rooted idea it had about durability. It could be done, he suggested, either by soft-pedaling durability or by deliberately promoting the idea of "non-durability." He worried whether such a campaign would have unanimous support of the marketers. "Will a few chiselers undercut the majority by screaming 'durability' to the public in spite of the general campaign?" he asked. In any case, he concluded that a trend away from durability had set in and would proceed with "gathering momentum." He said that it would take hard work and study to find the "right answers" to the many complex questions that are raised by this trend.

Meanwhile, there was evidence that some companies already were giving thought to modifying the expected lifetime of their products. Certain practices of General Electric came to light during a United States government suit involving General Electric's international agreements in the late thirties.[1] It should be stressed that the incidents that follow occurred during the thirties, when General Electric was under different management from what it is today.

In one memorandum introduced as an exhibit during the proceeding, a company engineer outlined to his superior a program for increasing sales by increasing the efficiency and shortening the life of flashlight lamps. He pointed out that progress already was being made. Originally the flashlight lamps outlasted three batteries. Then they were made to last only through two batteries. And now he was proposing that the lamp life be adjusted to last through one battery. "If this is done," he pointed out, "we estimate that it would result in increasing our flashlight business approximately 60 per cent." Another exhibit contained a message that a General Electric official wrote to an official of the Champion Lamp Works notifying him of a decision "to change the life of the 200-watt 110-120 volt PS 30 bulb lamp from 1,000 hours . . . to 750 hours." He added, "We are giving no publicity whatever to the fact that the change is contemplated."

And again, in 1939, an exhibit showed a General Electric official wrote to one of the company's licensees, Tung-Sol Lamp Works, notifying Tung-Sol of the following approved change: "The design life of the 2330 Lamp has been changed from 300 back to 200 hours. ... It is understood that no publicity or other announcement will be made of the change."

In the case of lamps it can be argued that one way to increase a bulb's burning efficiency is to shorten its life. (Another way is to increase the quality of materials and the workmanship.) It seems apparent, however, that officials in the cases cited were motivated not only by a desire for greater lamp-burning efficiency but also, quite possibly, by a desire to promote the sale of replacements. A letter was introduced in which a General Electric official pointed out that the customer "is prone to judge quality by life alone." And he added: "We realize that the constant reduction of lamp life that we have been in the process of carrying on has kept the volume of business up, but cannot refrain from giving a word of warning and a suggestion that it is about time to call a halt on this in view of the competitive situation."

Automotive designers, too, were apparently becoming intrigued by the possibility of practicing death control on their products. In 1934, two different issues of the *Journal of the Society of Automotive Engineers* quoted speculative comments by speakers at recent S.A.E. meetings. One stressed the "desirability of building automobiles with a limited life." Another suggested that all the parts of trucks might be designed for "controllable wear" as well as imperceptible wear.

The war years temporarily eased the "gathering momentum" away from durability noted by Mr. Kelley. But by the fifties the problem of mounting productivity of consumer goods was again bearing down upon producers. Many of their marketers began talking uneasily about the need for more obsolescence. And business journals pondered the problems involved. The February, 1959, issue of *Dun's Review and Modern Industry* carried an article by Martin Mayer, author of Madison Avenue, U.S.A. It was entitled: "Planned Obsolescence: Rx for Tired Markets?"

Mayer noted one of the discouraging facts in a manufacturer's life when he observed: "The more durable the item, the more slowly it will be consumed." He suggested that manufacturers could make some headway against this dilemma by making the older product seem obsolete (by creating obsolescence of material, function, or style). "The trick isn't foolproof," he warned, "but it ought to work a good part of the time—and perhaps can even be planned, assuring the manufacturer of a large, steadily increasing replacement market." Mayer observed that once the matter of subjective judgment is put aside, "it is clear that a pattern of successful style obsolescence must eventually be reinforced by a decrease in the durability of the product."

A number of designing engineers entrusted with shaping United States products meanwhile began showing acute cases of guilty conscience about some of the things they were expected to do. After all, they hadn't been taught during their idealistic days back in college how to build products that would fall apart after an appropriate period of service.

When members of the American Society of Industrial Designers met in the mid-fifties, Harvard Professor and Brigadier General George F. Doriot gave them something to chew on by chiding them because of the quality of their products. He told of his own sad experiences as the owner of an electric range that required servicing every six months, an electric hot-water heater that flooded his basement, and a washing machine that jumped and ran around. Professor Doriot charged:

"You have been called upon to put a varnish of appearance and attractiveness on things that are going down badly. . . . You are increasing the cost of things and their service. I call that cheapening design, and you will eventually lose your reputation."

The engineering journals uneasily mulled the pros and cons of planned obsolescence through materials failure. In April, 1956, *Electrical Manufacturing* ran a think piece called "Design for Planned Obsolescence." It said that the "lifetime" guarantee, once a potent sales appeal, was losing its charm as restless Americans faced with the need of an expanding economy were in a mood to accept planned obsolescence. "The hard logic of our national economy," it said, "would support the need for a broad policy of planned obsolescence in order to take the maximum advantage of our potential for productivity and technological progress."

What does this mean, it asked, "to those men who are responsible for the design engineering of these products? First of all, it means that design for planned obsolescence becomes a legitimate objective." It added that the customer today "will readily purchase an appliance say to serve him no more than two or three or five years, to be replaced at that time by a newer and presumably better model. But he will not accept this limited life for the appliance if he is to be burdened with service and maintenance problems and costs during the same period."

It suggested that "civilian" products should be designed the way military products are designed: for "a reasonably short life span" but for dependability during that short life.

Another journal which anguished over the problem of obsolescence, and more critically, was *Product Engineering*. Its editor charged: "The doctrine of 'planned obsolescence' is carried so far that the product can scarcely hold together for shipment. And maintenance is so difficult and unreliable that replacement is easier."

A reader of this journal protested planned obsolescence and offered a really drastic proposal. He wrote: "Let's stop all this researching and developing for a while! We're up to our glasses in 'progress' now.... We are inundating ourselves with junk. Science devises junk; industry mass-produces it; business peddles it; advertising conditions our reflexes to reach for the big red box of it. To be sure, we are skilled junkmen—but what of us? How far have we advanced? We are junkoriented cavemen!"

The most agonizing soul-searching, however, took place in the pages of *Design News*, a journal for "Product Designers and Engineering Management" during late 1958 and early 1959. And in the process a lot of cats came out of bags. It began when the editorial director, E. S. Safford, offered an editorial entitled: "Product Death-Dates—A Desirable Concept?"

Mr. Safford got right down to cases. "It is of marked interest to learn from a highly placed engineer in a prominent portable-radio manufacturing company," he began, that his product is designed to last *not* more than three years.

"Is purposeful design for product failure unethical? The particular engineer in question stoutly defends his company's design philosophy in two ways: first, if portable radios characteristically lasted ten years, the market might be saturated long before repeat sales could support continued volume manufacturing . . .; second, the user would be denied benefits of accelerated progress if long life is a product characteristic." The editor's informant went on to explain that it takes sales to get money in order to develop "better" performance, "better" styling, and "better" prices for products.

Editor Safford conceded that the consumer's "ten-year investment in portable radios was substantially higher than it would have been had his first radio lasted." But this "force feeding" of the consumer, the editor continued, had "contributed to progress." The contribution? The consumer had paid out over a ten-year period "three times the amount he would have voluntarily spent for this product— if the product had not been designed for short-term existence." How all this "progress" was producing a "better" price or "better" performance for the product was never quite made clear.

"Should engineers resist such a philosophy" if their management specified that it wanted a "short-term product"? Editorial Director Safford did not think they should. He said, "Planned existence spans of product may well become one of the greatest economic boosts to the American economy since the origination of time payments.

"Such a philosophy," he continued, "demands a new look at old engineering ethics. Respected engineers have long sought to build the best, or the lightest, or the fastest, or at the lowest cost—but few have been called upon to provide all of this with a predetermined life span.

"It is very possible that a new factor is entering the economic scene, through the skill of the engineer. This factor is Time, in a new costume, requiring new techniques, new concepts—perhaps new ethics.

"Is this concept bad? We don't think so. Progress in science is accelerating at an exponential rate, and the beneficiaries should be the underwriters."

This call for a re-examination of "old ethics" and the development of "perhaps new ethics" which would countenance death-dating of products hit some raw nerves and brought down a squall of comments on the editor's head.

Reactions came from all over the nation and from engineers and executives working with both large and small companies. (Some of the larger: Whirlpool Corporation, Remington Rand, General Electric, and Fairchild Aircraft & Missiles.) The General Electric man disagreed "in principle" with the editorial but liked it and called it "quite stimulating." On the other hand, the Remington Rand man expressed extreme annoyance. Another engineer congratulated the magazine for raising "this tremendously significant and important subject of product death rates. Whether desirable or not, everyone knows that the concept of limited-life product exists."

Several of the letter writers offered cautious agreement with the thesis of the editorial. They tended to take a let's-be-realis-tic attitude. The Fairchild man thought it "unfortunate" that the nasty phrase "planned obsolescence" had been hung on a type of engineering that "is practiced by nearly all design groups, in all fields, under the guise of economy or efficiency." In designing airplanes, he pointed out, "it is essential that the component or structure which has the least (but acceptable) expected service-life be used as the criterion against which the service life expectancy of every other component is judged. This may be termed 'planned obsolescence' or it may with equal honesty be termed 'Efficient Design.' In short it is wasteful to make any component more durable than the weakest link, and ideally a product should fall apart all at once. . . ."

The Whirlpool engineer-executive likewise made the point that "without a design-life goal, some parts of the product might last far longer than others and incur a needless cost penalty in the process. Setting the actual design-life objective is certainly a policy issue faced by a company's top management. . . . It would undoubtedly vary from one product to another and perhaps be reviewed and changed from time to time as economic or other conditions change. In my experience, a tenor fifteen-year design-life goal is much more common than the threeyear life mentioned for one product."

A reader might wonder why a product's life expectancy should change simply because "economic or other conditions" change.

Another let's-be-sensible letter writer pointed out that a major electrical company builds industrial fluorescent light bulbs so that all bulbs burn out at approximately the same time. "This makes it economically practical to change all the bulbs in one area of a building just before they burn out. It seems to me that we could use a lot more of this type of research."

The majority of the engineers and executives reacting to the editorial, however, seemed angry and bewildered. They appeared to have little enthusiasm for the "new ethics" they were being invited to explore. One said he was "shocked." Another said, "I boiled." A third snorted, "Ridiculous." A fourth called planned obsolescence "a spreading infection." A fifth said, "It is pretty sad when not only manufacturers but a nationally circulated magazine such as *Design News* takes a 'customer be damned' attitude." A sixth suggested, "It is even a crime against the natural law of God in that we would waste that which He has given us." And a seventh—an engineer of the Itek Corporation—sneered, "Please—let 'em last at least as long as the installments! Which they often don't."

The objections to designing death dates into products were primarily three:

1. Death-dating might give engineering a black eye. Jack Waldheim of Milwaukee—who, when the going got hot, was invited to write a "guest editorial"—said, "Such sophism on the part of the

spokesmen for our profession can kill with distrust the public respect for our skill. . . . We [would be] placing ourselves in the position of expertly skilled con men."

2. Death-dating would stultify imagination and creative ability.
Arnold Johnson of Loewy Hydropress complained that the United
States appeared to be turning "its engineers into destroyers; destroyers of their own creativity to satisfy the market. This surely will lead
to the destruction of the engineers' ability to create."

3. Death-dating was cheating the customers out of hard-earned
money. Harold L. Chambers of Remington Rand observed: "I
greatly doubt that any one of us [designers] would wish to apply
this 'principle' of planned short-term failure to his own purchases
of home, auto, piano, and other durable goods involving considerable expense. Why, then, support pressing this principle on 'someone
else'?" Another letter writer wondered how the death-date planners
themselves would like to find they had bought a pencil with one-
fourth inch of lead in it. Several expressed the opinion that if engineers did engage in designing products for a given life expectancy,
then ethics should compel them to insist that those death dates be
printed on the product. One was not optimistic that sales depart-
ments would permit that. Managements might fear, he said, that
such information would be "misunderstood" by consumers.

7. PLANNED OBSOLESCENCE OF DESIRABILITY

"Fashion is a form of ugliness so intolerable that we have to alter it every six months."—Oscar Wilde

THE TECHNIQUE OF MAKING PRODUCTS OBSOLETE by designing them to wear out or to look shoddy after a few years has limited utility. This limit on the usefulness of planned quality obsolescence inspired marketers to search also for other ways to render existing products obsolete. The safer, more widely applicable approach, many soon concluded, was to wear the product out in the owner's mind. Strip it of its desirability even though it continues to function dutifully. Make it old-fashioned, conspicuously non-"modern." As Paul Mazur pointed out, "Style can destroy completely the value of possessions even while their utility remains unimpaired."

Ideally, of course, it would be most satisfying to create this obsolescence in the mind by bringing out a substantially better functioning product. But in fast-paced modern marketing there is very often little new, basically, that can be offered. The manufacturer can't wait for the slow workings of functional obsolescence to produce something really better. Or he feels he can't. So he sets out to offer something new anyhow, and hopes that the public will equate newness with betterness. Fortunately for him, mid-century Americans are prone to accept that equation. The challenge in using this second form of obsolescence creation as a strategy is to persuade the public that style is an important element in the desirability of one's product. Once that premise is accepted, you can create obsolescence-in-the-mind merely by shifting to another style. Sometimes this obsolescence of desirability is called "psychological obsolescence."

Designer George Nelson bluntly summed up the challenge of producing the appearance of change when he stated, in *Industrial Design*: "Design . . . is an attempt to make a contribution through change. When no contribution is made or can be made, the only process available for giving the illusion of change is 'styling.' In a society so totally committed to change as our own, the illusion must be provided for the customers if the reality is not available."

Market researcher Louis Cheskin of the Color Research Institute is another knowledgeable observer who spoke frankly of the lack of significant improvement in United States products. He explained: "Most design changes are made not for improving the product, either esthetically or functionally, but for making it obsolete." Mr. Cheskin made what he felt was an important distinction between planned obsolescence of quality and planned obsolescence of desirability as far as conscience is concerned. He frowned on planned obsolescence of quality as antisocial and also dangerous. "We know a company," he continued, "that actually produced a product for the home to break down in two to three years. It broke down in less than a year. That was bad for the company."

On the other hand, he contended that planned obsolescence of desirability—or "psychological obsolescence"—was "socially justifiable because it redistributes wealth."

Industrial designer J. Gordon Lippincott, on the other hand, appeared less certain of the justification of planning obsolescence through such devices as the annual model change. "Industrial designers today," he said, "have become commercial artists rearranging a lot of spinach to come up with a new model. If we eliminate yearly models, we put a premium on better design. If you're going to live with something a long time, it has to be designed more subtly." In contrast, he said, contemporary gaudy styling "loses its glamour only one notch slower than a streetwalker at dawning."

All the emphasis on style tends to cause the product designers and public alike to be preoccupied with the appearances of change rather than the real values involved, and also tends to force more and more extravagance in the design as the designers grope for novelty. The famed Parisian couturier of the twenties, Paul Poiret, observed: "All fashion ends in excess." In countries such as Switzerland, where designers must still produce forms that are not quickly dated, they shun the excessive use of ornamentation or abstract form.

A producer of products can bring about a pronounced style change in several ways. For example:

He can change the predominant color used. In the late fifties, a great deal of work was done to groom colors for future leadership. In some instances, the "color forecasting" done by industry consultants strongly suggested collaboration if not conspiracy. *Consumer Reports* related, in the late fifties, the success that color consultants for a leading plastics producer had been having. In 1955, the consultants had "forecast that pink would be the leading color. It was. In 1956, turquoise was the predicted leader. It was. This year the prediction was lemon yellow," and it added that if the sale of lemon-yellow baby bathtubs, wastebaskets, bowls, and such could be trusted, then the forecasters were again right on top of the trend.

The producer can change the degree of ornamentation, as from severely plain to gaudy or ornate. A prototype for this kind of change was offered by the classic Greek columns, which evolved from the simple Doric through the slender, ornamented Ionic, to the excessively ornamented Corinthian. Or to take another classic model, after the Middle Ages the style of buildings and their furnishings moved from the bold, crude, clean-lined Renaissance style to baroque, characterized by elegant curves, and then on to rococo, with its fantastic mass of curlicues. These changes took centuries and evolved normally. Modern designers began striving to propel the public through comparable swings of style for their particular products within the span of a few years.

Or, finally, the producer can change the profile, as when he moves the tail fin or hemline up or down, or changes his basic emphasis from vertical to horizontal lines.

In the fifties, designers in a great many fields earnestly studied the obsolescence-creating techniques pioneered in the field of clothing and accessories, particularly those for women. Women's clothing and accessories, by 1960, had become a twelve-billion-dollar industry, much of it created by obsolescence planning. As Mr. Cheskin observed: "Every industry tries to emulate the women's fashion industry. This is the key to modern marketing."

The women's fashion field was ideal for leading the way in planned obsolescence of desirability because here psychological wants have been most rampant. Heine noted long ago that "when a woman begins to think, her first thought is of a new dress." For centuries women have craved for an excuse for a new dress, and so have become coconspirators with the dress marketers. Only those women in the very lowest and very highest social classes in the United States have actually come close to wearing out their dresses in recent years.

When a woman already has a closetful of good-as-new dresses, the best excuse she can offer her husband (who usually considers himself financially hard-pressed) for further splurging is that every dress she owns is out of style. In recent years the dressmakers have stepped up the pace of style obsolescence, so that by 1960 fashion ran through a full cycle every seven to ten years. Women's suits were following a fairly tight ten-year cycle. The seven-to-ten-year cycle was acknowledged by style consultant Tobé who is as close as anyone to being the dictator of style in the United States. Thousands of women's-wear stores depend upon her for guidance.

As early as the thirties, an executive of Filene's in Boston was calling for the creation of more obsolescence in women's clothing "to take up the slack." The most forthright statement of the widely felt need for stepped-up obsolescence of style was made in 1950 to several hundred fashion experts meeting in Manhattan. The speaker was B. Earl Puckett, chairman of Allied Stores Corporation. Basic utility, he said, "cannot be the foundation of a prosperous apparel industry.... We must accelerate obsolescence.... It is our job to make women unhappy with what they have. . . . We must make them so unhappy that their husbands can find no happiness or peace in their excessive savings."

And the following year, Alfred Daniels, merchandising executive for New York's Abraham & Straus, confided to businessmen in *The Harvard Business Review* that he had learned to promote, more or less continuously, new things for women. "Anything new," he said, just as long as it was in fair taste. In the trade, he said, this was called "running up and down stairs."

The trick, he explained, was to "get a lot of fashion cycles working" within the general trend, which some say is more difficult to manipulate. As an example he explained that there may be an "Oriental influence" taking place within the general trend in apparel design for women. The fashion merchant will know about this trend, but "he doesn't need to know how it came about. If he is curious he can call up some fashion expert, who may tell him it is a result of pressure by Mongolian idiots." Mr. Daniels added with no evident regret: "Today the fashion cycle moves so quickly it is a blur."

As for the practice of taking the hemline up and down, it is somewhat more difficult to create obsolescence by taking the hemline up than it is by lowering it. When you are going upward with the hemline, women who are durability-minded or who have stubborn husbands may get out their shears and each season take an inch or so off the bottom of their skirts. To cope with this tendency, a New York fashion advertiser explained to me, you need to do something else while you are raising the hemline. So you widen the waist. Thus American women had the "sack" look—or the chemise—while the hemline was being raised for them in the mid-fifties. Once the designers had reached the maximum height that decency permitted, they ameliorated the ghastly sack look by moving into the high-waisted "Empire" style and then started the hemline down again. And from the high-waisted Empire they quickly moved to the low-waisted look. Meanwhile, designers were broadening the shoulders to create obsolescence. Since shoulders had been narrow, with little material available, there wasn't much that a woman could do to fix over her existing dresses.

Bathing-suit makers had a somewhat different way of creating obsolescence. A buyer for Dallas' Neiman-Marcus explained why the bikini would be the big item for 1960: "The well-traveled waist-line has been going up and down since fashion de-emphasized the bosom, and the spotlight is now on the navel."

Women's shoemakers meanwhile were creating not only obsolescence but havoc by promoting the pointed-toe shoe with its accompanying manifestation, the spike heel. The pointed toe was deplored by doctors and the pin-point heel by the National Safety Council. An Oklahoma scientist has calculated that the spiked heel gives the woman's weight a focused impact equivalent to that of an elephant for a given spot hit by the heel. Tile floors began breaking up under the impact across the nation.

It might be noted that considerable success was also being achieved in creating obsolescence in the engagement and wedding rings that lovers give their betrothed. Old-fashioned people might still hold to the idea that such rings should be cherished till death parts the couple. But credit jewelers had different ideas and succeeded in persuading hundreds of thousands of married women to trade in their "old rings for new-styled ones."

Cosmetic makers, too, were busily introducing style concepts in their selling. One of the secrets of the success of Charles Revson, founder of Revlon, was that he brought fashion to nail polish with widely publicized changes of styles in shading every six months. The shades he unveiled every six months made his old shades obsolete. At one early stage, for example, he sold women on boldness in nail enamel, then subsequently unsold them on bold in favor of muted enamel.

Mr. Revson once explained to me: "Women can take to new things faster than men do. That spells opportunity to you." He said with some scorn that men are more stubborn about accepting style changes. Men have been the despair of aggressive marketers as they have, in vast numbers, dropped vests and hats and have insisted on wearing their shoes until they are literally worn out.

Now, the men's apparel industry has moved rather spectacularly to try to copy the obsoleting techniques used so successfully in women's apparel. The promoters of style swings for men had far to go to match the style change every three months achieved in the women's fashion field, but they had succeeded in achieving a major change for men once a year. It used to take four or five years to see a major change.

The growing preoccupation of the makers of men's wear with "forced" obsolescence was revealed in a report on the forty-first convention of the National Association of Retail Clothiers and Furnishers in 1959. It said: "Although only one speaker brought the subject into the open, forced obsolescence in men's clothing and accessories was a behind-the-scene issue. . . . Several representatives of clothing manufacturers suggested their industry could profitably follow the lead of the women's-wear industry and create obsolescence by more frequent style changes."[1] A few months later, the president of the Reliance Manufacturing Company, in a talk to his salesmen, stated that the "demands" of style obsolescence had become "the major marketing trend in men's wear today."

In fast succession during the mid- and late fifties and early sixties, men were led through the gray-flannel-suit phase, to the charcoal gray, to the Ivy League look, to the cutaway-style Continental look. Ties and lapels became visibly narrower, collars stubbier. Padded shoulders disappeared, as did the loose-falling jacket. An analyst for *The New York Times* concluded that by 1960 "a man wearing a suit and furnishings produced a decade ago would appear completely out of style."

One afternoon recently, your author had to buy a hat and raincoat. At the store where the raincoat was to be bought, the clerk purred: "Would you like the short new length, or the old regular length?" (I took the "old regular.") And at the hat store the clerk tried to explain to me: "Hat brims are shorter this year." A few days later, I read a statement by the president of the Hat Corporation of America, who said: "To make men part with their money, the only thing to sell is fashion. . . . We've got to keep them busy changing their hats."

Men's shoes, too, were finally being planned for obsolescence. *The Journal of Commerce* quoted shoe manufacturers as stating that "we will be making shoes for men, women, and youngsters so distinctive that anyone who clings to the old styles will be conspicuous." Low-cut brogues were being replaced by tapered high risers. The aim was to provide what the manufacturers called their first obsolescence factor in thirty years.

The Leather Industries of America, in fact, began a national campaign to persuade women to buy shoes as gifts for their husbands. Its director agreed that up until recently such a notion in gift-giving would have been inconceivable because men's shoes were "dull." But he added: "Today, men's shoes rival women's in fashion changes. A woman can be convinced that her husband is badly dressed if he wears conventional shoes all the time."

In 1960, the head of the House of Worsted-Tex, one of the nation's largest makers of men's clothing, happily reported that men had been given an entirely different look in a mere five years. He said, "They no longer want just a suit. They want a certain look of elegance, smartness, and success." He added that with the rapid acceleration of new models the industry was finally achieving the style obsolescence it had so long sought. And he concluded that the industry should be prepared to accept the increased costs "that go with such comparatively rapid style changes." Apparently, at least some of these costs were to be passed along to the consumer. The price of suits went up an average of five dollars within a year.

Even pre-teen boys' shoes were slated for obsoleting. They were being designed away from their "sexless" look to a "real nervous" look of flashy casualness. Meanwhile, the obsolescence planners were going to work on children's clothing. *Women's Wear Daily*[2] counted up three factors working to assist the marketers of children's wear at back-toschool season. Factor One was the growing birth rate. Factor Two was the fact that "children still outgrow their clothes." Factor Three was "the advantage of styling obsolescence." The last factor, the journal said, "must be dramatized, utilized, and publicized for all it's worth." And marketers "must pull out all stops."

Quite possibly the recent mood of the American people encouraged the promotion of forced obsolescence of desirability in a variety of fields. Louis Cheskin suggests that psychological obsolescence is a symptom of our times related to the prevalence of "boredom, lack of self-expression, absence of free and truly friendly communication between neighbors and friends, and a general lack of rational values."

The Chicago Tribune's market researchers in their studies of the people in the teeming suburbs found that "the inhabitants of new Suburbia are vitally concerned with taste and style." And housing consultant Stanley Edge observes that the new suburbanites "want to go along with the rest of the crowd."

On the other hand, the idea of promoting style obsolescence regardless of the public's particular mood undoubtedly struck some hardheaded manufacturers as dictated by logic. Periodic style changes in a product not only create new potential customers but put the nation's merchants on the spot to increase their sales of the product in question. The restyled product can have the effect of stimulating the dealers by persuading them that they have something new to sell. Also, periodic style changes enable the manufacturers to keep closer control over the sales quotas of their dealers and to force the dealers to launch crash selling campaigns to clear out their back rooms of old models during the last weeks before the new models are introduced.

For all these reasons the techniques of forced obsolescence of desirability pioneered in the apparel field were soon widely copied by the makers of an astonishing variety of goods, hard and soft.

We have, then, two controversial marketing strategies based on the creation of obsolescence. One is the creation of obsolescence of quality. The other is the creation of obsolescence of desirability.

(In addition, there is the obsolescence created by genuine gain in function, which, as noted, we all applaud.) Let us now look at two fields where the two controversial forms of obsolescence creation have been most energetically attempted. One is in the home and its furnishings. The other is in the motorcar industry. We will consider the motorcar industry first, since this industry is widely regarded as the keystone of the American industrial economy, and since literally billions of dollars a year are spent in obsolescence creation, particularly of desirability.

8. HOW TO OUTMODE A $4,000 VEHICLE IN TWO YEARS

"One of the strangest, yet best recognized, secrets of Detroit is 'planned obsolescence'—a new model every year."—Business Week

AN AUTO-PARTS DEALER IN SPRINGFIELD, ILLINOIS, offered me the opinion that as far as he could figure the United States motorcar had become "a women's fashion item." And an advertising executive working on a motorcar account confessed: "You want to know what sells cars today? It's style, period!" The advertisements certainly seemed to spell out his conviction. Some samples:

Ford: "Nothing Newer in THE WORLD OF STYLE"—or later, "*Vogue* magazine says Ford is a Fashion Success."

Chevrolet: "Styling That Sets a New Style"

De Soto: "Best Dressed Car of the Year"

Oldsmobile: "Start of a New Styling Cycle."

When the new 1960 Pontiac was unveiled, *The New York Times* described its sculptured lines—"a horizontal V front"—and added this observation: "Emphasis is almost entirely on styling, for there are no major mechanical changes."

The automobile industry was the first major group to become fascinated with the increased sales that might be achieved by imitating the women's-fashion stylists. Decades ago, General Motors took the automotive leadership from Henry Ford I by successfully insisting that competition be on the basis of styling rather than pricing. Mr. Ford in fifteen years had brought the price of his Model T motorcar down from $780 to $290, by sticking to a basic design except for minor changes. Such fanatical dedication to the ideal of an ever-lower price tag made competition on the basis of price most unattractive. Competitors such as General Motors did not relish trying to match Old Henry in either production know-how or pricing, so they emphasized a yearly change and a variety to choose from.

In the twenties and thirties, significant technological innovations such as balloon tires, shock absorbers, and four-wheel brakes were available almost every year to captivate the public. By the early fifties, however, the automobile industry was finding itself with fewer and fewer significant technological improvements that it felt were feasible to offer the public. Consequently, at all the major automotive headquarters—Ford now included—more and more dependence was placed on styling. One aim was to create through styling "dynamic obsolescence," to use the phrase of the chief of General Motors styling, Harley Earl. The motorcar makers began "running up and down stairs," as fashion merchandiser Alfred Daniels put it.

"New" became the key word as the manufacturers sought to make car owners feel like old fuds in any vehicle more than two years old. When the 1957 motorcars were launched, Chrysler revealed that it had "The Newest New Cars in 20 Years." Nash had "The World's Newest . . . Car." And Pontiac was "Completely New From Power to Personality." A columnist for *Advertising Age* noted that Buick—which he called the least changed of the new models—had used the word "new" twenty times in an advertisement. He added: "We find it difficult to assume that such complete and utter nonsense is justified by the need to sell 7,000,000 cars in 1957. If our national prosperity is to be founded on such fanciful, fairyland stuff as this, how real and tangible can our prosperity be?"

That, indeed, seemed a fair question. And glory be to an advertising-industry man for raising it!

The intensified preoccupation with obsolescence-through-styling brought new power to the automobile stylists and more than a little grumbling from engineers, who felt they were receiving less and less attention when it came to fixing the format of automobiles.

General Motors' Mr. Earl defined the stylist, incidentally, as "a man who is dissatisfied with everything." At Ford, styling was taken away from engineering and made a separate department. The $200,000-a-year head of this styling department, George W. Walker—"the Cellini of Chrome"—was at one time a stylist for women's clothing. When the 1958 models were launched, he frankly conceded that he designed his cars primarily for women. "They are naturally style conscious," he said, and even though they may not drive the car in many cases they seem to have a major say in the choice of a new car.

When the president of General Motors found himself testifying before a Senate subcommittee in the late fifties, he alluded to the "application of fancification to our automobiles." At another sitting he said, "Styling has become increasingly important in determining the share of the market."

Let us pause and examine in some detail just how "fancification" and other styling devices were systematized to produce obsolescence of desirability in the traveling machines made in the United States.

To comprehend the strategic mapping going on behind all the commotion about styling, we need first of all to understand the shell game Detroit plays with the public. The body shell is crucial to obsolescence planning.

If motorcar salesmen had their way, automobile makers would issue a vehicle that at least *looks* brand new each year or half year. Unfortunately for them, it costs many, many millions of dollars for retooling to overhaul a motorcar's physical form in any fundamental way. Consequently, even in seeking the superficial outer appearances of change, the motorcar makers have depended to a large extent upon illusion created by changes of decoration rather than of the body shell.

As recently as 1956, the Detroit motorcar makers customarily made a major overhaul in their shell only every third year. During the two intervening annual models they simply rejiggered grilles, lights, fenders, and so on. By 1957, the industry was heading toward an overhaul of the shell every second year. One year was becoming known as the year for "basic" change and the other the year for the "trim" change.

And by 1958, insiders were whispering the news—stunning to competitors—that General Motors was going to overhaul the shells of its five motorcars every single year. Each car was to be a new car each year. General Motors was able to achieve this break-through by an interesting expedient made possible by its gargantuan size. It chose to create a new look for its five cars each year by sacrificing some of the distinctiveness in the appearance of each of the five, Chevrolet, Pontiac, Oldsmobile, Buick, Cadillac. (This was before the compacts.) In short, all General Motors cars would bear more than a little family resemblance. The bold decision was made to bring out a brand-new shell each year and to use it for all five cars. Almost all models of all five cars each year would have substantially the same body. The basic body shell was to be stretched amidship about three inches for some of the big Cadillacs and Buicks. Later, there were reports that the three "luxury" compacts, which General Motors began unveiling in late 1960, would also have their own common body shell.

When General Motors' five standard-size cars for 1959 were unveiled, Joseph Callahan, the engineering editor of *Automotive News*, reported that "at least 12 important stampings are identical on all 5 cars."[1] Among the twelve he mentioned were a number of door panels, the upper back panel, three cowl panels.

"The big advantage of the common body," he explained, "is that the manufacturer of a multiple line of cars can save some of the millions it annually spends to create style obsolescence."

Obviously the major hazard in such an approach was the possible appearance of sameness in all General Motors motorcars. Action was taken to reduce this hazard by attaching different trimmings to the basic shell. Strips of painted metal were attached to the doors to produce distinctive sculptured looks. And Callahan added: "Differences also were produced by using a variety of chrome trim, rear deck lids, quarter panels, bumpers and bumper guards. Of course, many interchangeable parts are reworked for different cars and models. Reworking is achieved by changing the location of holes, making minor changes of shape, attaching extra pieces, etc."

Automotive insiders began speculating—and still are—whether the less gigantic Ford and Chrysler companies would be able to follow General Motors' all-new-shell-every-year program. A Senate subcommittee report on "Administered Prices" in the automobile field expressed concern about General Motors' move. It stated: "General Motors . . . alone has the financial resources to play this form of nonprice competition to the full: all other companies have good cause to be deeply alarmed over the future."[2]

Meanwhile, advertising journals surmised that eventually the automobile industry might be able to reach a new-car-every-six-months cycle of innovation.

How could the stylists know what shell to use when they had to design at least three years ahead of the car's unveiling? The styling experts at General Motors held an advantage in trying to anticipate— without exercising more than moderate clairvoyance—what shell or silhouette was likely to be considered smart-looking by the public three years hence. General Motors bought about half of all automobile advertising. Since the silhouette had to be frozen so far in advance of unveiling, General Motors was aided in securing a favorable response from the public three years later by its superior image-building power. As the Senate report pointed out: "Because of its great sales volume it [General Motors] has an immense impact in framing consumer attitudes toward style changes." During Senate hearings George Romney, president of the then-small American Motors, which pioneered the American-built compacts, testified to General Motors' power to mold public taste when he talked about the wrap-around windshield—and the "millinery" aspect of car making. He said that if a small company had introduced the wrap-around, it probably would have been a flop. It took a big company to swing it. Familiarity, he said, brings acceptance. Mr. Romney then made this remarkable comment:

"Now, Senator, in this millinery aspect, in the fashion aspect, a company doing 45 to 50 per cent of the business can make an aspect of car appearance a necessary earmark of product acceptance by the public just as a hat manufacturer—a woman's hat manufacturer—who sold 50 per cent of the hats would have a much easier time of making all other hat manufacturers put cherries on their hats if the cherries were decided by it to be the fashion note for this year." (Mr. Romney spent several heartbreaking years trying to interest the American public in the rationality of compacts and probably succeeded only because of the dazzling logic of his case—and the fact that many American sophisticates had turned to small foreign cars for relief from Detroit's gaudy giantism. This made it psychologically safe for Americans to be seen in small cars.)

During most of the fifties, the General Motors stylists decided that the trend in silhouettes should be toward cars that were ever longer, ever lower, and ever wilder at the extremities. By 1959, one automobile executive was confessing: "In length we have hit the end of the runway." A Chicago official estimated that just getting cars back to the postwar length would release eight hundred miles of street space for parking. There was no question, however, that millions of Americans still wanted the biggest-looking car they could get, particularly if they lived in wide-open areas where parking was not a serious and chronic problem.

Detroit producers who tried to bring out cars that defied the direction in styling General Motors had set—such as Chrysler in the early fifties—were badly mauled.

By the late fifties, Poiret's law that all fashion ends in excess was indubitably being demonstrated in the automotive field. The Big Three stylists were speculating how many more inches they could lower the silhouette before snapping human endurance and overstraining their own ingenuity. A four-wheeled vehicle can be squashed only so far. They used smaller wheels. They sacrificed rigidity. Some of them spread the wheels still farther apart as the only way left to get the engine lower. Meanwhile, the hump down the middle grew. The joke spread that the front seat of the new wide, wide cars could hold two grownups and a midget. One reason General Motors accepted the revolutionary idea of putting a rear-end motor in its Corvair was that this helped solve the hump problem.

As early as 1957, *Automotive Industries* reported that the low silhouette had become so low that "many people feel we have reached bottom." It added, however, "There is a feeling that stylists are aiming even lower." The sight line of drivers had dropped nine inches below the sight line of prewar autos. The following year, *The Harvard Business Review* carried an illuminating paper on product styling by Dwight E. Robinson, professor of business administration at the University of Washington. His investigations had taken him, among other places, to Detroit's secretive studios for styling. He reported: "Stylists recognize that the extreme limits on lowness imposed by the human physique are only a few inches away and [will] come close to realization in the 1960 models."

By 1959, Pontiac's Bonneville hardtop stood just four and a half feet high, a full foot lower than the Pontiac of a decade earlier. Some drivers of late-model makes of cars—where seats were nearly a half foot closer to the floor than they had been a decade earlier—reported they were wearing bicycle clips to keep their pants cuffs from dragging on the floor. People also began discovering that sitting in a low-seated car throws more of the weight onto the end of the spine, a more tiring position for long trips.

In July, 1959, *The Wall Street Journal* reported an astonishing incident that indicated the style swing must certainly finally be approaching its nadir. At General Motors' own annual meeting, shareholders stood up and lamented their personal difficulties in trying to work their bodies into late-model General Motors cars. One man from New Jersey exclaimed, "I bumped my knee and my head getting into" a 1959 Oldsmobile. He was received by a burst of applause. An average-sized man from Massachusetts exclaimed that he found he couldn't sit in a 1959 Buick with his hat on. And he added: "It's a disgrace for a woman to have to get in and out of such low cars."

The reporter commented that General Motors' Chairman Frederic G. Donner "listened impassively and without comment" to these laments.

Six months earlier, the same Mr. Donner was quoted in *Sales Management* as supporting what it referred to as "artificial obsolescence." Mr. Donner was reported stating, "If it had not been for the annual model change, the automobile as we know it today would not be produced in volume and would be priced so that relatively few could afford to own one. Our customers would have no incentive or reason to buy a new car until their old one wore out." He clearly was concerned about giving car owners "an incentive or reason" to turn in their old cars before they wore out physically.

Meanwhile, stylists were striving to justify the new low, low cars on high philosophic or sound functional grounds. A Chrysler stylist told a Detroit gathering of the Society of Automotive Engineers that the low silhouette was all a part of a broad trend to the "low look" in contemporary design. He cited everything from ranch houses to sofas. Others cited the low center of gravity in the new cars as a great aid in cornering. Actually, the banked curves of most of the recently built highways made this a puny plus factor.

As for the trend to wildness at the extremities, this was evidently related stylistically to squashing down the midsection. If you believed the motorcar advertisements, you assumed there was sound functional reason for the fantastic outcropping of tail fins on motorcars in the late fifties. The fins were said to stabilize a moving car in a crosswind. Professor Robinson commented: "I found few designers in Detroit willing to say there is much scientific support for these claims."

Instead, Professor Robinson concluded that the fins began jutting up on the drawing boards as the stylists sought to push the midsection lower and lower. He asserted: "The analogy between this squashing effect and tight lacing at the waist and expansion of the skirt in the crinoline era is almost irresistible." He went on to say, "The tail fin— supposedly derived from the airplane tail—may be interpreted as the last resort of over-extension, an outcropping that quite seriously serves much the same purpose as the bustle or the train."

By the time the 1961 models were appearing, the retreat from the long, low look had begun. Tail fins on almost every make of car—evidently by common consent of the stylists—became visibly smaller. Flared blades gave way to rolled edges.

The groping by automobile stylists for cheap ways to make their new-model cars look different also resulted in a fascination with adding lights during the late fifties. General Motors cars, which once had managed to get about at night with only three lights (two in front and one in the back), began carrying up to fourteen outside lights fore and aft. Apparently the automobile stylists couldn't agree whether all these banks of lights were most needed on the front of the car or on the rear. Some stylists placed them mostly on the front (Cadillacs, Chevrolet Impalas had eight there), whereas others loaded the lights mostly on the rear. On some cars some of the tail lights were dummies, or nonfunctioning.

By 1960, however, anyone who owned a two-year-old car with a dozen or more outside lights could reasonably be expected to feel his car had been dated in an uncomfortable way. Now the designers were achieving a new look by subtracting lights! Likewise, the millions of two-toned and three-toned cars stamped out by the Detroit automobile makers in the mid- and late fifties had become sirens old before their prime. Detroit began promoting monotones. Only on the rooftop was a second color now occasionally permitted. Even the swing of a portion of the market to compacts was not an unrelieved disaster from the styling standpoint. The compacts made the long, fat, gaudy makes of the late fifties—especially those in the lower-prestige lines—seem terribly gauche. Every swing, whether seemingly sensible or seemingly insensible, helps create obsolescence. It is the swing that counts.

It should be noted that Europeans had less and less basis for feeling smug about the way Americans were being enticed by "dynamic obsolescence" in the automotive field. Until 1960, most European makers took pride in their refusal to make changes just for the sake of change. But as the Europeans built up their auto-making capacity at a furious rate to cash in on the opening in the United States and around the world created by Detroit's commitment to gargantuan vehicles, these Europeans found themselves—with the introduction of American compacts—hustling to build markets. This led them to begin making more frequent visible changes in style, in the Detroit manner. Their problem in thus creating obsolescence of desirability in their home markets was, however, complicated. Most European car buyers still had the idea that a motorcar should last a good long time. A sales official of the British Motor Corporation, Ltd., was heard to complain[3] : "All you've got to do is drive out on a Sunday and have a look. You'll find people out washing and polishing cars that are twenty years old. Why, the blighters think more of their old cars than they do of their wives!"

American automakers, when they would talk about their strategy of planned obsolescence of desirability at all, insisted that the annual model switch was essential to the American way of life. A Ford executive argued: "We are confident that the annual change cycle has advantages for the national economy in terms of employment, and it is essential for competitive reasons. The change in the appearance of models each year in creases car sales."

The Big Three of Detroit were spending more than a billion dollars a year to put a new dress on their cars each year. To put it another way, since the consumer of course pays in the end, the average new-car buyer was paying more than two hundred dollars extra to cover the annual cost of restyling the cars. And this did not include the actual cost of the non-functional "bright-work" or "goop" placed on the cars. That added at least another hundred dollars.

A further cost of the annual styling was the loss in quality. Laurence Crooks of Consumers Union put it this way: "The annual model change has a great deal to do with lack of quality in cars, and any speeding up of this changing . . . always redounds to the discredit of the cars. It takes a long time to perfect a car and get the bugs out of it."

Because of all these factors related to style change, American cars were declining in value at a precipitous rate. The Federal Reserve Bank of Philadelphia made a study of this aging problem of "second-hand sirens" and concluded that motorcars were depreciating twice as fast as they reasonably should. It explained:[4] "Because yearly model changes make a car look older than it actually is, mechanically speaking, the price drops faster than the remaining mileage potential. . . . A car four years old with roughly two-thirds of its active life left usually sells for about one-third of its original price. Variety and change accelerate obsolescence." (This calculation assumed a potentially "active" life of twelve years. Actually, that figure appears to be out of date. By 1960, the tendency to junk cars before they were ten years old had become the prevailing pattern. Runzheimer & Company, the expert on fleetoperation costs, found that Detroit-made cars were depreciating almost twice as fast as the little snub-nosed Volkswagen, whose manufacturers consistently scorned the annual model change. While keeping the same profile over the years, however, it quietly introduced hundreds of small changes.)

American motorists by 1960 were trading in their "old" car by the time it reached an average age of two and a quarter years. The Ford Motor Company in one of its advertisements said this showed how smart and shrewd the average motorcar owner was becoming. At that age, it pointed out, the car starts showing minor ailments and dents. Further, it stated, "The car is two years old in style. Its fine edge is gone."

For many of the cast-off beauties produced in the late fifties the "fine edge" certainly was gone. Used-car dealers were calling them "Jonahs." Their heels now seemed run over, their mascara was running, and their chrome jewelry tarnished; their bulk was excessive and their power windows, brakes, and steering wheels frequently malfunctioning.

The styling trend in American automobile design as 1961 approached was away from pink dinosaurism, and toward a more formal design. A design consultant for one of the Big Three automobile producers confided to me what the "main styling stream" was likely to be in the early sixties. He said that a more upright, classical, and austere look was in the works.

Professor Robinson gained much the same impression in his chats with Detroit designers. The trend, he gathered, would be away from the squashed-down, streamlined look to a more "squared-off, boxy look." (There was also at least a promise of more "functional innovation.") He found designers showing fascination with models of early American cars, with their boxy, squared-off looks. Professor Robinson commented: "None of them expressed any astonishment when I raised the question of the likelihood of a revival movement."

The motorcar profile was not only destined to become more upright, but it evidently was essential that any change in profile should be quite drastic. Professor Robinson explained why the change would have to be made abruptly rather than gradually: "Having utilized gradualcompression and lengthwise expansion of the body as a means of differentiating new models from old for so many years, it would be entirely self-defeating for the industry to start building them [just] a few inches shorter or higher. . . . The reason? It would be tantamount to repeating the dimensional style characteristics of 1957-58. The cars would then be duplicates of silhouettes already cluttering up the usedcar lot. . . . A fashion can never retreat gradually and in good order. Like a dictator it must always expand its aggressiveness—or collapse."

Eric Larrabee found in the late fifties that harassed motorcar designers were wondering how much longer their magic would continue to work. However, they were alone in their uneasiness. He related: "Everyone else in Detroit seems to believe that the designers will be able to go on pulling new models out of the hat indefinitely." In mid1960, a spokesman for one of the Big Three was hinting that "specialized vehicles" were being carefully considered—presumably to promote the more-cars-per-family trend. And he suggested that because of the staggering costs and diminishing effectiveness of resculpturing cars each year, the annual model changes would start involving less "massive and exotic changes." It turned out, however, that even the compacts that appeared in 1960 were being drastically restyled for 1961.

Earlier, as the sixties loomed, *U.S. News & World Report* carried a report for its business readers on "The Big Changes Coming in Autos." A subhead read: "Ahead: Much Restyling."

Let us look next at evidences of obsolescence in quality in the motorcar field. Some of the evidence of quality loss can be attributed, as indicated, to the frequent shifts in design produced by the straining to create obsolescence of desirability. But there is also some evidence of quality loss that cannot be explained by frequent styling changes.

9. AMERICA'S TOUGHEST CAR—AND THIRTY MODELS LATER

"Letting his fins down, Clare Briggs, Chrysler vice president, last week . . . said, auto service is bad, and the quality of cars is 'not as good as 10 years ago.' The auto industry, admitted Briggs, 'has treated the public badly, to say it mildly.'"—Time, June 2, 1958.

A FRIEND OF MINE WAS INTERESTED IN MR. BRIGGS'S candid observation that he wrote asking Mr. Briggs to amplify why he felt this drop in quality had occurred. Second thoughts or more cautious counsel had apparently persuaded Mr. Briggs to put his fins back up. He replied by sending a clipping in which an automotive driver praised the Chrysler Corporation's then-current Imperial. In the article, the Imperial was hailed, but for reasons that had little bearing on durability. Examples: the car's pick-up, looks, deep door pockets, deep carpeting, big trunk, maneuverability, quiet motor, brakes, turn indicator switch, side mirror.

In fairness to Mr. Briggs it should be stated that his own company has had a reputation for being more engineering-minded than some of its major competitors. But still his observation about the general decline in the quality of cars was a squalid commentary on an industry that boasts of spending hundreds of millions of dollars each year on "research and development." Little of the money appears to have gone to improve the longevity of motorcars. In 1956, the motorcars being led to the scrap-yard chopping blocks were three years younger than the motorcars being scrapped in the late forties. The Automobile Manufacturers Association chose to explain away this awkward fact by asserting that motorists in the fifties coddled their cars less than those in the forties, when motorcars were in short supply, and when Americans found how surprisingly long a car could be kept running. The association preferred to compare the 1956 longevity with the prewar 1941 longevity. Even here, however, it had little to shout about. In the fifteen-year span, the automakers had managed to add only a fraction of one year to the life expectancy of automobiles. During the same fifteen years, medical science had added many years to the longevity of the nation's human beings. It should also be added that in those fifteen years there had been a great increase in smooth, paved roads. Meanwhile, the major motorcar makers had almost entirely stopped stressing durability in their sales appeals.

In late 1958, *Printers' Ink* conceded that "there is a widespread feeling that 'they don't make cars the way they used to'—either mechanically or from the point of view of interior decor." And an official of the Automotive Finance Association in testifying at a Senate subcommittee hearing told of a survey he had conducted with association members on the state of the automobile industry. He quoted one member as responding: "The quality of today's automobile does not compare favorably with past years. . . . The price of the product continues to go up and the quality continues to go down. Improvement in automobiles in the past few years has strictly been tinsmith work."

Meanwhile, *Automotive News* reported charges that new cars were missing bolts, that they suffered from malfunctioning parts, squeaks, rattles, and other maladjustments that had become "the rule and not the exception in present American cars." The charge was made that motorcar manufacturers had been resorting to "slipshod assembly method" and that the "poor quality of mass production cars" was becoming evident.

The American Automobile Association released some figures on automobile breakdowns which indicated that the mounting garage bills of individual motorists were not isolated cases. It disclosed that although motorcar registrations rose by less than one million from 1957 to 1958, the number of motorcar breakdowns leaped upward by five and one half million!

Sale of automobile parts soared year after year. Partly, of course, this was caused by the increase in the number of cars on the road. But partly, the executive vice-president of a Long Island ignition parts manufacturing firm told *The Wall Street Journal* in 1960, it was because "manufacturers are building them so they'll get to the junk pile faster.... But they're compensating," he added, "by making them give better performance." As an example, he said, the shock absorber was currently being designed to give more cushioning but not to last as long as older types. Also, he observed, "today almost as soon as new cars hit the street they need replacement parts for all the gadgets they are loaded with."

How much of this evident obsolescence of quality was planned? Certainly, as indicated, some of it was due to the industry's haste in rushing out its annual models each fall with rejiggered trimmings and added accessories. But some of it also undoubtedly was due to the reluctance of many of the manufacturers to make a car that would hold the affection of its owner for more than a very few years. In all of the arguing about motorcar design, the makers kept their eye on the ball. And that ball was their total annual dollar volume in sales.

If maximum dollar volume was their goal, then the temptation was great to do three things: upgrade the price of the car; sell the car to as many people as possible; and make sure the buyers would be on the market again before too long to buy another car. The inevitable result of such thinking was best summed up in a letter to *The Wall Street Journal* in the late fifties by Mr. Glenn Ashworth of Morgantown, West Virginia. Mr. Ashworth was critical of current automobile design. It was apparent from his technical discussion that he was knowledgeable on the subject. He attributed the current state of motorcar design to this factor:

"Maximum sales volume demands the cheapest construction for the briefest interval the buying public will tolerate."

In one succinct sentence Mr. Ashworth enunciated what appears to be an Iron Law of Marketing in mid-century America.

Willingness to follow the dictates of the Iron Law seems to vary by divisions within an automobile-making company. Engineers tend to resist the law more than stylists, who are much more sales-oriented. This difference in willingness to bow to the law has produced significant differences in the rate at which quality deterioration appears in different sectors of the motorcar.

The parts of the motorcar still clearly controlled by the engineers— those out of sight under the hood—have tended to maintain their quality longer than the visible parts more fully controlled by the stylists. The chief of Runzheimer & Company, which specializes in estimating costs of automobile fleet operations, takes a dim view of some aspects of recent automobile design, but he has found that the innards of motorcars have shown consistent improvement. "Mechanical dependability, reflecting design of the vital motive and transmissions parts and quality of metals used, has greatly increased during the past twenty years." And he offered the interesting incidental information that "noticeable deterioration in over-all car performance, and the consequent increase in over-all operating costs, usually begins somewhere between 45,000 and 60,000 total miles." It is during this mileage span, he indicated, that it makes sense to think about turning in your car on a new one.

One engineering journal carried the charge in 1959 that engineers were falling down on the job because little was being achieved in prolonging the life of engines and improving their thermal efficiency. At least, however, the engineers were not charged with building engines for shorter life spans than formerly.

Laurence Crooks, the chief automotive expert at Consumers Union, has concluded that today's engines are "very good." However, his comments became scathing when he talked about the trend of automobile design as a whole. His auto-testing experience has convinced him that "the quality on the whole has been going downhill. . . . Stuff keeps falling off."

Mr. Crooks spoke nostalgically of the 1941 Chevrolet as a motorcar that really had built-in quality and sensible proportions. To cite another example, he said that few cars today were as solidly and sensibly built as the postwar Hudsons. And the 1952 Chevrolet is a car he remembered with fondness. He felt that the 1959 Chevrolet was no match for the 1956 model. Speaking of the quality of cars in general, he told me in 1959: "Cars were better built five years ago for the state of the technology existing at the time than they are today. The cars then were more honestly built."

The bodywork of motorcars and their structural rigidity were not as good as they had been a decade ago, he felt. And this widespread lack of structural rigidity had played a major role in promoting "creative obsolescence." Nothing makes a car seem old faster than rattles. And motorcars produced in recent years have tended to develop rattles faster than they did a decade earlier. Further, he said, "the rattling gets worse as the car grows older. With the vogue for hardtops—into which less structural stiffness can be built—this characteristic is getting worse." In 1959, *The Wall Street Journal* took note of all the complaints about late-model cars by conducting a survey. It quoted the owner of an automobile repair shop in Detroit as saying that engine quality was commendable but that "the bodies today are cheesy. They're full of rattles."

Another thing that makes a fairly new car seem cheesy and old— regardless of its dependability in transporting its owner—is exterior rust and corrosion. In the late fifties, many models developed mottled looks with a rapidity that appalled their owners. Some motorcar makers such as Oldsmobile installed corrosion-resistant aluminum grilles as a sales feature because of all the unhappiness, but others evidently were content to let the discolored splotches appear. Frequent resculpturing of the exterior was said to be one cause of the difficulties. The widespread use of salt on roads might also be a factor. But some of the corrosion, it was charged, was being deliberately encouraged. Financial writer Sylvia Porter quoted officials of an industrial-design firm as asserting that "alloys are designed to rust instead of last."

Consumer Bulletin, published by Consumers' Research, Inc., took note of all the complaints about quick-rusting bodywork by reporting: "There seems to be no doubt that bodies of present-day cars could be made to last much longer than they now do, but manufacturers are fully aware that if they make their cars too durable, future sales will suffer; consumers will naturally tend to keep their cars longer before turning them in if bodies have well resisted corrosion and other types of damage that mar appearance."

These "other types" of damage that mar appearance with distressing frequency often appeared inside the car: tattered floor mats, sagging springs, grimy or worn upholstery. A new-car dealer told *Automotive News* in 1957 that he was "ashamed" of most of the recent models he had sold which then had up to 20,000 miles on them. He said, "The interior trim looks as if it may have been dragged behind for at least half of the miles. . . . The upholstery in the cars today may be fancier and have the 'metallic buildup story' but brother, watch out! If the manufacturers cannot sell with the new cars a good, durable, longwearing upholstery, why not send the new cars out without the seats upholstered and let us install good seat covers?"

In considering the shrinking durability of modern cars, we should also take note of the shortened life span of a number of individual parts.

Take tires. A leading chemical scientist working for a tire company told me in the early fifties that he had high hopes a tire would be developed that would last 100,000 miles. Perhaps he was just being woolly-headed, but at any rate in the following years when technological miracles were said to be happening on all fronts, the life expectancy of tires kept going down and down. *The Wall Street Journal* reported in 1959 that "tire company engineers privately concede tires are wearing out faster these days." The manager of the American Chicle Company's fleet of 430 cars told *Journal* investigators, "We've not only noticed that we get less mileage, we've computed it to be 25% less." He added that his tires were now averaging about

15,000 miles. A few months earlier, the *Journal of the Society of Automotive Engineers* carried a report by an official of the Goodyear Tire & Rubber Company stating that in three recent years treadwear life on American tires had dropped 18 per cent. A comparative analysis of tread-mileage on *first-line* 6.70-15 tires of various makes tested by Consumers Union in two different years showed these spreads from best to poorest:

1954—The range was from 22,000 to 31,000 miles.

1958—The range was from 18,000 to 27,500 miles.

Conditions for the tests can never be precisely duplicated, but still these figures would suggest a sharp downward trend was occurring in tire tread-mileage.

One explanation offered by tire-company officials for the decline in the life expectancy of tires has been the trend to smaller fourteen-inch wheels as a styling feature. But note that the above comparisons were all made on the basis of a fifteen-inch wheel! Undoubtedly, the trend during most of the fifties to higher-powered, bulkier cars and power brakes helped the decline along. *The Wall Street Journal's* report on the tire situation included two observations of particular interest. It said that "auto companies generally maintain a stony silence when questioned about complaints of declining tire mileage." And what about the tire companies? *The Journal* reported:

"Of course there's no reason to believe that the tire companies themselves are particularly upset about faster-wearing tires, although it's a blow to their engineers' professional pride. Tires which wear out rapidly mean more sales."

Or take the mufflers. We noted in Chapter 4 that they have been burning out faster than they did a decade ago. This shortened life span, in fact, could be stated quite precisely. Automobile mufflers in 1958 had only one half the life expectancy of mufflers bought a decade earlier. *Design Sense*, published by Lippincott & Margulies, the industrial-design firm, took note of the shortened life span of mufflers in calling on industry to take advantage of new technologies to give longer life to products. "To take just one example," it said, "a major steel company has had available for some time—with no takers—a lead-coated steel which, for *just 8 cents more* per auto muffler, would give a product that would last the life of the car. Instead, automakers are still installing mufflers that must be replaced on an average of once every two years at a cost to the consumer of $18 to $27 per muffler."

But perhaps a change was coming. At least American Motors—which was leading the fight against obsolescence planning in both the automotive and appliance fields—announced a ceramic-coated exhaust system for both muffler and tail pipe of its 1961 Ramblers. The process was first developed by the military for jet planes and was said to make exhausts virtually impervious to corrosion. The company said in making the announcement that, while the process is more expensive, it is in line with the company's policy of seeking greater product durability.

Motorcar makers interested in building a more durable vehicle might well examine for inspiration Citroën's "Deux Chevaux," which reportedly often runs 100,000 miles over all sorts of roads with practically no maintenance. It has an eighteen-month waiting list of eager Frenchmen.

Or better still, the motorcar makers might try copying some of the features of the Model A Ford, perhaps the most rugged motorcar ever built. Many hundreds of these four-bangers are still getting daily use in North America three decades after they were built. They have been used to tow cars two decades younger to the scrap-yard crushing machines; and are eagerly sought by collectors and hot rodders alike. The Model A's straightforward frame (a simple set of rails with three connecting members), its rear end, its differential gears, and its engine have proved in thousands of hot-rod races to be very rugged indeed.

One of the happiest motorcar owners I know is a sales representative who must often travel fifty thousand miles a year and has long felt bedeviled by the high maintenance cost of his cars. He heard that the Checker company—maker of taxicabs—was starting to make a few thousand extra cars each year for sale to the general public. Every time he went to New York, he made a point of riding in Checker cabs and pumped the drivers on performance. He relates, "They always gave it high praise for durability, and seemed unanimous that it goes one hundred thousand miles without a valve or ring job." He encountered several drivers whose cars had passed the two-hundred-and-fifty-thousand mark in mileage. The simplicity of maintenance also appealed to this man. Quickness of repair is vital for cab operation. He points out, "The four fenders are bolted on, and when they are damaged the replacement cost is only about twenty-five dollars."

Several months ago this man bought a Checker Superba and has become very fond of it. He explains, "We all love the level floor in the passenger compartment—no hump—and the wonderful visibility, the headroom, the wide doors, and the short turning radius." (It can turn around in a thirty-seven-foot circle.) Now let us turn from the American motorcar to the American home and explore the extent to which obsolescence through deterioration of quality is promoting sales of the products that go into the home. Here, the evidence of deterioration is substantial indeed.

10. THE SHORT, SWEET LIFE OF HOME PRODUCTS

"My mother had the same washing machine for twenty years. She has the same refrigerator now she had when I went to high school thirty years ago. . . . We [my own family] built a 'leisure house' five years ago. . . . We're on our second washing machine and our second drier. . . . We threw out the disposal. . . . We're on our third vacuum cleaner."— Industrial designer J. Gordon Lippincott

PROBABLY WE ALL TEND TO LET NOSTALGIA COLOR our recolections as to the durability of our family possessions in earlier decades. Still, the trade press in the home-furnishing field is not given to nostalgia, and all during the past decade it reported evidence of a lowering of quality of such goods as rugs, furniture, upholstery, television sets, refrigerators, stoves, and lamps. One retailer was reported observing: "There's no such thing any more as a consumer durable. They are all semi-durables, with the accent on the semi." He found the serviceable life expectancy of a range then to be about seven years, and some of these new automatic washers not even three years.[1] (Other sources gave longer life expectancies.)

One of the trade journals that carried discussions of quality deterioration in some lines was *Home Furnishings Daily*. In 1957, it carried two articles on lower quality found in house-wares (such as toasters). Its investigator reported: "Many housewares manufacturers are cheapening the quality of their products, and are likely to step up this process even more in the months to come." Later that year, the journal made a survey of 127 appliance dealers and reported finding increasing difficulties caused by faulty appliances and television sets being sent back by customers, often a few weeks or months after purchase. According to the dealers, their worst problems came in these fields, listed in descending order of aggravation:

1. Washing machines
2. Refrigerators
3. Driers
4. Television sets
5. Washer-dry combos
6. Ranges
7. Air conditioners
8. Freezers.

The particular parts that were reported causing the most trouble were, first of all, timers. Others cited were controls, motors, cabinets, finishes, components and soldering, tubes, thermostats, pumps and switches, wiring and defrosters, transmissions and valves. Behind the difficulties, the dealers felt, were such causes as lack of quality control, poor inspection, poor craftsmanship, poor engineering, and "workers who don't care."

Other complaints focused on the word obsolescence. A financial columnist for *The New York Herald Tribune* grumbled about the fascination with "dynamic obsolescence" being shown by appliance makers and said, "The only dynamism we've spotted in the appliances around our house is the way they deteriorate after not too much use." And the chief of the product-testing department of a business firm complained to an appliance technical conference of the American Institute of Electrical Engineers in 1958: "The poor consumer is really the fall guy! Year after year this consumer copes with appliances that cost more and more and, in many cases, give less and less satisfactory service. . . . The rumor that appliances are being built for only a limited life—to serve the great god, obsolescence— does the industry harm."

A part of the breakdown pattern apparently was the loading of the appliances with gadgets that often immobilized the whole machine when they failed. Another aspect of the high breakdown rates was the growing use of plastic parts that snapped or warped. Often the plastics were not intended for the usage to which they were put. And then there were charges that appliance makers were cutting down on the gauge of steel, the size and number of bolts, and the quality of interior finishes where corrosion protection is important.

In addition, there was specific indication that evidence of quality obsolescence was not unconnected with the drive to increase replacement sales as the industry fought off glut. An appliance buyer commented on the glutting of the market for appliances in 1956 and wondered if the makers would try to get out of this mess by deliberately producing for "a short life in order to keep it turning over." An electrical manufacturing company official, obviously aware of the same temptation, warned the following month in the same journal (*Retailing Daily*), "If we are to create obsolescence . . . and find ourselves making products that last too long, we must rely on something besides mechanical deficiencies to create a replacement market."

Possibly some manufacturers were not too careful about finding "something besides mechanical deficiencies" to move goods. As the appliance industry began pulling out of its severe recession in 1958, a business writer for *The New York Times* reported:[2] "Spokesmen for stores say the recovery may be due to obsolescence or breakdown of appliances, combined with a spurt of confidence in the general economy. Manufacturers add that an increase in residential building recently also is a factor."

Was something more than reasonable wear and tear involved in creating this "obsolescence or breakdown"? Perhaps not, at least in many cases. But let us look at reports on the trends in quality for some specific products that are supposed to help make a house a home.

THE FAMILY WASHER. This, as we have indicated, leads the list of the home appliances most likely to cause trouble soon after purchase. Monte Florman, chief of the appliance-testing division at Consumers Union, said: "These are the biggest offenders in my experience and also on the basis of the relatively larger volume of mail that Consumers Union receives from dissatisfied users." He said they should be planned for heavy use, but often are not. A substantial percentage of the new machines fail in some way during the months the Consumers Union test them. He feels there is no question that home washers could be made more durable, but that it might involve leaving off some of the gloss and gadgetry to maintain the present price level.

Many complaints by consumers seem to center on the malfunctioning of plastic parts of the washers. A *Wall Street Journal* report on consumer dissatisfaction with modern home products reported a number of complaints about grief caused by plastic parts.

The chief of a market-research firm told me that some of the embarrassingly early and conspicuous breakdowns of appliances were due to errors in estimating the product's death date; they broke down before the warranty period was up. On the other hand, some of the breaking down undoubtedly resulted from simple corner-cutting or haste to get out a new model, with the companies that were driving for increased sales showing less concern about durability of their product than the public might assume it deserved. When the Philco Corporation bought a washer-producing company, it inherited a tub full of trouble in the form of rusted bearings in the inherited company's washing machine (Power-Surge). It seems that a plastic device in the base of the tub of many of these washers would not withstand the heat of wash water. The device cracked and let water seep down into the bearings. Philco finally felt obliged to offer to pay owners their full purchase price if the owners would turn in their Power-Surge on a current model.

Some Hotpoint models made in 1955, 1956, and 1957 proved so troublesome that sales for its home-laundry appliances slipped for a while. Citing Hotpoint's tribulations, a business writer for *The New York Herald Tribune* made this interesting comment:[3] "Distributors were getting six or seven repair calls a year on these Hotpoints, compared with a national average of two or three repair calls." Note that national average!

In order to get back in the good graces of its buying public Hotpoint announced a $10,000,000 repair and replacement program. Soon, however, *Sales Management* was reporting that Hotpoint had stopped publicizing the program. It surmised that too many people were applying for replacement and sending costs "right through the roof. Hotpoint service departments tell us they are flooded with demands for new machines." The moral of all this, the journal admonished its marketing readers, is "Don't jump into a replacement or repair program. Carefully evaluate the cost, the customer response. One-tenth of your products may be defective, but nine-tenths of your customers might like new models at your expense."

One company that had been very slow to change its models was Maytag. Consumers Union reported a few months ago that the basic form of the Maytag washer had not changed in many years. Perhaps it was no coincidence that Consumers Union tests regularly showed the Maytag washer as being of consistently high over-all quality. And when I asked my local repairman—who has been at the bedside of our fouryear-old washer three times this year—to name a really well-built washer, Maytag was the one that occurred most emphatically to him.

THE FAMILY REFRIGERATOR. Here, too, gimmickery has seemed to fascinate many producers more than durability. The 1958 appliance technical conference of the American Institute of Electrical Engineers was scolded about the "flood of flimsy gadgets and accessories [mostly plastic] that plague the user." An example cited was the snapping of the plastic handles of crisper drawers. Plastics have appealed to producers not only because they are usually cheaper than metal but also because their built-in colors help promote selling on the basis of style and impulse.

It should be noted, of course, that plastics can vary considerably in ruggedness. They can be heavy or thin. Plastic dials and knobs can have a metal sleeve to take the screw, or they can be just plastic. The latter are the more likely to pull off in your hand. Also plastics can be tough or fragile. *Appliance Manufacturer*[A] pondered the "oddity" that the manufacturers were frequently not using the most durable plastics available. It talked about "parts and accessories in refrigerators that looked fine in the showroom, but discolored or cracked under normal home use . . . [yet] there were plastics available which would have cut costs—maybe not quite as dramatically—and performed adequately in the application." It chose to blame this "oddity" on the industry's headlong, single-minded rush to cut cost.

THE TELEVISION SET. A few years ago a guided-missile expert named Fred Stevens working for Northrup Aircraft, Inc., said there was no technological reason now why television sets could not be built that would run for eight years without a single repair call. This could be done, he said, if television makers used techniques employed in building missiles.

Such a statement simply revealed that Mr. Stevens, with his head buried in defense work, was badly behind the times. As *Consumer Reports* pointed out, he "hasn't heard of the emphasis among manufacturers of consumer goods on built-in obsolescence."

At Consumers Union a majority of the 1958 test samples of portable television sets bought developed failures within a few weeks of being purchased, while being tested, and had to be repaired. Consumers Union reported it had also been encountering an increasing number of set failures in twenty-one-inch table models.

Karl H. Nagel, head of Consumers Union television testing division, told me that despite all the miraculous claims made in television advertising, a television set made in 1952 offered a "nicer picture" than sets made in 1959. He said: "There has been no major advance in terms of the quality of the received picture since the early 1950's." And he felt that sets made in 1947 were better constructed than those being offered for sale a decade later. In 1947, television sets were able to reproduce all the picture components contained in the "signal" sent out by a broadcasting station. In 1956, not a single one of the sets tested could reproduce the transmitted picture!

Mr. Nagel pointed out that skimping had been taking place particularly in tubes, both in number and quality. A television set made in 1947 had more than thirty tubes. By the late fifties, some sets had only half as many because the makers had been designing multiplefunction tubes. When such a multiple-function tube goes bad in one part, you must throw the whole thing out. Furthermore, he said, "Tubes just don't last as long." Most of them today don't have the life that earlier tubes had, so that they can't take the continuous use the earlier tubes could take. They are built "too close to operative limits."

A number of other competent witnesses have also remarked on the declining quality of modern television sets. Testers at Consumers' Research, for example, found that the 1957 television receivers were in general not as good as the 1956 models in quality and performance. And, in 1957, a spokesman for the National Appliance and Radio-TV Dealers Association lamented that the quality in television sets had become so poor that dealers couldn't make a "decent profit" if they tried to make good on all complaints. He said: "It is not enough that 80 per cent of the TV sets sold function normally. We all know that one rotten apple can spoil the whole barrel."

Don Baines, a columnist for *Home Furnishings Daily*, noted uneasily in the late fifties that many appliance manufacturers were rushing to get into the field of servicing their equipment. He asked: "Why all the rush to get into the servicing angle? Is it because the appliance won't stay in A-1 working order too many days after it is installed in the home?" He added that a suspicious person might begin to wonder "just how good the appliances are." And he concluded: "I'm beginning to suspect that the manufacturers know something consumers don't know and frankly I'm worried. Is that blasted little TV set of mine due to conk out again?"

Some companies, it should be noted, show a greater dedication to the ideal of quality than others. Zenith is one company that has gone slowly in embracing innovations and cost-cutting short cuts. And it has fought to build and maintain a "quality" image. In 1959, Consumers Union listed seventeen television sets in the twenty-one-inch category and found only one that deserved to be check-rated. It was a Zenith.

SMALL APPLIANCES AND OTHER HOUSEWARES. Trade reports commented throughout the late fifties on an upsurge of early breakdowns of some types of household electric wares. In many brands returns were running up to half of all items sold. And, of course, many people who had bought "lemons" or won them as trading-stamp premiums didn't bother or weren't able to return them. *Retailing Daily* reported that those returned by indignant customers demanding replacement were usually replaced. The defective ones were repaired and then "resold during storewide clearances or at special sales for 'demonstration and floor models.'" The most troublesome electric housewares, it said, were toasters, irons, and percolators. All three use thermostats, which often failed.

In 1957, the same journal (which had changed its name to *Home Furnishings Daily*) reported that manufacturers were "watering" their products in dozens of different ways to cheapen them. It mentioned reduction of the thickness of plating, substitution of cheaper materials, and reduction in the size of products. It concluded that in some cases the "high end of the line"—or the highest-priced models offered by a manufacturer—were "no better quality-wise than the low end was a few years ago." Consumers Union expressed its disgust with the quality of toasters being offered the public. It pointed out in 1956 that although pop-up, self-timing toasters had been on the market for several decades, only three out of a sample of twenty-two tested were high in quality. Many of the test samples were defective, and some were downright hazardous. At about the same time, *Retailing Daily* noted that "switches on rotisseries have been turning bad lately."

In 1960, *Home Furnishings Daily* reported that breakdowns on electric housewares were setting an all-time record. Significantly, however, there was now a reduction in the breakdowns that came under the warranty guarantees. Manufacturers had been straining mightily to relieve themselves of responsibility for breakdowns, which they found "very expensive." They evidently did this by (1) making sure the products would outlast the warranties and (2) cutting back the warranties. Many dealers in the San Francisco area lamented that they often could not return merchandise to manufacturers when the item proved defective after a few weeks' use.

If cost cutting was behind much of the deterioration in the quality of appliances, how much more would it cost to make more rugged appliances? There was testimony that it would not cost much. In 1958, the director of product engineering at Whirlpool Corporation told appliance engineers meeting in Chicago, "If we would look closely at our products, it would be apparent that improvements can be made at little or no expense." An official of the Electrical Testing Laboratories in New York offered the opinion that many improvements could be made in electrical appliances without undue cost which aren't made. He expressed belief that the industry feels products should be made with only the "required utility" to keep pace with competitors.

Laundromat washing machines usually are more rugged than machines sold to the home user, and last many hours longer without breaking down. Their cost of manufacture is comparable to that of the home machines because they come without the jukebox effects and gimmicks felt to be desirable for the home market.

So much for the quality of appliances. Let us now examine the obsolescence in quality observable in several categories of home furnishings. The philosophy guiding many manufacturers was described to me by Louis Cheskin of the Color Research Institute. It was his conviction that the public was largely responsible for encouraging the philosophy. He put it this way:

"Why make the handles on cups so that they won't break off? Who wants to pay 10 per cent more for dishes so that the dishes will last a lifetime? Most housewives want or welcome an excuse to buy a new set of dishes every year or so. Who wants furniture to last forever? The large American middle classes do not. They want furniture to be in style, not outdated. . . . Furniture, clothes, dishes can all be made to last longer at very little additional cost. But neither the maker nor the consumer is interested in this."

The makers of home furnishings might be cheered by such a rationale as Mr. Cheskin offered, but they felt that American consumers still had a long way to go in shedding old-fashioned ideas about durability. Many felt that—unfortunately for them—most North Americans still tended to think of homes as symbols of permanence. Thus prospective customers seemed to feel vaguely guilty if they weren't assured that the carpet or chair they were buying would last a lifetime. A trade journal noted this lack of reasonableness when it contrasted the attitude of the typical mattress buyer with that of the typical automobile buyer. The motorcar buyer, it said, cheerfully pays $4,500 for a motorcar that he expects to get only two or three years' use out of, and yet the same man "practically demands a gold-plated guarantee that the new luxury mattress [costing only two hundred dollars] will be good to his dying day."

Such consumer attitudes as these, it said, "have been bedeviling the entire home furnishings industry." Here, then, are some comments and facts concerning the levels of quality that have become widespread in the past few years for specific home furnishings.

FLOOR COVERINGS. During a panel discussion in Atlanta between housewives and rug merchants, one housewife asked a question which trade-press reports called "the bombshell question." She began by pointing out that sixteen years before she had bought a rug for eighty-five dollars, had given it hard use every day, and it "has not lost any of its color." Further, it showed no worn spots and no worn nap. Her "bombshell" question was this: "Do any of the carpet companies make any such quality as that now?" It was unanswered.

The trend in rug quality was summed up by Mildred E. Brady, editorial director of Consumers Union, in these words: "There is no doubt whatever that until recently very good rugs have lasted from generation to generation. Today, ten years is the commercially promised life for a good wool rug."

A multitude of the rugs being sold were far from being "good" by even the lowered standards prevailing. Carpet mills received so many complaints from customers about poor-wearing carpeting in the late fifties that they tightened up their complaint procedures to protect themselves. Very quietly the rugmakers began putting a two-year ceiling on the period that they would listen to grievances. *Retailing Daily* reported that the retail rug dealers were uneasy about this twoyear ceiling the manufacturers had imposed even though it was generous by appliance or automotive standards. They felt that the manufacturers "would have to begin to educate consumers to the idea that carpeting of today will not wear as long as the floor coverings that their parents had." The journal continued:

"As one furniture dealer states it: Today's consumer expects carpet to last as long or longer than her mother's because she is paying three times as much for it. She knows her mother's carpeting lasted between ten and fifteen years. This was said to be not an unreasonable expectation but also one which the consumer had to be educated away from. The buying public does not accept readily the idea of obsolescence in carpets and rugs."

The same journal quoted the owner of an interior-decorating shop in Birmingham, Alabama, who voiced considerable distaste for products that would last twenty years in view of all the easy credit available. Speaking of floor coverings, he asked: "Why should it last forever, or even ten years for that matter?" He urged manufacturers to forget about how long a product would last and to concentrate on getting out good quality fashion merchandise. His main interest, presumably, was on the word "fashion."

A part of the trouble with modern carpeting was that the manufacturers had downgraded quality and fought off quality standards. Another problem was the introduction of tufted carpets, which could be made much faster and cheaper than woven carpets. The makers of woven rugs reduced the quality of their rugs in order to compete more effectively with the tufted rugs. Another reason for the deterioration was that much of the carpeting was being bought by big housing developers who tended to install the cheapest floor covering they could in order to increase their profit margins. Still another problem was that the long-wearing wool from wild sheep—which helped make grandma's rugs so durable—was becoming difficult to procure.

Meanwhile, customers were being lured by promises of miraculously long-wearing rugs in sales messages that stressed the nylon content of the new offerings. Such promises were in large part illusory. This was demonstrated when the du Pont Company reduced the price of nylon to rug manufacturers. An industry poll was taken to find out whether this lowering of nylon costs would be reflected in either lower prices for rugs or in better quality in rugs. The majority opinion was that there would be no change whatever! *Retailing Daily* explained why in these words: "It was frequently pointed out that there is so much misrepresentation on nylon blends in the retail field that many customers buying them actually think they are getting all-nylon carpets. Under these circumstances, obviously there is no merchandising advantage in increasing the blend. . . . To get a significant improvement in performance beyond the standard 10% blend, one must get to fifty percent or more." And Consumer Reports commented on the "standard 10% blend" by saying, "The rug industry is frank to say that the percentage of nylon is too small to amount to any improvement in the quality of the rug. It is there as a sales pitch hook and, of course, an excuse for a higher price."

The widespread deterioration in rug quality could not be attributed to any growth in desperation to eke out a few pennies' profit. In 19S9, when complaints about deterioration in quality of rugs were running high, *U. S. News & World Report* published a table showing how sixtynine groups of stocks had fared in Wall Street during the general climb in stock prices of the preceding year. Stock prices do not necessarily reflect earnings, but still it is noteworthy that the stocks of the rugmakers led the entire pack with a rise of 154 per cent. In second place among the sixty-nine profit makers, incidentally, was "Radio, TV manufacturing." Its rise in value was 116 per cent.

FURNITURE, INDOOR. Throughout most of the fifties,

charges that the quality of American-made furniture was degenerating were aired in the trade. Returns in upholstered furniture rose sharply. In the midfifties, a trade wrangle developed because furniture makers refused to make even a one-year guarantee on the wearing quality or permanency of color of upholstery fabrics. The head of one upholstering company said that major troubles were with fabric shrinking, stretching, and fading. In 1958, a Chicago dealer charged that defects were increasing at such a rate that most of the stock arriving was in need of some repairs. The most resounding blast at the furniture industry was aired in a letter to *Retailing Daily*[5] signed by "A tired complaint adjuster" who said that "for obvious reasons" he did not dare to sign his name out of fear that his store would be blackmailed by the furniture manufacturers. He began:

"If there is any industry on earth that has reason to hide its head in shame it is the furniture manufacturers group who have literally 'gotten away with murder'... in hiding the defects of their products. ..." He charged that makers were indifferent about inspection. "I can show you half a dozen makers of upholstered pieces who won't even bother to reject a sofa if the material is cut too short and pops loose after a few weeks of wear." He said he was recently "horrified" while visiting one of the Midwest's leading makers of medium-grade living-room furniture to notice how many frames made of knotty wood were being used. "No wonder the epidemic of broken-back sofas that have to be returned," he said. "Have manufacturers no conscience any more?"

Even the National Retail Dry Goods Association blasted manufacturers in 1957 for their "faulty manufacturing." The chief of one manufacturing firm conceded that the association's charge of sloppy procedures was well founded. And an officer of the National Association of Furniture Manufacturers warned at a trade convention that if the furniture makers didn't "give heed to the quality problem the public is going to be convinced that modern upholstered furniture is inferior to that of twenty-five years ago." Apparently it was not only the public that might be convinced. A partner in the Crown Upholstering Company lamented: "I have been in the furniture-making business for almost thirty years and I can honestly say the fabric situation has never been worse." All this is not to indicate that durable furniture has disappeared from the American landscape. When the United States Air Force Academy was furnishing its buildings, it specified that equipment should be designed to last for fifty years with a minimum of upkeep. The designer, Walter Dorwin Teague, designed and selected furnishings accordingly. He advised: "That means that we try not only to give durability to the furniture and equipment, but to give durability of style as well."

FURNITURE, OUTDOOR. A sharp downtrend in the quality of aluminum summer furniture produced many angry outbursts and defenses in the trade press during the late fifties. One store owner complained: "Standards have gone to the winds." Specific grievances of dealers centered on the trend to use more and more insubstantial material in the chairs. Dealers alleged that:

Manufacturers increasingly were using a gauge of aluminum only one half as thick as the .065 material they had used a few years earlier.

The breadth of the tubing itself was being narrowed as much as a quarter inch.

Webbing was thinner and contained fewer strands. Some webbing had as few as nine strands; and one merchant said such webbing would quickly give way when people weighing more than 140 pounds sat on it.

Stainless-steel bolts were giving way to aluminum rivets.

DRAPERY FABRICS. In the summer of 1959, *Home Furnishings Daily* reported: "Claims of an all-time low in quality of drapery fabrics on the market today underlie growing discontent among local dealers and cut-order jobbers. Sources are deeply concerned over what was reported to be a staggering amount of poor fabrics coming from converters and mills." It said complaints seemed to focus most on misprinted print goods, misweaves in plain goods, and problems with synthetics, which some dubbed "test tube" fabrics. Meanwhile,

Better Business Bureaus were receiving a flood of complaints about new fabric combinations which were said to dissolve into their separate parts in the first dry cleaning.

Many manufacturers of hard and soft goods of the American home still were striving to increase the durability of their products. But in general it would appear that durability was knowingly being nibbled away. The ideal of a "lifetime" product, which once was the shining goal of makers of a wide range of home products, was reduced for most to a memory. When we asked Mrs. Brady of Consumers Union for a list of the products still designed to last a lifetime, she responded: "I can think of only one—the piano."

Finally, let us note the efforts being made to create the other controversial kind of obsolescence—obsolescence of desirability—in the home. Here the obsolescence creators have come up with some of the most interesting and nonrational results of all.

11. FASHION LINES FOR THE KITCHEN

"If we could get people trading appliances the way they do automobiles— we'd have it made."—An appliance dealer at a Raleigh, North Carolina, conference which heard a clamor for more style changes.

THE SUCCESS OF MOTORCAR MAKERS IN PUTTING more cars on the road by using the strategy of styling attracted the envious interest of people trying to sell all sorts of goods for the home. That pioneer of automobile fancification, General Motors' Harley Earl, turned marketing statesman in the mid-fifties by inviting other industries to share in the automakers' wonderful formula for everlasting prosperity. "The bringing about of 'dynamic obsolescence' in other industries," he stated, "represents one of the greatest challenges to industrial designers."

His challenge was quickly accepted. *Business Week* reported that "other industries—notably electrical appliances—are bringing themselves up-to-date on the styling concept of Detroit. General Electric Company representatives spent considerable time at Ford this summer and fall inquiring into the Ford technique of organizing and operating a styling department and merchandising the stylist's products."[1]

Another thing that created envy in the appliance industry was the way the rival motorcar manufacturers managed—despite all the talk about secrecy—to stress the same new features each year, whether they be tail fins or eight headlights. Was this the result of clairvoyance, massive inter-shop spying, or quiet exchange of views at industry-wide meetings? Some sort of exchange certainly seemed to be involved. *Home Furnishings Daily* reported a widespread yearning in the homefurnishing field for more co-ordination in springing innovations on the public. "There are some who believe the industry's product improvements have been dissipated because they are too widespread," it reported. No one firm had all the new features, and rival advertising was pulling the public in many different directions. It added: "They compare the appliance business in this case . . . to the car business, where the big improvements are usually general in any given year, and not limited to only one firm."

So it was that what industrial designers called the "Detroit Influence" began spilling over into many lines of marketing. The head of an institute of appliance manufacturers admonished his members, "We have got to develop dissatisfied customers."

News began leaking out that appliance makers were attempting to systematize the creation of obsolescence of desirability. The business journal *Forbes* commented in 1956: "Keeping-up-with-the-Jones rivalry will be exploited by home appliance makers in an upcoming campaign to convince Americans they should replace refrigerators, ranges, and washing machines every year or so. . . . Front-running Frigidaire has already kicked off its sales campaign with a slogan: Planned Product Obsolescence."

Frigidaire, it should be noted, is a division of General Motors.

Newspapers began carrying reports that soon the housewives of America would be renewing their kitchens every two or three years with sparkling-new appliances. When financial columnist Sylvia Porter heard reports that Frigidaire was embarking on a campaign of obsolescence creation, she called the head of Frigidaire to ask about rumors that Frigidaire would have an entirely new trade-in formula. The Frigidaire chief confirmed the rumor and, she reported, explained: "We have committed ourselves to a program of Planned Product Obsolescence." The replacement revolution was on.

A number of months later, during the 1958 recession, *Home Furnishings Daily* carried this headline: "Planned Obsolescence

Creates Sharp Rift in Appliance Industry."

It said no other area of the major-appliance business was commanding so much disagreement as that of the program of planned obsolescence "under which the industry has been working." The main grievance causing the "rift" was the widespread feeling that the industry was still not doing enough to create obsolescence. And the next year the same journal carried this headline:[2] "Obsolescence to Key Westinghouse Drive."

Dealers, it explained, were being urged to point out to prospects "how obsolete 1949 appliances are." In 1960, *Consumer Reports* quoted a Westinghouse official on the need of a "new look" every year in order to assist sales. Complete redesign each year, he said, would be too costly. "But changes only in decorative trim will satisfy the dealer, please the customer, and effectively 'obsolete' the previous year's model."

The home builders and home furnishers, too, were eager to nibble at the tempting apple of obsolescence creation. When I spoke before a meeting of a national association in the construction field, a home builder from central Texas who preceded me shook his fist at the several hundred builders in the room and told them to get out there and create more obsolescence. One of the nation's largest mass builders, John Long of the Phoenix area, began offering new models every six months. And builders across the land began trade-in plans to encourage owners of "used" homes to switch to their new homes. *Business Week* reported: "The home building industry is finally taking a cue from the auto industry. . . . Like the auto makers the home builders are trying to foster 'planned obsolescence' by putting more emphasis on styling, etc." People who couldn't afford an all-new home were urged at least to spruce up by buying new fixtures for their "used homes."

Home builders began talking excitedly about the House of Tomorrow, which will come in sections, and all or part of the house can be traded in for a new model. The kitchen of tomorrow is to be bought as a unit, with annual model changes available for the dis-

contented. Appliance companies were reported considering building entire prefabricated walls and even rooms with their appliances
built in. The whole wall could be traded in. *Business Week* reported
that homeowners would be encouraged to trade in a room just as
they now trade in their car on a new model. And it added that there
would be "national brand advertising to see that they do."

As for home furnishings aside from appliances, here are a few of
the specific home furnishings where plans for obsolescence creation
were going forward:

CHINA AND GLASS. *Retailing Daily* reported: "Take a hint
from the auto manufacturers: play up newness; make the public con-
scious of their old glass and china. Let them know it is stylistically
obsolete."[3]

FURNITURE. *Home Furnishings Daily*, quoting the counsel of
Louis Cheskin of the Color Research Institute: "The manufacturers'
next step is to promote psychological obsolescence . . . promote one
specific design—possibly limited to one or two pieces of furniture
every year . . . [this] should be promoted in conjunction with a brand
image as a symbol of up-to-dateness for that particular year. Every
five years a completely new grouping should be promoted. . . . In other words, a minor change every year, a major one every five years."[4]

BEDS. United States Steel, a major producer of bedsprings, in
1960 prepared a massive campaign to change American ideas about
the right size for a bed. It hoped to swing North Americans away
from the longstandard fifty-four-inch double bed to oversized and
twin beds. United States Steel was reported prepared to spend a
million dollars to put consumers and retailers into a mood to yearn
for larger beds. Its campaign was called "Space for Sleeping." In this
drive it had the cooperation of bedding manufacturers, who also
would benefit by any outmoding of the standard bed since there
would be an increased demand for larger mattresses, frames, sheets,
and all the other fixings.

SEWING MACHINES. A letter written by the public-relations consultant of a major sewing-machine company revealed the

president's plans for launching new models. It said: "The regular introduction of a new line ought to lead, he feels, to the obsolescence psychology so important to autos, refrigerators, etc."

FLOOR COVERINGS. The assistant general sales manager of Armstrong Cork Company was reported as stating: "[his] company has developed a program of planned obsolescence designed to bring a change in product acceptance every five years."

BATHROOM SCALES. One major manufacturer of scales was reported to be embarked on a plan to come up with new designs that would make obsolete the scales that are already in 60 per cent of American homes.

The specific styling techniques that were perfected to out-mode the home products already owned by Americans were interesting for their ingenuity and bore more than a little resemblance to the techniques used by the automobile designers.

For one thing, they sought to modify the profile or silhouette of many of their products, just as automobile designers had squashed down their product during the fifties. The automobile designers had stumbled upon the streamlined, teardrop shape as a symbol of modernity. This shape, which came from the discoveries of aircraft designers, had less but some plausible functional relevance in automobile design. But the relevance of the teardrop look became completely unclear when applied to such things as refrigerators, stoves, meat-grinder handles, electric irons, orange juicers, and radios. Wind resistance seems a strange preoccupation for the designers of such products.

By the late fifties the teardrop had run its course. Very shortly after refrigerator makers began talking about the imperative need for planned obsolescence to cope with mounting inventories, refrigerators abruptly received a new shape. Suddenly they no longer seemed designed for flight with rounded corners and oval contours. The new refrigerators were boxes again, with sharply squared corners. With impressive unanimity the major refrigerator makers discovered the square look. I have before me pictures of seven major brands in 1959.

All seven have the severely straight lines of a rectangular slab with sharp, square corners. By the spring of 1960, a trade journal was reporting that appliance makers were starting to push two-door refrigerators in "their efforts to break up the growing log jam of refrigerator inventory," The log jam amounted to nearly 800,000 unsold units on hand.

The television manufacturers sought to modify the profile of their product by a different approach. In 1957, when sales turned sluggish, the cry went up for a drastic change that would outmode existing sets or would persuade people to buy a second set. The industry responded by unveiling the new Slim Look. Sets abruptly became—or seemed to become—shallower. To achieve the slim profile, the makers used a squat 110-degree picture tube instead of the regular 90-degree tube. Companies competed to see which could get out the slimmest set.

By 1958, Sylvania was promoting in large advertisements its "Sylouette," which it claimed had a "cabinet only ten inches deep." Technically that was correct. But the tube mask bulged three inches out in front of the cabinet, and the tube guard bulged three inches out to the rear of the cabinet, to give the set itself a total thickness of sixteen inches.

The functional excuse for this race to a new slim profile was that it would permit the set to fit into a bookcase. This, however, hardly seemed to be a crying need, since most television-set owners did not own bookcases. Karl Nagel, chief of television testing for Consumers Union, said the Slim Look was "only to create obsolescence." When I asked an engineering executive of one of the largest television-set manufacturers about the trend to slim sets, he shrugged and said, "Just style."

Mr. Nagel pointed out that the slim set with its squat 110-degree tube did not produce as good a picture as many 90-degree tubes, since certain types of 110-degree tubes developed considerable optical distortion. Furthermore, all the components of the chassis had to be specially mounted for slim sets, so that they became much harder for a serviceman to get at.

Another tack taken in producing obsolescence was in the use of colors. The chairman of the Color Standardization Committee of the Institute of Appliance Manufacturers helped lead the way in this by pointing out in 1956 that color could be the "greatest technique for creating obsolescence in the major appliance industry."[5] He suggested that the appliance industry get behind a program of color changes, and that the members "quit having a guilty complex" about the idea of finding an orderly and economic method for satisfying consumer desires. He added, "That is to say, if color will help sell goods, let's use color and use it as an efficient sales tool."

For a few years appliance showrooms became a riot of pastel colors. The white refrigerator left in a home began looking like a relic of a bygone era. The stylists' fascination with pastels exhausted itself before the fifties ended, and the trend in color went right back to white, with some venturing into fancification with tracery effects. Left in the backwash of the change were several hundred thousand homeowners who had believed pastel to be the wave of the future.

The marketers also made heavy use of gadgets and trim to create a new look. Stoves and washing machines were emblazoned with control panels suggesting they were prepared to take off for outer space. I counted thirty-five buttons and dials on one Hotpoint gas stove. Others had almost as many. Consumers Union found instances, upon dismantling stoves, where certain of the dials had no connection underneath the cover. They were dummies.

The complex panels also served another purpose. They flattered the housewife's ego. Only she, it was implied in the promotions, was capable of mastering such a magnificent scientific instrument. This motivation was pointed up in Product Engineering in a discussion of the guilt feeling many homemakers had nowadays because homemaking was being made too easy for them with all the easy-does-it automatic appliances. The report explained that this "guilt feeling has been overcome in designing automatic appliances by putting great emphasis on complex-looking dash-panel assemblies to house the controls. Through such design techniques we compensate for the latent 'guilt feeling' of the user by giving her controls and push buttons she alone can use creatively."

Or take two other innovations that were hailed as steps forward but might just as properly be characterized perhaps as planned obsolescence by running up and down stairs.

In the early days of television all sets had transformers. Around 1951, sets were unveiled without transformers, and this "advance" was proclaimed as making the sets better, more modern, and more fashionable. Then in 1959, several major companies began proudly unveiling new sets that had transformers again. These new sets were said to be safer and better performing than the old-fashioned transformerless sets!

The other example is the turn-around shelf in refrigerators. General Electric introduced such a feature as a great boon to the housewife. Then in December, 1958, a trade journal carried this complaint made by an appliance dealer: "We were just getting a tremendous public acceptance on the GE turn-around shelves when GE dropped them. We're getting tired of building up a demand for new gadgets only to have the manufacturer drop them for another gimmick."

Mass home builders, too, were experimenting with the possibilities of creating obsolescence of desirability through the development of styling trends. During the late fifties, lattice windows and other smallpaned windows were being introduced in mass-produced homes in many parts of the nation. In the West and parts of the Midwest, a Cinderella house was being promoted. It had latticed windows, steeply pitched roof, scalloped eaves. James Mills, who serves as a consultant on marketing strategies for builders throughout the nation, told me that builders are not unaware that small windows and steep roofs, if widely accepted, can create obsolescence in existing houses. The trend to small windows might, for example, outmode every home in the nation with a picture window.

As for the steep roof, many builders hope that, too, is a trend. A number of builders hoped or anticipated that the exterior profile of homes would shift away from the horizontal look exemplified by the ranch house of the fifties to more upright lines, just as the motorcar was moving toward verticality. David Muss, who had built nearly a quarterbillion dollars' worth of homes, announced firmly in 1960: "The two-story house is coming back."

In the appliance field a good deal of uneasiness was developing about the growing reliance upon planned obsolescence of desirability. Some within the trade castigated "phony obsolescence" and "warmedover face-lifted phonies." Still, as E. B. Weiss of *Advertising Age* pointed out, the resistance to bringing out a new model annually in both the appliance and automobile field was but "a tiny trend." He felt that despite all the lip service "in the end, competitive necessity calls the tune." Still, he hoped some progress could be made against some of the "chicanery," "fluff," and "nonsense" during the sixties.

We now say farewell for the moment to planned obsolescence both of desirability and of quality. The best brief summary of the cost of all this built-in obsolescence to the public is offered by Dexter W. Masters, director of Consumers Union, who states:

"When design is tied to sales rather than to product function, as it is increasingly, and when marketing strategy is based on frequent style changes, there are certain almost inevitable results: a tendency to the use of inferior materials; short cuts in the time necessary for sound product development; and a neglect of quality and adequate inspection. The effect of such built-in obsolescence is a disguised price increase to the consumer in the form of shorter product life and, often, heavier repair bills."

The repair bills Americans were encountering—as they reflected an effort to keep the nation's output of goods and services mounting— deserve a separate brief inspection.

12. THE REPAIRMAN'S PARADISE

"When a $300 fully-automatic washer with whistles and bells on it won't run properly, it's not as effective as the medieval practice of beating clothes on rocks."— George Young, president of the Cincinnati Better Business Bureau.[1]

AMERICANS WHO STILL BOTHERED TO KEEP BOOKS on their spending were finding that a greater portion of their income each year was going to repair their cars, appliances, furniture, and other possessions. In hundreds of American cities, people had become so harassed by the problems of coping with a variety of repairmen that for an annual fee— and 10 per cent of all the bills— they were channeling their calls for help through an intermediary or clearinghouse.

As automation wiped out hundreds of thousands of jobs in goodsproducing industries, the slack was being taken up to a large extent by new openings in the service industries. One of the great and growing service industries was product repair. By 1960, the nation had twice as many repairmen—or about two million—as it did before World War II. And companies building replacement parts frequently were enjoying a greater volume of business than the makers of the products. Sylvania's director of research predicted in 1960 that within three years Americans would be spending two and a half times as much a year for television service, parts, and installation as they would be paying for new television sets. An official of Kelvinator estimated that Americans were paying sixteen billion dollars a year for service on all products—and would be paying nearly twice that by 1975.

In 1960, a spokesman for Kelvinator, announcing his company's determination to concentrate on making basic improvements as they could be developed and to avoid making an annual overhaul, observed that such a course would enable Kelvinator to slash in half its rate of service calls on automatic washers during their first year of operation.

The large makers of motorcars, appliances, and other products moved in to share in this exploding field by setting up servicing organizations—and thus expanding their total volume of business. The servicing organization affiliated with a major television manufacturer, as an example, began handling nearly half of all calls for servicing ailing color television sets. The head of this group pointed out to a convention of dealers in Chicago that the more money people can be persuaded to pay for a new television set, the more freely they will be willing to pay for servicing without haggling. One reason that charges for service on a color set can be higher than on a black-and-white set, he explained, "is [that] the customer has paid more for his set and, therefore, is adjusted to pay more for servicing that set." He concluded by saying, "The future of the servicing industry is extremely bright and profitable."

There were charges that some manufacturers were encouraging their dealers to sell the products themselves at cost if necessary in order to make their real profit out of their servicing operation. A car dealer complained to a Senate subcommittee that an official of the company producing the cars he sold had criticized him for not finding more things wrong with the cars brought into his garage. He wasn't doing enough to promote the sale of parts.

Many repairmen, whether company affiliated or independent, were developing a zest for repairing and replacing parts that became a phenomenon of the times. The president of a national electronic servicing association observed (possibly in a jovial mood) a few years ago: "What we'd evidently like to see is a TV set that works perfectly for the first thirty days but breaks down regularly every thirty days thereafter" (after the warranty is up).

Another amiable comment worth noting on the attitude of many repairmen was that offered by the chairman of a national association of dealers. In the late fifties he said:[2] "Unfortunately we have forgotten how to charge for service." He then told how an optometrist he had heard of worked. After the optometrist had fitted a customer with glasses, he would tell the customer that the charge was ten dollars. If the customer didn't blink, he followed with, "For the frames, and ten dollars for the lenses." He added, "We should learn from this how to inform our customers of service prices." (Later the same year, *Time* magazine carried a report that in Detroit twenty out of twenty-two repairmen spot checked had proved to be overcharging for work.)

Automatic washers and dishwashers were requiring an average of two service calls during the first year of operation. Television sets were requiring 1.4 calls the first year, and electric driers and refrigerators were quite likely to require at least one call the first year. On some "epidemic items"—brand models rushed into production with little testing—breakdown rates ran much higher. Behind much of the product failure was lack of quality control—or quality deliberately controlled to a short-life level. And behind much of the high cost of product maintenance were buck-happy repairmen. In many communities, however—and my own included—the repairmen are mostly competent, conscientious, and dedicated.

Beyond all these factors of debasement of quality and banditry by repairmen there were several objective factors about modern appliances that helped make them expensive to maintain and that helped increase the business volume of servicing agencies or replacement-parts manufacturers, and, in some cases, the manufacturers hoping to sell new replacement units. For example:

There were more things to go wrong. Those added luxury features that so delight copy writers were adding to the prone-ness of products to break down.

The rush to extras on washing machines in the form of cycle

controls, additive injectors, increased the number of things that can develop ailments. *The Wall Street Journal* noted: "Parts and accessory dealers naturally are pleased with the added extras put on new cars." They should be. I have two neighbors who bought station wagons in 1956. One bought a model with power steering, power brakes, automatic shifting, power windows. The other—a curmudgeon type who doesn't think that shifting gears and raising windows by hand are too much of a strain—bought a car without any of the extras. His years of ownership of the car have been relatively trouble free. (And by spurning the extras he saved several hundred dollars at the outset.) The other neighbor who bought the car with all the extras moans that he got a "lemon." His car, he states, has been laid up at the garage seven times, usually because of malfunctioning of the optional equipment.

Replacement parts were costing more. The gismoed motorcar was a good case in point. A creased fender that in earlier years could be straightened for a few dollars was now, with "integral paneling" and high-styled sculpturing, likely to cost $100 to correct. The wrap-around windshield was likely to cost three to five times as much to replace as the unbent windshields that motorcars had before the fifties.

Ailing parts were increasingly inaccessible. In their preoccupation with gadgetry and production short cuts—and perhaps obsolescence creation—manufacturers often gave little thought to the problem of repairing their products (or deliberately made them hard to re-pair). *Sales Management* commented that "products are not designed for service." It told of a steam iron that could be repaired only by breaking it apart and drilling out the screws. Some toasters were so riveted together that a repairman had to spend nearly an hour just getting to the working part. And many complex appliances had to be largely dismantled in order to replace a fifteen-cent light or a ten-cent spring. Product analysts at Consumers Union told me that air-conditioning units in automobiles were often cluttering up the engine compartment so badly that it took an hour or two to remove a rear spark plug. Built-in appliances—which were being hailed as the wave of the future—had to be disengaged from the wall before repair work could begin. Many of these built-ins were simply standard units without coasters and could be repaired only from the rear.

Repairing had come a long way from the day when Henry Ford I built his cars so that any owner could handle all repairs with the help of a simple set of tools that Mr. Ford provided. A Ford dealer in the late fifties complained to a Senate subcommittee that he often had to buy up to three hundred dollars' worth of special tools every time a new model came out. A television repairman who arrived at my house with a vast kit of equipment told my wife he couldn't even carry all he needed these days because of all the changes in component design, which he felt were often pointless.

Necessary parts were often hard to obtain. An acquaintance told me she had to get along for nine years with a plastic control knob missing from her gas range because she couldn't buy a replacement. Finally, out of embarrassment, she got rid of the stove even though it still worked satisfactorily. The plastic knob had snapped off soon after the stove was purchased. A man on Long Island related angrily that his $2,000 pump became useless within two years because a two-dollar part that had broken was no longer obtainable.

Some companies have gone to great lengths to keep supplies of replacement parts. Maytag boasts that it can replace any part on any washer it has made in the past thirty-three years. But only a few companies could make the same claim, or probably would care to. When I have questioned them, they have usually responded that they maintain replacement parts "as long as a demand for them exists." The demand, however, was likely to mean a profitable demand. Another problem was that the wave of mergers, especially in the appliance field, had left many products orphaned. The company absorbing your brand usually has no more than nominal sympathy for your troubles with the product that was made before they took control of the company. Still another problem was the bewildering variety of models that each major company produced each year. In the jungle of similar-but-different models it was often extremely difficult for even the most conscientious repairman to stock knobs or timers for every variant.

Manufacturers often failed to provide information that would facilitate repairs. Recently, *The Boston Herald* editorially protested that appliance manufacturers were getting so "cozy" with service manuals that customers seeking them got the impression they were "censored as if they contained obscene material." *The Electric Appliance Service News* likewise expressed indignation on behalf of servicemen, or at least independent servicemen. It said, "Our mail is loaded with gripes daily from servicemen throughout the country lamenting their inability to obtain service manuals from certain manufacturers." Often this coziness has sprung from the desire of the manufacturer to keep the repair business to itself and out of the hands of independents. The News charged that "some manufacturers do not make service manuals available to all independent repairmen and therefore it is almost impossible to make repairs easily and properly—and at a time-saving expense."

Another problem was that the manufacturers often hid the model number near the bottom of the refrigerator or in the pit beneath the burners in a gas stove. The manufacturers of many products have never even bothered to agree—in all their trade meetings—where the model number should be placed. And no replacement of parts can be made until the model number is located.

The trend was to encourage customers to replace parts rather than to bother repairing them. If the manufacturers could not persuade people to throw away the whole product and buy a new one, then the next best thing was to persuade them to throw away parts. The high cost of repair work was also a factor here. *Business Week* reported that "garages, service stations and dealers now have the attitude that it is much cheaper to replace a defective carburetor, say, with a new or rebuilt one than to fix it." A television announcer extolling the wonders of the sponsor's cigarette lighter stated that if the lighter became defective it could be fixed in a jiffy just by replacing the entire lighter mechanism. On the other hand, it should be noted that one of the very few companies left in North America that offer an absolutely unconditional lifetime guarantee on their products for both parts and labor is the ZIPPO lighter manufacturer.

The increasing difficulties of the housewife in keeping her multitude of products in good working order were perhaps best summed up by the late Bernard De Voto when he said: "If a 50-cent belt in the vacuum cleaner wears out, the agency will not replace it in less than six weeks and not then until a series of young men have tried to sell her a new machine, alleging that hers is antiquated."

13. PROGRESS THROUGH PLANNED CHAOS

"We get our best prices on sales days. With the sales spirit in the air the customer usually assumes your prices are real low. . . .I make this mass sales hysteria work to my advantage."—An appliance dealer in Astoria, New York.[1]

THE DICTIONARY ON MY DESK DEFINES RAZZLE-dazzle as a "state or event of confusion, bewilderment, bustling." Marketers concerned with developing strategies for expanding sales in the face of the specter of satiation were finding that a state of "confusion, bewilderment, bustling" was often the ideal one in which to operate. They were not just negligent in not giving consumers information needed for making prudent purchasing decisions. Frequently they engaged in deliberate obfuscation of values.

Most Americans above the really poor like to splurge and can splurge most easily if they can assure themselves that somehow they are getting a bargain. And some could vent their latent sadism by taking advantage of the dire circumstances forcing the merchant to make a sacrifice. The merchants accordingly placed themselves in the posture of desperation. The "bargains" they offered were in many cases the kind that would enable the customers to turn in their old power cruiser on a new bigger one complete with sundeck and ship-to-shore telephone.

In such situations it was essential that the customer not have any easy way of knowing how much real value was promised by the price tag. Two informed comments suggest the state of affairs that has developed in the modern American market place:

"We have reached the point where price lists are no longer prices; they are simply advertising devices."—An official of the Federal Trade Commission.

"For a widening range of goods only a sucker pays list prices."—*Consumer Reports*.

Value had become the hidden ball, and sometimes the seemingly irrelevant factor. The product analysts at Consumers Union who judged the performance of twenty-two automatic electric toasters a few years ago found that the best buy at that time for over-all quality was a $14.50 toaster. On the other hand, a toaster priced at $39.50 ranked twelfth among the "acceptable" toasters. And of the three toasters rated as "unacceptable," all three cost considerably more than the $14.50 "Best Buy." (In a subsequent test toaster qualities seemed more in line with price differentials.)

Colston Warne, Amherst economist and president of Consumers Union, has concluded that there is slight if any correlation between the price and quality of much of the branded goods offered on the market. He pointed out that "one may, for example, buy inferior margarine at any price between 22 cents and 44 cents a pound; one can buy the highest grade on the other hand for either 23 cents, 27 cents, or 40 cents." The cost of manufacturing a product had less and less relation to the price that marketers might decide for strategic reasons to set on the product.

Much of the obfuscation of value was created behind the screen of the trade-in lure. The high trade-in had proved to be enormously effective in luring prospects who already owned the product being offered. In many lines, however, offering to accept trade-ins raised a problem. There was little demand for used refrigerators, washing machines, electric razors. In some lines the goods accepted in trade were widely regarded as nuisances that had to be endured. Yet the pretense had to be maintained that the trade-in was valuable.

An anonymous salesman who discussed selling strategies in a *Home Furnishings Daily* series told how to cope with the prospect who springs a trade-in on you unexpectedly. He wrote: "In case someone walks in practically wearing a badge proclaiming 'I have a trade-in' naturally I boost my prices to accommodate him. [However] If a customer should hit me between the eyes with his 1947 Frostcool just when I've got a deal clinched I have two choices. First is to allow no more than $10 or $15 for the old box, then try to add it back in as service and delivery charges. Second is to tell him pointblank that the old box is worthless and that I am doing him a favor taking it away."

The strategy of upping the price to cover the trade-in allowance— called "the packed price"—was, of course, widely used in automobile merchandising until a federal law required the posting of a "suggested" price at the factory, which made packing more difficult. However, price packing was still widely used in the appliance field.

An example of the chaos that could be achieved by the trade-in device occurred in the electric-razor field. One firm was offering a fivedollar trade-in allowance for "anything that shaves." And a trade journal reported that many outlets offering to take the trade-ins on the various brands of razors they were selling "will easily oblige without a physical trade-in." The trade-in, in short, had become a price-juggling device. And one New York discounter ran advertisements offering Remington electric shavers that carried a list price of $29.50 for $10.97 if the customer had a trade-in, or for $15.47 if he didn't have a trade-in. By 1959, several of the major shaver makers were quietly withdrawing their trade-in offer. Sunbeam, which led the withdrawals, explained that the trade-ins had become a nuisance to dealers and distributors.

A young New York City housewife, Jean Banks, described to me her bewilderment regarding values in supermarkets as she pushes her little cart through miles of aisles. She explained: "If my grandma wanted to know anything about what she was buying, she would ask her grocer. I've never seen my grocer. I think he lives in Scarsdale. Grandma paid the same price whenever she bought a particular product. I have to be a mathematician to figure out if it would be cheaper to buy two packages for the price of one; to buy one package at the full price but use my 25¢-off coupon; to buy three packages and get my purchase price for two of them refunded by sending in three boxtops; to buy two for 29¢ or three for 44¢; or to buy one package at the full price and use the boxtop entry blank to enter a contest where I may win my height in silver dollars. It's all very complex."

The editor of *Progressive Grocer* confided to his grocer readers that "goods we want to push are priced 'two for,' 'three for,' or 'ten for.'" And he added: "Some women even think that's the only way the store will sell the item."

Dial soap manufacturer proclaimed a "½ price sale" for a three-bar package. It turned out, if the buyer read the small type, that he was really being offered two of the bars at full price and the third bar at the half price.

Housewives across the nation were becoming so overloaded with dinnerware that came in detergent boxes—and displacing needed detergent—that they were running out of shelf space. A Ford dealer in Westchester County, New York, was offering free mink stoles with each automobile sold. Perhaps the most astounding offer, however, was that of an appliance store in Lafayette, Louisiana. To each person willing to buy certain of its deluxe electric ranges at the regular suggested retail price, it promised to furnish three rooms of the customer's home. It would give away free a living-room set, a bedroom set, and a dinette set! With this and other lures the store sold $42,000 "worth" of major appliances in four days. In the late fifties reports circulated that in central Ohio morticians were offering green stamps to clients; but there is no evidence that such offers are being made today.

The game of printing price tags and price lists consumed a great deal of the marketers' creative thinking. So much "pre-ticketing" was being done that the Federal Trade Commission expressed concern. In pre-ticketing you print price tags with blue-sky prices and then slash them with a heavy black pencil to emphasize your desperate state. A new bargain price is entered. In 1958, *Printers' Ink* carried this headline: "FICTITIOUS PRICE ADVERTISING IS LIKE SIN—EVERYONE'S AGAINST IT, BUT ALMOST EVERY-ONE ENGAGES IN IT OCCASIONALLY."

The ads were likely to use such phrases as "regularly——," "usu-ally——," or "made to sell for——." Watches were an example of products that seldom sold for their supposedly regular price. A blan-ket distributor provided tags on which the merchant could print whatever list price struck his fancy, but the blankets were to sell for $8.95. The Federal Trade Commission issued a complaint against Howard Stores Corporation, a nationwide clothing chain, for using such advertisements as "$49.55, usually $70." It said, "Howard nev-er sold any of the advertised merchandise at the purported regular price." A survey of appliance prices that covered nine famous name-brand items showed that none of these items were being sold at the list price in any of thirty stores checked in eight cities.

When the Federal Trade Commission singled out a furniture store in Washington, D.C., for advertising to consumers that they could "save $80" from regular furniture prices, the store offered an interesting and belligerent defense. The store contended that the term "regular" as used in the trade didn't really mean the regular price charged but meant the price the furniture could be sold for if the "regular" markup was applied. It proceeded to blast the meddling Federal Trade Commission for being so "overprotective" of consum-ers that it would ultimately produce a "race of idiot consumers" who would be at the mercy of sharp sellers if they ever stepped foot out-side the protected shores of the United States.

Another selling strategy that had become so prevalent that the "overprotective" Federal Trade Commission was disturbed was the practice of proclaiming "bargains on a string." A seemingly fantastic bargain is advertised to lure prospects when there is no intent of actually selling such a product. The bargain offered has disappeared by the time prospects begin beating on the door. Or the ten-cubic-foot refrigerator offered for $119 to attract prospects turns out to be a discolored box made by a firm that disappeared in a merger some years back. But the store does just happen to have some really excellent bargains just marked down from a fanciful regular price.

In the wilderness of tire marketing, obfuscation of value was additionally produced by the strategy of planned chaos of nomenclature. The industry refused to set any standards to control what tires could properly be labeled "first line," "second line," or "third line." And the names the tire marketers dreamed up for their various "lines" of tires often offered the tire buyer no clue to the quality he was buying. Here, for example, were three tires offered by Firestone in 1958: Firestone Super Champion, Firestone Deluxe Champion, Firestone Deluxe Super Champion.

Which would you say was the first-line tire? Number three? You are wrong. That was the second-line tire. The first-line tire was number two.

One basic measurement of the quality of a tire is the number of miles its tread will last. Analysts at Consumers Union found that there was only a general likelihood that first-line tires would give more mileage than second-line tires. In 1959, one of the four tires found to give the most miles per dollar was B. F. Goodrich's second-line rayon tube-type tire. And among thirteen first-line nylon tires of one size tested, the amount of miles that could be expected ranged from 28,600 down to 18,400.

A second basic measurement of tire quality is carcass strength, a safeguard against blowouts. Consumer Bulletin reported in 1958 that Motor Vehicle Research, Inc., found in testing three hundred tires that "the cheapest lines of the makes tested were found to have better carcass strength than so-called 100-level or first-line tires. In one make, the first-line tire was the poorest of all tested while its third-line tire was the best of all tested in strength of carcass."

In some fields where prices had only slight relation to quality or cost of production, the prices were set on the basis of psychological considerations. Many marketers in the Alice-in-Wonderland economy of modern-day America found they could raise their total number of sales by raising the prices they charged. Marketing strategist Louis Cheskin warned producers that "many a product fails because . . . the price was too low."[2] It doesn't have a "quality" image that a higher price tag can give. A Western manufacturer of cosmetics who acknowledged marking up some of his products 900 per cent was quoted as explaining: "A cheap line wouldn't do well. Women wouldn't be caught dead telling their friends they bought cheap cosmetics."

The cost of the lipstick sold in a fashionable store often is only a penny or two more than the lipstick sold in a five-and-ten-cent store; yet the fashionable store may charge $1 or $2 more for it. In one case a company offered two brands of lipstick. One cost the buyer twice as much as the other. Both lipsticks used the same formula. A cosmetics company expanding overseas is finding that it can sell nail enamel to natives of the Congo. Many of the native women can afford—at the prices charged—to buy only enough enamel to cover one fingernail. But that seems to give them pleasure. Perhaps they will hound their husbands to work harder so that they, the wives, can cover more of their nails with enamel. Still another company was hailed in a marketing journal because it had succeeded in raising the price level of all cosmetics. For example, it boldly began selling nail polish at a price 500 per cent higher than its competitors. This, one gathered, was real marketing statesmanship.

In general, the trend was toward competing in such factors as image building, styling, packaging, preferred shelf position, and premiums rather than on price. According to one estimate, half of all small electrical housewares manufactured in the United States were being bought as premiums by the trading-stamp companies. All these promotional approaches, of course, raised the price of food sold in supermarkets. They also gave the big company—as in the automotive field—an edge over the challenging newcomer who didn't have the resources to hammer home an image. As economist Colston Warne has pointed out, "One of the important functions of advertising is the creation of a haven from price competition."

Possibly some of this general disdain for price competition that has developed simply reflects the prevailing mood of a people in an era of abundance and abandon. Some marketing experts argued that as a society attains more and more abundance price as a decisive factor tends to retreat into the background. Pierre Martineau, research and marketing director of *The Chicago Tribune*, reports that a survey made for one national chain suggested that only a third of the women shoppers studied were economy-minded, while almost as large a group saw the shopping expedition as "fundamentally social."[3] They were looking for a friendly, congenial environment. Many were newcomers in the areas studied; and the stores and their personnel were becoming substitutes for the friends they had left behind.

Whatever the reasons, startling similarities in the prices charged by supposedly relentless rivals began appearing. This would suggest that prices were chaotic only when the marketers desired them to be. Consider the evidence of groupthink in the tire market, which appeared a few pages ago to be so chaotic. The tire makers could not agree on minimum standards for a "first-line" tire; yet in their list prices they showed astounding unanimity of thought. *Consumer Reports* noted in July, 1959, that despite extreme variations in tread wear found in first-, second-, and third-line tires "the Big Four manufacturers' suggested list prices for these lines were phenomenally similar. On first-line nylon tubeless 6.70-15 blackwall tires the list price for each of these brands was $37.06. In the 7.50-14 nylon tubeless versions the list price of $38.81 for these Big Four brands also did not vary by even so much as a penny."

The Report of the Senate Subcommittee on Antitrust and Monopoly of the Judiciary Committee (85th Congress) on administered prices in the motorcar industry noted a similar extraordinary coincidence. It observed that "differences in price for comparable models of the major producers have been all but obliterated." It found a "striking uniformity" of prices among the three major producers. In some cases it related, there was actual identity in price to the last dollar; in the majority of cases, the companies were within a few dollars of each other. This was particularly true of General Motors and Ford; in the case of Chrysler, a traditional margin of about $20 usually prevailed over the prices of its competitors, it said.

The president of General Motors announced in the mid-fifties that "price cutting should not be a factor in competition." His views prevailed. When the 1957-58 recession developed, and the motorcar market was glutted, the major motorcar makers chose cutting production to cutting prices. And this was the general pattern set by American marketers.

Historically, recessions have corrected the inflationary prices that have developed in times of rising prosperity. But in the 1957-58 recession the marketers refused to let prices follow the normal downward adjustment to lessened demand. And after this recession had ended and businessmen were congratulating themselves for holding prices firm, *Sales Management* asked its marketing readers:

"Did you prolong the recession? That's a nervy question, isn't it? But seriously, now that most of the panic is over, do you feel that you did the right things . . . ? Did you cut prices below a sensible level? Did you try to sell your product or simply undersell competitors? Did you emphasize price above product? Or did you justify your fair price to your customers? Did you cut advertising to save money?"

Quite possibly, in an era of abundance, cutting production rather than prices is a justifiable response to lessened demand. It at least reduces the drain on resources. But the head of the Federal Reserve Bank of Chicago commented that the new ability of industry to increase prices in the face of falling demand meant that industrial leaders were embracing "a new, a novel and a frightening theory of consumer demand."

There was widespread acceptance among marketers, at least until the sixties began, that creeping inflation—or ever-higher prices—had become a permanent part of the American way of life. And consumers had learned to agree. Inflation was accepted as "normal" as long as the nation had full employment and an ever-increasing man-hour productivity rate, with labor and stockholders splitting the benefits of the man-hour gain rather than passing them on to the general consuming public in the form of lower prices.

And this general resignation to price upcreep became in itself a significant sales goad to keep customers coming. The public was told—apparently correctly—that nothing would ever again be as cheap tomorrow as it was today. So hurry, hurry, hurry. A housing developer on Long Island warned prospects to hurry because his houses were being raised $1,000 in price a month hence. And the appliance salesman-author who did a series on sales techniques confided how he worries an undecided prospect by disclosing that "prices are going up on these goods." As a convincer he pulls from the drawer a handful of undated manufacturers' bulletins announcing imminent price rises. He has saved them over the years for just this use.

There was, by late 1960, the possibility that overabundance of goods—plus the pressure of foreign price competition—would ultimately force a halt to reliance upon creeping inflation. But this possibility remained to be tested. As the sixties were about to begin, *Sales Management* advised its readers that for better or worse they should assume that they would "have to increase the price of their product one or more times *a year* during the next decade." (The italics are mine.) And it warned: "You will probably want to consider frequent introduction of new models with new price tags so that you can argue that the higher price is buying superior features."

14. SELLING ON THE NEVER-NEVER

"Instant Money-Cash Loans within 20 seconds"—An advertisement on behalf of Georgia's Citizens & Southern National Bank system.

AS THE WANTS AND NEEDS OF MOST AMERICANS became less and less insistent owing to the general upsurging of material abundance, the mass sellers achieved new break-throughs in devising techniques to make the buying of products "easy." Spectacular gains were made in perfecting ways to help—and induce—Americans to buy more and more against future earnings. Admen began referring to the strategy of selling on credit as one of the great "creative" forces in the American economy. An official of the National Retail Merchants Association asserted that credit was becoming "a way of life in this country."

When the American Bankers Association met in Chicago during the late fifties, a principal speaker was Charles H. Brower, head of the Batten, Barton, Durstine & Osborn advertising agency. Sales were then lagging. He stated: "If we are to break the present economic log jam, you installment-credit bankers and we in advertising must do it by working together." He urged the bankers to get into the swing of advanced merchandising techniques in order to make borrowing from them both moral and fun. The lending man, he said, should "get up from his desk, and smile and shake hands with the prospective borrower, no matter how poor a credit risk he appeared to be."

Loan-company officials at a conference were admonished by

a psychological consultant to use "positive" rather than "negative" appeals. They were told that the average American still had old-fashioned puritanical ideas about money and going into debt. This prospective borrower must be assured that what he is doing in seeking a loan is not shameful but is rather a forward-looking step. The borrower must feel "I am on my way up. I am taking out an advance payment on my invested earning power next year."

Under the new pressures, credit changed from being a simple financial aid to being an active sales tool. More and more retailers were discovering that it was no longer enough merely to have a credit plan available for consumers. It was also considered imperative to promote the use of credit. An appliance center in Albuquerque, New Mexico, began requesting that credit applicants list the names and addresses of three friends or relatives. These references named soon received a letter from the store stating: "Dear Friend: Yesterday we had the great pleasure of opening an installment account for——. When they were here in the store we asked them for the names and addresses of any of their relatives whom they thought worthy of inviting to our store. May we at this time, etc., etc., etc... . No obligation, nothing to buy. Our coffeepot is always hot, etc. . . . Sincerely,——."

The possibility of buying on the never-never—as the British so quaintly call going into debt to buy—makes people into better prospects. The selling task is eased. Less persuasion is required. An official of the Institute for Motivational Research has explained that people generally are afraid of making a purchasing decision of major importance. The possibility of buying on credit, however, seems to postpone the necessary decision. "It removes the air of finality inherent in a cash transaction. In a sense the credit buyer makes up his mind to buy while he is still paying for the item."

To the seller, another major appeal of selling on credit is that customers tend to buy more when they discover they don't have to put up the money immediately, and they are less apt to look hard at the price tag or haggle for a lower price. It should not be overlooked, furthermore, that many retailers were discovering to their pleasant astonishment that they could often make more money on the interest charges in financing a purchase than on the sale of the item itself.

For all these reasons the public began being assaulted with a massive barrage of gay invitations to go into debt. The growing dependence of the economy on credit buying became painfully evident for example in 1959, when the nation was starting off on a new buying binge, after the recession. *The Wall Street Journal* cited these three among many comments from across the country. A department-store credit manager in Fort Worth, commenting on his store's recent sales gain, said, "Every dollar of the increase came from credit sales." A banker in Elwood, Indiana, said his bank had experienced an "astronomical" increase in consumer loans in the past two months. And an executive of the J. C. Penney chain of variety stores commented that never have people "been so conditioned to buy what interests them on credit."

During the fifties, consumer indebtedness rose three times as fast as personal income. The average American family by 1960 was taking on about $750 of installment debt alone each year—and paying it off at the rate of $650 a year. Millions of Americans were embracing never-never buying with zest. The chairman of General Foods cited this new zest of consumers to buy on credit in talking of the "creative" possibilities in modern merchandising. He explained: "Today's consumer insists on having whatever he or she wants at once, whether it be a house, an automobile, an electric refrigerator, a power mower, a suit of clothes, an Easter bonnet, or a vacation trip, and paying for it out of income yet to be earned."

His emphasis was on the words "at once." The president of a bank in Rutland, Vermont, commented less enthusiastically. "The young people here are the same as everywhere else. They have to have a house and a car right away." He added that in recent years the whole idea of indebtedness had changed. Author William Attwood in surveying American attitudes reported encountering a truck driver near San Diego who lamented: "The more money I make, the more payments I seem to take on. There's no letup."[1]

Whatever the hazards to the consumer, a great many Americans were finding that the fastest way to build a fortune was to deal not in products but in money itself. Mildred Brady of Consumers Union remarked to me that "the most profitable product sold today is money." The truth of this could be observed by standing at the main intersection of just about any American small or middle-sized city. The majority of neon signs to be seen are likely to be pulsing or blinking messages such as "LOANS" or "CREDIT." And the changing tenor of the invitations to seek loans could be seen in New York's subway trains. They carried posters showing "Mr. Consumer" as "king" being eagerly offered a cigar by a moneylender of the Beneficial Finance System. The lender gaily welcomes the "king" with the remark: "CASH? Just say the word. Get your budget in good shape with a Beneficial bill clean-up loan___We like to say Yes!" A good many debt-ridden Americans were being attracted by the idea that they could somehow "clean up" all their debts by taking on one new master-type debt.

Once-lofty banks were joining in the scramble to ease the public into indebtedness. They complained that the retailers who were happily and profitably selling money were intruding on their territory. They tried to outbid the other lenders with coaxing messages on billboards and over the airways. Hundreds adopted the idea of issuing credit cards that permit a person to go into any branch or into just about any store in town, flash the card, and say, "Bill the bank." In Dallas, Texas, some of the banks have been opening branches right on the floor of appliance stores. And in some cases these bankers-on-the-spot have been rebating to the store owner about a third of the interest charges they collect from financing appliance sales.

Meanwhile, millions of Americans began stuffing their billfolds with other kinds of credit cards that enabled them to buy baseball tickets, perfume, old master paintings, men's suits, bedrooms, and meals. Analysts at the Institute for Motivational Research had little difficulty figuring the secret of the appeal of credit cards. They explained: "Credit cards are symbols of status. They are also magic, since they serve as money when one temporarily has no money. They thus become symbols of power and inexhaustible potency."

And these magic symbols of potency were not hard to come by. The Diners' Club regularly had men handing out application cards to passers-by on both floors of Grand Central Station in New York.

In the early days of the Diners' Club, co-operating restaurants could justify the extra 7 per cent service charge they had to pay the club on the ground that it brought new business. But when in many cities most of the major competing restaurants joined up with either the Diners' or other dining credit clubs, membership then became a necessary expense to keep from losing business. It didn't take the restaurants belonging to credit clubs long to decide who should bear the burden of the 7 per cent assessment. A great many passed the charge on to the customers in the form of higher prices for food and drink.

Still, restaurateurs felt the credit cards were good for business. *Restaurant Management* surveyed the credit-card situation and concluded credit-card customers were much more likely to be big spenders. In large restaurants "the average check that is charged through a major credit-card company will be from 20 to 25 per cent higher" than the check paid by the cash customer. It noted that some restaurant owners were fearful that the increased prices on the menu might be disastrous to the industry, but it counseled such timid operators to be of good heart: "We sincerely doubt that the customer will even notice— particularly the credit-card customer."

Several of the nation's larger variety-store chains began giving trial runs to "charge-it" plates. Many department stores came up with revolving credit schemes. And automobile credit rose 800 per cent during the decade ending in 1957. When a motorcar merchant advertised "100% financing plus easy terms," it usually meant a small loan would be arranged on top of the maximum installment loan. The profits to be made in financing motorcar purchases became so inviting that many car dealers fought as hard to get the financing as they did to clinch the sale of the car itself. A St. Louis dealer pointed out in *Automotive News* that selling the financing and insurance could bring as much as $146 extra profit on each sale.

In home buying, more and more millions of cash-short prospects were being persuaded to take a second mortgage or to "buy" their home on a "contract" basis. Under the common contract, the would-be homeowner pays a very high interest—7 to 13 per cent a year—and doesn't really take possession of the home until the contract is paid off. He is allowed to live in it just as if he were renting it. In some parts of Michigan, I found most of the new homes were being sold on "contract."

Meanwhile, two novel types of mortgage were being pioneered to lure the hard-pressed and the imprudent. One was the "open-end mortgage," which becomes a sort of revolving charge account. As you pay off some money, you can keep going back for more with little red tape—and if you're not wary, you keep yourself deeply in debt for life.

The other tantalizing new deal in mortgaging was the "package mortgage," which has become immensely popular with both sellers and buyers. Under this "package," the mortgage covers not only the cost of the home but also many of the extras, such as laundry and kitchen equipment. Builders in St. Louis reported that the "package" helped them double their sales. And a Fort Wayne, Indiana, builder told me that a third of his home buyers were buying their appliances in the "package." Appliances were included in the twenty-year mortgages. Some were even buying intercom systems for their homes with speaker attachments in the breezeway and ordering that the cost of them all go into the "package." Builders found that offering the package mortgage not only eased the financing but helped promote sales. Women were more easily sold on a house if it already contained many sparkling appliances.

And few computed the cost. Buying a refrigerator as a part of a package mortgage with the cost of the refrigerator being paid over a thirty-year period almost doubles the cost of a $400 refrigerator.

Rug manufacturers tried to get wall-to-wall rugs into homes under a package mortgage. The Federal Housing Administration finally balked at this. One reason for the balking was the obvious one that few rugs made today can be expected to last the life of a thirty-year or even a fifteen-year mortgage.

Investigating home-buying habits in the Midwest, I found that most home buyers do not compute the burden they are undertaking when a home is offered to them on a long-term mortgage. In Toledo, Ohio, a salesman and his wife proudly showed me their custom-ized pre-fab ranch house which they said they had just bought for $19,500. Did they have a mortgage? Yes, it was a thirty-year kind for $17,000. How much was their interest rate? The husband said, "Gosh, I don't know . . . 4½ per cent, I think." His wife thought it was 6 per cent. Their difference in guesses could make a difference of nearly $6,000 in the total cost. Actually, it turned out, they were paying 5½ per cent interest. The one thing they did know was that their monthly payment was $96.53. We quickly multiplied that fig-ure by the 360 months they had committed themselves to pay it, and added on the $2,500 cash down payment. The result was a figure that plainly dismayed them: $37,250.80. That was the real price of their home, not $19,500.

As the sixties began, the American practice of buying posses-sions on the never-never began spreading on a large-scale basis to several other parts of the world. Conservative British banks entered the installment-lending business as goods became more plentiful in that country. Joseph Wechsberg reported that in Yugoslavia *na ot-platu* (buying on installment) was becoming the new passion. He related: "Everybody I know in Belgrade is falling hopelessly and en-thusiastically into debt. They can plunge to one third of their income and the monthly payments are automatically deducted from their pay check."[2] (This automatic deduction might ultimately have to be-come the only feasible solution to the problem of collection in the United States.)

Radio Moscow chided the Yugoslavs for becoming slaves to a

"degenerate capitalistic habit." But this just proved that sometimes the propagandists in Moscow don't know what Soviet planners are up to. Within a few weeks after Radio Moscow sneered at Yugoslavia, the Soviet Union began offering her citizens products not in short supply such as cameras and radios on an installment-plan basis.

How far Americans could continue running up debts against future income without inviting disaster during an economic turndown was not clear. The typical American family was several thousand dollars in debt, counting both short-term and long-term commitments. On the other hand, marketers claimed, Americans had a wider margin of income left after the real necessities of life were provided than ever before—though the definition of necessities was continually being upgraded by the managers of the Labor Department's Cost-of-Living Index. Thus the argument depended somewhat on whose definition of "necessity of life" you were using.

The Federal Reserve System's Board of Governors observed that "relatively little is known about the safety margins in the finances of consumers who borrow on an ... installment basis." It added that the evidence suggested the margin of safety was getting narrower.

A survey by insurance companies revealed that the average American family was about three months from bankruptcy. That was its cushion against disaster after two decades of unparalleled prosperity. For millions of families—especially for many living in suburban subdivisions—the brink of disaster was much closer. They were so pressed in meeting their host of monthly installment charges that they were stopping smoking temporarily or putting their wives to work or seeking debt-consolidation loans, or all three.

A number of members of the National Retail Merchants Association began voicing apprehension about the mounting level of installment debts. The controller of a Midwestern firm said he was now watching collections more carefully than sales. And the controller of a Pittsfield, Massachusetts, store said: "One really bad year in business and this whole credit setup will fall like a card house."

In early 1960, bankers in many areas of America were reporting a notable increase in requests for loans on motorcars that were not up to their usual standards for risks. And the bankers were also uneasy because the amount of money they had tied up in installment loans had risen four times as fast as their deposits during the past decade.

By the spring of 1960, the Federal Reserve Bank of New York was expressing concern that too many consumers were getting too deep into debt. It noted that half of all American families were being forced to devote a fifth of their income to meeting commitments on regular payments and stated that this was a "very real reason for concern" and that a continuing of the borrowing trend would "result in an unduly heavy burden on the borrowers—particularly in the event of a more serious recession than those experienced in recent years."

Other reports noted that the average American family was now forced to set aside 18 per cent of its after-taxes income to pay its consumer debt and monthly mortgage charges, whereas ten years ago the figure was only 11 per cent. Meanwhile, the chief economist of a leading advertising agency was predicting that in the coming decade the proportion of family income going to pay installment debts would keep rising.

If debt collection does become a plaguing problem, American creditors might consider the idea of using conspicuously painted debtcollection trucks to call on the homes of the delinquents. The dread of neighborhood gossip would inspire debtors to exert themselves more to make repayment. Such trucks were under consideration by a merchants' association in Great Britain.

Whatever their ability to repay, American consumers were spending an ever-larger share of their income in meeting interest charges. The bewitching new credit-card plans of banks were usually costing the users 12 to 18 per cent interest. In addition, the banks were often collecting 5 or 6 per cent from the stores for providing the business. And the stores in many cases were raising their prices to the customers in order to cover this expense.

Banks with such plans were often disguising their stiff interest charges by advertising that their loans cost 1 per cent or 1½ per cent a month. Any interest charge not translated into true annual cost is meaningless. Yet many stores were specifically forbidding their sales personnel to talk about true annual interest. Many short-term loans were offered the public as 3 per cent. The fine type disclosed that they were 3 per cent a month, so that they were actually 36 per cent loans. In 1960, Senator Paul Douglas began pressing a bill (S.27S5) that would require moneylenders of all kinds to disclose in writing to consumers exactly how much interest the borrower would have to pay on a true annual basis. *Sales Management* pointed out that the bill might send "buyerson-the-cuff into a tailspin." And an executive of a national merchants' association argued that people expect to pay more when they buy on credit, but that "to give them too much information about financing costs would only befuddle them."

As millions of American citizens began adjusting to spending more than they earned, living in the red was glorified as not only fun but patriotic. *Sales Credit News* printed a parable about the wise and foolish lovers. The foolish lovers—in its version—decided they still couldn't afford to get married, so they both set out on a systematic program of saving until they could unite and establish a home without going into debt. They were foolish, the journal explained, because they were postponing and thus missing a portion of the pleasure of living life together. And, further, they "deprived the national economy of two or more years of family consumption."

The wise lovers, in contrast, were not deterred from uniting in matrimony merely because they had no savings. They got married immediately, took their honeymoon on credit, bought a car on credit, bought a home on credit, and furnished it on credit. These heroes of the consuming battle line, the journal said, "stimulated production, created employment, increased purchasing power, raised the standard of living."

The journal didn't say whether they lived happily ever after. Chances are, they didn't. Living close to insolvency with unpaid bills pressing creates marital strains between husbands and wives. This, of course, is a matter of common observation, but it has also been substantiated by a survey made for a group of insurance companies.

When investigators for *U.S. News & World Report* sought to diagnose the mood of America by nationwide interviewing, they asked many people what their biggest worry was. The answers predominantly were "money" or "making ends meet." The report stated: "It's a worry that cuts across all income groups, all occupations, and all ages."

A minister in Cedar Rapids, Iowa, reported that "in 75 per cent of the cases where people come to me with marital problems, money enters in." And a doctor in the same city said many of his patients' aches and pains were caused by money problems.

"You buy a car on time and stretch the payments over thirty months, and you've got a chronic pain. You really have."

A Long Island kidnaper explained his rash act by stating he had lately been harassed as a result of trying to meet installment payments for thousands of dollars' worth of gadgets and accessories he had bought for his little home.

Still, as the sixties have begun with something less than jet-powered take-off, most American citizens are not particularly apprehensive that they would fall into really serious trouble because of their debts. They feel that the federal government—whether Democratic or Republican— is emotionally committed to make it safe for them to continue spending. And it has become increasingly probable that if a notable lag in consumption does develop the federal government will be under massive pressure to manipulate interest rates in such a way that saving will be discouraged and spending encouraged.

When worried economists urged the curbing of easy credit, merchants and manufacturers protested that it would slow down sales and invite a depression. They quite probably were recalling the admonitions from Washington to buy instead of save during the recession of 1958. One business analyst reported then that "evidence is mounting that people are saving instead of spending, and the Administration doesn't like it." The headline over his analysis read in part: "RISE IN THRIFT SPOTTED AS DISTURBING ADMINISTRATION."

William Whyte, Jr., in *The Organization Man*, cited an unforgettable comment he frequently encountered in the new suburbias when the people talked about the possibility of a depression. He found that they refused to believe it could happen because "They can't dispossess everybody."

Meanwhile, at least one marketing consultant was speculating that the great forthcoming crop of new babies—so eagerly awaited by marketers (see Chapter 16)—might well be financed on credit.

15. HEDONISM FOR THE MASSES

"Why Deny Yourself?"—Headline of an advertisement for John David men's wear.

IN THE BROADWAY PLAY, "A RAISIN IN THE SUN," THE son imbued with modern ideas voiced a lament that would delight most marketers. He cried:

"I want so many things, it drives me crazy. . . . Money is life!"

His old-fashioned mother, sad and perplexed, replied: "You can't be satisfied just to be proud. . . . How different we've become!"

The marketers of the United States, in addition to developing specific strategies for moving goods, sought to develop an overall strategy that would make all the others more effective. They sought to generate a love for possessions and a zest for finding momentary pleasures. They sought to encourage Americans to break out of their old-fashioned inhibitions and to learn to live it up. All this, it was hoped, would produce a permissive mood for carefree buying.

Americans traditionally have liked to think of themselves as a frugal, hard-working, God-fearing people making sacrifices for the long haul. They have exalted such maxims of Ben Franklin as: "A man may, if he knows not how to save as he gets, keep his nose to the grindstone."

Puritanical traits were esteemed necessary to survival by the settlers struggling to convert forest and prairie into a national homeland. By the nineteenth century, however, a flamboyant streak was beginning to emerge clearly in the American character. Emerson observed that Americans, unlike Europeans, exhibited "an uncalcu-lated, headlong expenditure." As more and more Americans found themselves living in metropolitan areas, hedonism as a guiding phi-losophy of life gained more and more disciples. People sought pos-sessions more than formerly in emulation of, or competition with, their neighbors. Quite possibly, the environment of thickly settled areas brought a lessening of serenity and a feeling of being swal-lowed up that impelled the people to strive for distinctive emblems and gratification through consumption. The growing availability of manufactured goods undoubtedly had a great deal to do with the rise in hedonism. The upheaval of wars and the uncertainty of life in an atomic era also contributed to the live-for-themoment spirit.

During the fifties, however, another force came powerfully into play in the promotion of hedonism. Many marketers, as a calculated strategy, sought to promote a mood of self-indulgence in order to promote sales. The puritanical inhibitions of Americans were seen as blocking consumers from enjoying the wondrously rich, full new way of life that marketers were ready and eager to provide.

Advertising agencies in their house organs declared that the pu-ritanism still lurking in many Americans should be a major target. Admen were exhorted to re-educate people's thinking into "health-ier channels." Ernest Dichter, head of the Institute for Motivational Research, was in the forefront of marketing consultants who spelled out for sales managers the opportunities provided by the new mood of selfindulgence. He reported to them that "America is experienc-ing a revolution in self-indulgence." People, he said, were more and more prone to ask, "Why shouldn't I?" They were increasingly willing "to give vent" to their "whims and desires." And he added: "We've learned that one rarely makes one's ultimate goal—so why not enjoy life now?"

At other times he seemed a little less certain this mood had become general and pointed out why it should prevail and how it could be made to prevail. Americans had been "caught in a cobweb of tradition and moral concepts which . . . have portrayed life as a sequence of misery, worry, and toil." What was needed, he said, was a more reasonable attitude toward life, with fun and pleasure and happiness no longer considered unethical. "Learning to accept the permanent 'burden' of a good life is one of the most challenging psychological problems of our age." His publication *Motivations* said that one of the central problems of the day was to give people permission to enjoy their prosperity, to feel moral not immoral in their hedonism. Advertising displays and sales promotion plans should be geared to this theme.

Many marketers joined in the game of tearing away the puritanical cobwebs and educating the public away from being old-fud Prudence Pennies. Professor Otis Pease, Stanford University historian, took a comprehensive look at advertising in the late fifties and concluded that advertising was seeking to discredit thrift and was working to whet the acquisitive impulse.

Here is one kind of problem they tackled. Furniture makers were annoyed by the persistent old-fashioned habits many parents exhibited when their children married. These parents still thought they were helping the newlyweds by giving them hand-me-downs, pieces of furniture they could spare from their own homes. Some furniture men began urging at trade-association meetings that the furniture industry sponsor an advertising campaign designed to shame both parents and the young couples away from such a practice.

The joys of self-indulgence were stressed, consciously or unwittingly, in many sales messages. A New York department store told women in a full-page advertisement: "Even If You Own a Dozen Coats, You Can't Afford to Miss. . . . " A San Francisco store featuring luxurious fixtures and accessories for bathrooms beckoned passers-by with the sign, "PAMPER YOURSELF!"

Sales experts began searching for occasions to provide the public with an excuse for splurging. Holidays took on ever greater importance in their planning. A bed merchandiser cried out that he was offering "BIGGEST WASHINGTON'S BIRTHDAY SALE IN OUR HISTORY—ONE DAY ONLY!" A New York department store ran a full-page advertisement showing children's shoes with the headline: "EASTER IS A NEW PAIR OF SHOES." An appliance store in Erie, Pennsylvania, sold $30,000 worth of goods in a giant three-day St. Patrick's Day sale with prizes. On the second day of the sale, members of a local church held a cake sale in the store. Many who came for cake also bought appliances.

By the beginning of the sixties, Mother's Day was computed to produce $17 worth of purchases for every mother in the land. Father's Day produced $7 worth of buying per father. And Graduation Day assured $10 worth of purchasing per graduate.

The most cherished splurge day, of course, was Christmas because that was not just a day but a whole season. Spending per family ran into hundreds of dollars. An average teen-age girl could be counted upon to make at least $55 worth of purchases in anticipation of Christmas each year. The main streets of some Midwestern cities were draped with Christmas decorations by the second week in November. Several weeks before a recent Christmas, the Arthur Murray organization in New York proclaimed: "Hurry: Special pre-Holiday Arthur Murray Offer! GIVE YOURSELF THIS CHRISTMAS GIFT . . . Now!"

The Christmas gift ahead-of-time that the reader was invited to give *himself*—in this notable interpretation of the traditional Christmas spirit—was a dancing lesson.

Two advertisements within a few feet of each other in a New York subway car indicated pretty well what was happening to Christmas under the pressures of consumerism. One showed Santa Claus holding on his lap a cutie wearing du Pont nylon stockings. The other showed a different Santa happily smoking Kent cigarettes. On television, on the other hand, a third Santa was expressing his preference for El Producto cigars. To a child it must have all been very confusing.

An appliance retailer confided to *Consumer Reports*: "If you have to hit a guy [customer] with higher prices, do it during the Christmas selling season when he feels good." Merchants were doing such a good job of promoting the giveaway spirit around Christmastime that attorneys for defendants in claims cases maneuvered to try to keep their cases from coming before a jury in the latter half of December.

As sales planners searched the calendar for possible splurge days, they found that the calendar revealed poor planning. There were no really good holiday excuses for splurging between Father's Day in June and the Christmas season. A movement began to set aside August 1 as "Friendship Day." On this new holiday each citizen could show— through purchasing gifts—how much he cherished his really good friends.

We shouldn't overlook Valentine's Day. It has become one of the big newcomers in the eyes of marketers. It is in fourth place among the holidays producing significant increases in sales. A New York department store filled its many windows with merchandise, and over each it placed the sign: "HOW DO I LOVE THEE? LET ME COUNT THE WAYS." The ways, as enumerated in the window displays, included mink stoles, copper frying pans, ties, and negligees. As Valentine Day, 1960, approached, the publication Sales Sense for druggists called Valentine's Day "a real sweetheart of a day to increase sales" for those stores "alert to cash sentimentality into dollars."

Sad days as well as glad days could be the occasion for giving. Billboards in some parts of the United States showed a bouquet of flowers with the admonition not just to send sympathy.

Another approach used in promoting hedonism in the United States was to encourage, to a state of chronic itch, the tendency of Americans to love change in their lives. Anything "old," "used," or "permanent," was to be disdained. A marketing expert counseled the home-furnishing industry: "Make people discover for themselves that there's fun and pleasure in changing their decor. Establish a standard based on changeability and not on permanence." All this helped provide a philosophical base for the throwaway spirit, already discussed.

Home builders succeeded during the fifties in insinuating a new and odious word into the language of home merchandising. That word was "used." A new house became a "used" house if the buyer decided a month after moving in that he wanted to sell it. Any used house was to be viewed with suspicion if not contempt. It was soiled merchandise. (Your author should confess that in his entire lifetime he has never lived in anything but very used houses.)

The executive marketing board of the National Association of Home Builders was admonished by the president of an advertising agency in late 1959 to set up a multimillion-dollar advertising fund to make Americans want to get rid of old homes. He proposed that the association make the average American as dissatisfied with an antiquated house as he would be with a twenty-year-old automobile.

John and Mary Drone, the chronically overstrained subdivision dwellers in John Keats's *The Crack in the Picture Window*, were caught up in the organized scorn of the used house. Keats related: "The Drones never once considered anything but the purchase of a new house. Not for an instant did either entertain the notion of a spacious—and far cheaper—older house. . . . Newness became a criterion surpassing cost and, in some cases, need. Second-hand development houses were sold to the kind of people who buy second-hand automobiles solely out of need."

Pierre Martineau, research and marketing director of *The Chicago Tribune*, observed much the same wariness of the old in his *Motivation in Advertising*. He reported: "Tradition bores us now. Instead of being an asset, it is virtually a liability to a people looking for the newest—the newest!—always the *newest!*" A survey made by a magazine for the mechanically inclined revealed that the typical American changed his or her car mainly for the sake of change. He wants a new one. General Motors in 1960 began running double-spread advertisements glorifying the general idea of new-car buying. It proclaimed. "THERE'S NOTHING LIKE A NEW CAR TO ENRICH YOUR FAMILY LIFE."

Hedonism was also actively promoted by campaigns to persuade the American people that they deserved to enjoy the pleasures of enriched living *instantly* and without lifting a finger. "Instant" and "ready" became the magic words in marketing everything from soda pop, whipped cream, and cherry pies, to headache remedies. The noted business philosopher, Charles G. Mortimer, chairman of the board of General Foods, lectured businessmen that one of the great challenges of the day was promoting "creative convenience." He pointed to the "tidal wave of craving for convenience" sweeping the country and stated: "Today, convenience is the success factor of just about every type of product and service that is showing steady growth." He continued, "Just about everything we buy today must be ready to use, ready to wear, ready to plug in, ready to turn on, ready to take home . . . ready to serve. This aspect of our national impatience represents probably the greatest challenge to marketing creativeness that American businessmen have ever faced." Tomorrow, he predicted, even the home would be prepackaged and sold "almost ready for a family to move in and start living!"

According to one joke, maids considering the possibility of favoring a family with their services were likely to inquire cautiously: "Do you peel or thaw?"

An elderly supermarket operator in Indianapolis shook his head sadly as he pointed out to me all the "convenience" foods he was selling to bridge-playing wives. He muttered: "The husband works all day and then comes home to a dinky little precooked pot pie." He said he would not permit them in his own home. Ready-to-serve meals are likely to cost up to 50 per cent more than home-prepared meals.

He told of jesting with one young redheaded wife who was inspecting his bakery-made cherry pies. He asked her why she didn't make one herself. She replied: "I wouldn't know how to begin." This elderly man began showing her by listing the ingredients. When he said "shortening," she asked, "What's that?" He explained and began showing her how to roll out the crust. She wrinkled her pert nose and said, "It sounds terribly messy. I think I'll take this one here."

Hundreds of wives, he told me with a shrug, buy his expensive jars of chicken a la king every week when they could make it themselves from leftovers for less than a third the cost. Yet these same wives, he said, see themselves as frugal, thrifty guardians of the family's dollars and keep complaining to their husbands about the terrible time they have making ends meet because of the high cost of food.

Recently businessmen have discovered that the United States is embarking on a "new age of elegance." Women's clothing is becoming "casually elegant." Merchandisers of furniture have become obsessed, in their talk, about the public's new craving for elegance. Gold-plated bathroom faucets are soaring in popularity, as are gold-plated toothbrushes. Jewelers have joined in hailing the new era of elegance. And the food marketers have decided that the United States is becoming a nation of elegance-loving epicureans. The sale of luxury foods doubled in four years as North Americans were persuaded to nibble $3,000,000 worth of caviar a year, and the more brave of them to stomach such delicacies as chocolate-covered ants.

A domestic champagne producer, in its advertisements, has begun urging married couples to break out champagne for breakfast. It calls breakfast the "critical time in matrimony." And it proposes that the spouses "face up" to each other with champagne whenever they begin feeling that "the bloom is off the marriage."

Still another aspect of the promotion of hedonism, we should note, has been the drive to make Americans more impulsive in their shopping habits. Du Pont found that impulse buying in supermarkets had soared nearly a third in a decade. Supermarkets changed from being simple, stripped-down marts designed to pass on the economies of mass buying to the consumer. Originally they had operated on a slim 12 per cent markup. Now the supermarkets have become shimmering carnivals offering free automobiles as prizes, offering premiums, trading stamps, soft music, and hundreds of packages that have been shrewdly designed, at considerable expense, to present an imagery that will cry out to the passing shopper: "Grab me!" The result of all these changes in the supermarkets is that markups have risen on the average to nearly 20 per cent.

The family's apparel items also have become impulse items. *Modern Packaging* reported that shirt manufacturers felt it was no longer sufficient to wrap a shirt in a transparent, protective film. The package had to be upgraded by creating more invitingly printed transparent packages.

Louis Cheskin, director of the Color Research Institute, meanwhile reported to marketers: "The consumer does not judge the product, he judges the package." Men's belts might be a case in point. Traditionally, belts offered for sale simply were hung from a store rack and presented as a utilitarian item. However, marketers were finding that men's belts could be sold to both men and their wives as impulse items if adroitly packaged. Mr. Cheskin pointed to the experience of the makers of Paris belts. Mr. Cheskin was invited to address a conference of the top management of the Paris company on the subject, "Why Should Belts Be Packaged?" He summed up his advice to them in his book, *Why People Buy*. He said that for the wife in this era of abundance "the mere act of buying a belt for [her] husband . . . is filled with deep psychological implications." Here is the surprising analysis of these implications as they were turned up by his researchers:

"Marketing tests and experience have shown that normally a woman will not be attracted by belts hanging from a rack. Hanging belts do not arouse a woman's interest. A hanging belt has no attraction power. It is limp, unstimulating, and undesirable. To the normal, healthy, energetic woman a hanging belt is not a symbol of virility or quality. It cannot possibly be associated with her man. It is not an appropriate symbol. It presents a negative image." On the other hand, "a belt that is encased in a psychologically potent package" has favorable symbolism and "is naturally assigned the role of symbolizing respect, affection, and even great love." The potent vessel chosen to house this love symbol was a chaste white cardboard container with a transparent plastic dome appropriately called "Vista-dome," perhaps because it resembled a vista-dome bus. The success of all these strategies for promoting hedonism was apparent from a number of reports. *Printers' Ink* reported that a new type of feminine customer in supermarkets was evolving. This customer, it reported, "is constantly looking for something new."

An editor in Pittsburgh observed: "The people who are complaining about high prices are the ones coming out of supermarkets loaded with bottles of cocktail cherries, goldfish in plastic bags, frozen foods, TV dinners, phonograph records—all sorts of things you really don't have to have so fancy." Sociologists reported finding that American families, regardless of their income level, tended to wish they had about 25 per cent more than they had.

As the sixties opened, the business and financial editor of *The New York Herald Tribune* summed up for businessmen what prevailed by saying: "If a whole people can be said to wallow in prosperity, Americans will do it in 1960 as, uninhibited, they gluttonously reap the fruits of 183 years of free enterprise." He said that the Luxury Life had become the goal of most Americans.

Perhaps the most impressive report on the swing to hedonism was made by the research division of *The Chicago Tribune*. Its study, entitled *The New Consumer,* was based on a $100,000 study of homemakers from three different social layers in the suburbs of Chicago. At all three levels a trend toward hedonism was evident. Mr. Martineau, director of research and marketing for the *Tribune,* summed up the findings of the investigators as they related to this trend in these words:

"There has been a shift from the philosophy of security and saving to a philosophy of spending and immediate satisfaction ... more selfindulgent spending, a tendency to equate standard of living with possession of material goods. ... "

Consider the change in attitude toward spending money. At the upper-middle-class level, a wife in the town of Golf recalled the simple, frugal pattern of life that her own parents had maintained and then exclaimed: "We're so different. We are absolute spendthrifts. We don't have a dime. We live for today. ... " Another wife in this same town asserted: "You must spend just a little more than you can afford to progress higher in life." The reports noted that the wives at this level tended to see "conspicuous consumption" as investment, not waste. One wife in Golf, the daughter of a prosperous, self-made lumberman, said: "My father feels it is disgraceful the way we spend money—he feels we should save for a rainy day; but I feel I may not live for the rainy day, so I'm going to enjoy each day to the full *now*. . . . My parents did not decorate their home every four or five years, as we do."

At the somewhat less prosperous suburb of Park Forest, wives showed the same restlessness and pleasure in spending. One wife said that the difference between herself and her parents was that she buys "new furniture and lamps because we get tired of looking at them any longer." Another woman said: "Today, we're always looking to buy something that's a time saver so that we can have more time to relax and enjoy life." Still another woman said that when she and her husband buy draperies, rugs, and furniture they hope the goods "don't last as long as our parents' did."

Women in the third community of Home Town, primarily a working-class and lower-white-collar suburb, revealed this same fascination with accumulating material things. The report stated that in Home Town "the gadget . . . becomes the symbol of 'finer living.'"

16. PROGRESS THROUGH PROLIFERATION OF PEOPLE

"A Bonanza for Industry-Babies. Sixty Million More U.S. Consumers in Next Nineteen Years."—*U.S. News & World Report,* January 4, 1957.

IN THE LOBBY OF THE UNITED STATES DEPARTMENT of Commerce building a giant "clock" is running which brings joy to the American marketers who watch it ticking. It is one Washington frill they heartily endorse. Every seven and a half seconds a blue light flashes, as on a pinball machine, to indicate that a new baby has been born somewhere in the United States. Much more slowly, a purple light flashes—every twenty seconds—to indicate that some unfortunate American citizen has died. Another flashing light indicates the occasional arrival of an immigrant.

The key light is the white one, which shows the net results of all these changes. It flashes every eleven seconds to indicate that in that period one more human being has been added to the total United States population. Thus every eleven seconds marketers have gained one new prospect who will need food, clothing, shelter, and later on toy pistols, motorcars, hi-fi sets, powerboats, mixers, and casket. A large sign beside this clock during the late fifties read:

MORE PEOPLE

mean

MORE MARKETS

A soft-drink party was held in the lobby in October, 1958, when the tote meter flashed past 175,000,000. Heady predictions were made about the prospects opening up to marketers as a result of the fantastic population explosion in the United States.

U.S. News & World Report, which is read primarily by businessmen, stated: "America's greatest boom is in people. Business, workers, government will be kept busy providing for an exploding population."

Actually, the United States population was exploding much more violently than that publication realized when it forecast in 1957 that the nation would have "Sixty Million More U.S. Consumers in 19 years." Later census estimates indicated that nearly one hundred million more consumers might be added to the United States population in the next twenty years. People were living longer and longer. Couples were marrying younger and younger—and setting their sights on larger families. Girls now approaching the marriageable age expected to have one more child than their mothers did. The bumper crop of babies born after World War II would soon be marrying—in the mid-sixties—and were expected to produce a prodigious increase in the population.

The nation's growing population was widely perceived by exultant businessmen as a built-in guarantee of long-term prosperity and as a main prop of the expanding economy. And to some extent they sought to promote the idea that having big families was a fine, wonderful thing.

Americans were prone to deplore population expansion in faraway lands. The fact was, however, that the United States was going through one of the greatest population explosions in the history of mankind. Its rate of population increase was as high as that of India and Italy, if not higher. Nearly three million people already were being added to the United States population each year, and that rate would grow. This was equivalent to adding annually a dozen brand-new cities the size of Omaha. If current trends continued, quite likely the United States population by the end of the century—or within the lifetime of most of us—would more than double the present population.

All this was viewed as progress. Babies by the millions would eliminate the possibility of serious depressions and serve as a backstop against possible miscalculation in overexpanding the capacity of factories. A few weeks after the stock market went into a slump at the beginning of 1960, financial analysts advised nervous investors to be of good cheer: with the population growth in prospect, stocks just *had* to go up in the long run.

The Advertising Council took the lead, appropriately, in spelling out the happy implications of the baby boom. To put consumers in a mood to step up their spending—and stop worrying—it organized a multimillion-dollar pepping-up campaign. One of the advertisements it prepared showed the picture of a stork—symbolizing population growth—on its nest. The caption read: "THIS BIRD MEANS BUSINESS."

Such ads not only would help put the public in a confident buying mood but might encourage American families to feel they were being patriotic if they had large families, as well as proving their virility and old-fashioned Americanism. During the 1958 recession, the Advertising Council drew up seven basic reasons why Americans should be confident about their future. The Number One reason cited was "*more people.*"

Here are a few other samples of the kind of exulting businessmen were doing at the prospect of multiplying the number of humans in the United States.

Printers' Ink: "Marketing opportunities are unlimited.... It will mean that in the next ten years the rate of new home production will have to be doubled."

Sales Management quoted a marketing-research director as exclaiming, when the United States Census Bureau revised upward its projection of future population growth: "There is gold in them thar years."

Engineering News Record: "NEW POPULATION SCORE CARD CAN HELP YOU STRIKE IT RICH—The country's booming population growth spells money in the bank for the alert construction man. . . . It means

> More homebuilding
> More community facilities
> More roads
> More commercial buildings
> More factories
> More transportation facilities."

The views of marketers that more babies could be the basis for national rejoicing became widely accepted or seconded by the public.

The number of young families hoping to have four or more children doubled during the postwar period.

To marketers the vast emerging "youth market" was particularly tantalizing and challenging. For one thing, there were so many prospective customers involved. A vice-president of an advertising agency, McCann-Erickson, pointed out that by 1965 there would be 77,000,000 young people in the United States under the age of twenty. As a businessman and I drove past a new schoolyard filled with children, he joked: "Look at all those happy little dollar signs."

Furthermore, these young people were becoming significant spenders. Most estimates agreed that teen-agers alone had become a ten-billion-dollar market just on the basis of their own spending power. And by 1970 they would be a twenty-billion-dollar market. Already each teen-ager could be counted on to spend more than $400 a year. It was no longer a market to be scorned as a nickel-and-dime thing.

Marketers were admonished to remember that all these millions of youngsters would one day marry and become really big spenders if properly nurtured. Catch them while their buying habits are forming! "GET THEM AT THE GET AGE!" one network trumpeted as it urged advertising men to consider its heavy juvenile audience in buying time. And *Seventeen* magazine stressed that its teen-age readers were at the "motivage" in acquiring lifetime buying habits.

A firm called Teenage Public Relations, Inc., emerged to guide advertisers in tapping the teen-age market. And *Teen* magazine set up a Teen Consumer Testing Board to help advertisers make sure they were playing the right "tune" to lure teen-agers to their products.

Finally, the youth market was receiving new respect because marketers were realizing that youths are perhaps the most tempting target of all for selling because they tend to be even more impulsive, unskilled, and manipulatable than their parents. And parents are more prone than in the past to indulge their youngsters in whatever fads the marketers are able to stimulate. Teen-agers proved to be excellent prospects for deodorants, breast-developer hormones, hair dyes, home permanents, pimple removers, and pep pills. An executive of the Institute for Motivational Research pointed out that while teenagers might not believe in authority, they did believe in advertising.

The new mood of parents in wishing to indulge their children's whims was noted several times by researchers for the *Chicago Tribune's* study of attitudes of suburban homemakers. One mother in Park Forest explained: "My teen-age son likes to wear off-color sweaters and shirts with socks to match. Elastic belts are the fad now. My daughter must have a leather parka jacket. We want our children to enjoy life. Therefore, if they want something the other children have, we buy it for them."

The *Tribune's* report on Park Forest observed: "There is much buying for the children, and the things bought are determined by what the child wants, rather than what the parents want for him. What the child wants, in turn, is determined either by what the other kids have or by a particular item seen in advertisements. The parents see 'giving the child what he wants' in the way of material things as a positive thing."

The great baby boom—or "population bomb," as some preferred to call it—put marketers in many dozens of lines to mapping plans to "cash in" on it.

First, of course, there was the obvious tot and toddler market for baby powder, nursery furniture, soft foods, nipples, etc. *Sales Management* reported in 1960 that new baby foods were being researched and launched at "a frantic pace."

Then there was the booming youngster market for ice cream, soda pop, phonograph records, and toys—not to mention school desks, rubbers, etc. American youngsters by 1960 were receiving a billion and a half dollars' worth of toys each year. During a good December day, American stores were jingling up six million dollars' worth of toy sales every hour. The average American child received $26 worth of toys a year. In my own state of Connecticut, where toy consumption is highest, the average child received $36 worth. The head of a firearms manufacturing firm observed that by the time a boy is fifteen he has had between fifteen and twenty replicas of guns—and so is now a prime prospect for a real bullet-firing one.

Most of the major manufacturers of brassieres—and many minor ones—began promoting and selling bras to nine-and ten-year-old girls. By 1960, this had become an important market, as thousands of little girls had been conditioned by the emphasis on bosoms in advertising and elsewhere to worry about their flattish chests or to see bras as status symbols. The 28AA bra especially built for moppets was described by New York women's editor Eugenia Sheppard as "a limp white object that looks like a dead rabbit and is positively the No. 1 gift, except for nylons, that ten-year-olds . . . crave these days." She quoted a bra executive as explaining, "Of course, it's all in their minds, since most of these bras have hardly any shape. . . . A few are padded for little girls with an inferiority complex about being flat."

The really lush youth market, however, was the teen-age group. Its members were likely to have big wants, big allowances; and often they had their own earned, big-sized spending money. *Life* magazine surveyed the teen-agers' spending habits and concluded that they were surrounding themselves with "a fantastic array of garish and often expensive baubles and amusements," including 1,500,000 motorcars and $20,000,000 worth of lipstick. It cited the case of a seventeen-year-old girl in Van Nuys, California, as a "seller's dream." The consumption habits of this girl, Suzie, while high, were said to be fairly typical of girls in "upper-middle-income families in her town." In the previous year, Suzie had received $1,500 worth of clothes and $550 worth of entertainment and $102 worth of beauty-parlor treatments. She owned seven bathing suits and had her own telephone. On summer-vacation days she loved to wander with her mother through department stores, picking out frocks or furnishings for her room or silver and expensive crockery for the hope chest she had already started. The publication said some people might think that American teen-agers were being spoiled to death, but it suggested that it was too late for parents to revolt. "Teenage spending," it said, had become so important that "such action would send quivers through the entire economy."

In its predictions of things to come as the sixties began, *Printers' Ink* carried the headline: "AD AGENCIES WILL SET UP TEEN-AGE SECTIONS." The publisher pointed out that teen-agers constituted the fastest-growing market in the United States today, "offering astounding sales potential." But, he added, "special advertising techniques must be developed to meet the challenge."

One group of marketers making great gains with teen-agers was the cigarette makers. *Fortune* magazine, commenting on the way the cigarette industry had managed to bounce back from its slump following the cancer scare as it related to cigarette smoking, observed: "In part this [bounce back] is due to population gains, particularly in the big increase in the number of teen-agers, who appear to be smoking more furiously than ever before."

Coffee makers meanwhile were working to recruit teen-agers. The National Coffee Association placed a sixteen-page insert in *Scholastic* magazine, which is geared to teen-agers. It gave tips on such commendable things as studying, safe driving, grooming, dating, health, and popularity, but printed a coffee recipe at the bottom of every page.

Perhaps the most significant—and, to me as the parent of three teenagers, most disquieting—move the marketers made to tap the teen-age market was to issue "junior" credit cards. Many department and other stores across the land have begun inviting Junior to wave his credit card and say, "Charge it!" Stores of one major chain began taking young debtors on the cuff even before they were old enough to shave—at the age of fourteen. Some stores made it clear that parental approval was not necessary in order to open a junior charge account. A department store in Iowa began advertising: "TEEN-AGERS! HAVE YOUR OWN CHARGE ACCOUNT!"

An official of the National Retail Merchants Association exhorted department stores to open up junior charge accounts and contended: "Teen-agers of today are America's greatest natural resources" and offer a "made-to-order opportunity for the sales-minded credit executive."

The stores inviting Junior's patronage on a credit basis usually professed to be utterly uninterested in him as a customer. They just wanted to help him become a more prudent citizen by offering him an educational program in money management. A department store in Iowa heralded its junior credit plan by saying, "Its purpose is to give these young people experience in managing their budgets and to promote their early appreciation of good credit standing in their community." On the other hand, the Council on Consumer Information commented on some of the plans that stores were making for Junior by asking: "Are they attempting to follow the Biblical admonition: 'Train up a child in the way he should go: and when he is old he will not depart from it'?" The president of New York's Bowery Savings Bank said that teaching the young to spend on credit "is something like teaching the young to use narcotics."

This training of the young was also being pressed by one association of finance companies with the rather amazing cooperation of a national association of school officials. A booklet entitled *Using Consumer Credit,* widely distributed in American schools, upon inspection turned out to have been prepared with the help of two publicists working on behalf of this association of finance companies. It urged its student readers: "Don't be afraid to use credit."

A further development pleasing to marketers was that young people were marrying at an earlier age. The most frequent marriage age of girls had dropped to eighteen. And more and more college students were marrying instead of waiting until after graduation. This meant they usually were permitting their early years of marriage to be subsidized by parents. A young man no longer needed to establish his capability to be a breadwinner before marrying.

When a lad and lass prepare to marry, something pretty wonderful happens from the marketers' viewpoint. Spending—by cash or credit—shoots up at a dazzling rate. The bride and groom spend, their parents spend, and their well-wishers spend. The couple of 1960 needs a shimmering brand-new home instantly, fully equipped. *U.S. News & World Report* put "new demand resulting from a marriage at about $13,600." And it stressed that that figure was conservative. It broke down this figure as follows: A house costing an average of $10,000 was required—whether purchased or rented. Then there was at least $500 required for a car, and an average of $2,500 for equipping the new household with furniture and electric appliances. Finally—and this seems most conservative—there was $600 required for expenses incidental to the wedding such as ring, clothes, catering, and honeymoon. An enterprising sample-distribution outfit, Bridal-Pax, began handing out kits at marriage-license bureaus. These kits, distributed to hundreds of thousands of brides-to-be, contained samples of brand-name furniture polish, household cleaner, etc.—and, of all things, headache pills!

And so it was that most marketers were elated by the prospects of an additional hundred million consumers being added to the United States population within about two decades. Some alarmists wondered where jobs, resources, and living space would be found to support these additional hundred million people. These, indeed, were prickly problems to be pondered tomorrow. To talk about them today might jar consumer confidence. But could such questions wait?

PART III

Implications

17. EVER-MOUNTING CONSUMPTION?

" . . . we may not be able to get rid of the mess without also getting rid of the abundance."—John Kouwenhoven in a *Harper's* article entitled "Waste Not, Have Not—A Clue to American Prosperity."

THUS FAR IN OUR EXPLORATION WE HAVE NOTED the developing dilemma posed by ever-mounting productivity in the United States, and the very logical or human responses that marketing people have made in coping with this new kind of national dilemma. We have examined the strategies devised to encourage individual Americans to buy more goods and services each year. And we have noted the growing reliance of marketers on the willingness of Americans to keep their population expanding.

The results might be characterized in various ways. But certainly one result is a force-fed society with a vested interest in prodigality and with no end in sight to the need for ever-greater and more wasteful consumption.

Now we come to the harder part of the book from the author-analyst's viewpoint. It is far easier to try to diagnose a developing situation than it is to assess what this situation implies for the future, or suggest what if anything can or should be done about it. In this instance it is particularly true because the situation developing in the United States appears to be unique in the history of mankind. There are no obvious precedents to cite as guide marks for present or future action.

In a most tentative mood let us try to comprehend the implications of a system that demands that its people engage in ever-greater consumption.

First of all, we should note that this system, despite any current excesses, has brought the American people to one of the highest levels of physical well-being the world has ever known, exceeded only, perhaps, by New Zealand's. And this is no mean accomplishment to be deprecated. Haunting anxiety about where one's next meal or pair of shoes is coming from has become but a memory for all but a small proportion of the population that is unemployed or lives in rural slums or is engaged in migratory work. A Negro boot-black in Oklahoma proudly showed me his pair of thirty-dollar cowboy boots. Further, we must recognize that every operating system devised by man has its shortcomings and unpalatable aspects. It is no accident that all economic Utopias have remained ideals. Any real-life economic Utopias that man could devise quite probably would soon prove to be dull, if not unworkable, to consumer and seller alike.

And, then, there is the uncomfortably challenging point to be recognized that perhaps the United States has no acceptable alternative to ever-rising and wasteful consumption. I don't agree, but this viewpoint deserves respect. Mr. Kouwenhoven, cited at the outset of this chapter, is a dispassionate social observer, not an overheated marketing man. He tells of seeing American national forests strewn with beer cans. The beer cans are to him symbolic of the thoughtless, throwaway wastefulness of Americans in regard to the nation's resources. He suggests that there may well be "a rather tricky relationship between waste [symbolized by those beer cans] and abundance." Can the United States have one without the other? Is such wastefulness becoming a major factor in keeping the wheels turning? The *Wall Street Journal* commented on the acknowledged wastefulness of the United States economy by arguing that the real waste would be to kill the goose.

Some economic analysts and marketers shudder at the mere thought of American consumers returning to a prudent, rational approach to buying. They are not sure what might happen to the national prosperity. The Wall Street analyst Paul Mazur, in *The Standards We Raise*, asks: "Just suppose that ... the factor of obsolescence were to disappear from the scene?.... What would happen to a market dependent upon new models, new styles, new ideas?" *Retailing Daily* quoted an appliance dealer as expressing fear that his annual sales would be slashed drastically if he couldn't lure prospects with frequent changes in color and gadgetry.

A number of economic writers have argued that the annual style change in motorcars, which we have discussed, has become essential to the economic well-being of the entire nation. When the 1959 model motorcars were unveiled, the most notable changes were stylistic. Tail fins jutted in every direction. The dual headlights were shifted into new positions. The silhouettes were made still lower, still wider, still longer. And there was still more unneeded horsepower. Also, as usual, the price tags were higher than the year before. In short, these motorcars represented the high point of progress through styling obsolescence. The offerings might well have been considered an affront to the intelligence of the American people. Yet in announcing these motorcars, responsible magazines carried such somber headlines as: "THE FATE OF OUR ECONOMY RIDES WITH THE 1959 CARS."[1]

And respected economic writers offered such observations as "The response to the new cars this fall will be of enormous importance to the nation's economy." Writers pointed out that one American worker in six now owes his job, in one way or another, to the motorcar industry. Even drive-in theater owners and owners of roadside motels are dependent upon Americans having a superabundance of motorcars.

Perhaps the most vigorous stand ever taken to justify the consumption of unneeded goods came back in the thirties, when marketers were first perceiving the challenge of the need for evergreater consumption. A writer discussing the new concept of "obsoletism" in *Printers' Ink* made a comment that sounded startlingly like a line that might have been in Huxley's *Brave New World*. He stated earnestly:

"Any plan which increases consumption is justifiable. . . . People are persuaded to abandon the old and buy the new to be up to date. Does there seem to be a sad waste in the process? Not at all. Wearing things out does not produce prosperity, but buying things does. Thrift in the industrial society in which we now live consists in keeping all the factories busy."

Even assuming that force feeding has become inevitable, Americans still do not have to like it. And it seems reasonable that they should at least understand the price they are paying for the force feeding and the attendant preoccupation with consumption. Let us look, then, at a few of the prices that Americans appear to be paying:

The preoccupation with consumption is starting to make Americans look a bit fatuous in the eyes of the world. A few years ago, the industrial designer Raymond Loewy commented that nothing about the appearance of the nation's fat, gleaming automobiles "offsets the impression that we must be a wasteful, swaggering, insensitive people."

When the United States opened up its gigantic 1959 exhibition in Moscow's Sokolniki Park in an effort to win the admiration of Russia's people, a *New York Times* reporter called it "a glittering, colorful acclaim of consumer America. It is chock-full of the frills of American life." The reporter expressed his puzzlement that amid all the dazzle no unifying theme or overall message seemed to emerge.

Other reports indicated that many of the millions of Russian citizens viewing the exhibit likewise were puzzled by the American sense of values. They kept asking why so little stress was placed on such things as education and medicine. Some of this may have been deliberate heckling, but the reporters suggested that a genuine mood of puzzlement seemed to be involved.

The wastefulness of the United States has made its market more open to goods produced abroad. In earlier years, when North America's advanced technology was the wonder of the world, foreign manufacturers usually relied largely on lower-cost labor to enter the United

States market. And American industrialists still justify the use of more and more labor-saving automation as their way to meet foreign competitors who have a seeming edge because of their substantially lower labor costs, even though their labor costs, too, are rising as their productivity rises. One American steel company, which has been having difficulty selling barbed wire for farm use because of low-priced European wire available, hopes to use technology to maintain a competitive edge. It is perfecting a machine that will go onto a farm and lay fences automatically for the farmer. In this way it hopes the farmer will find that the total cost of wire and installation will be less if he orders this company's wire.

Today, however, the United States has lost most of the edge it held in technology, skills, and resources. Vice-Admiral Hyman G. Rickover has observed that the notion that modern technology is a unique American achievement is an "illusion" that has been "nourished by our mass media, advertising having made of bragging a fine art. To look at the ... jubilant reports of new inventions, discoveries, gadgets, and nostrums one would never guess how much we owe to Europe in basic research—that fountainhead of technology."

Many American companies have weakened their competitive position by their preoccupation with producing obsolescent goods and devoting ever-greater amounts of their budgets to sales promotion and advertising. Overseas producers have discovered that they can often beat the American competition just by providing a better product— better in quality, function, and durability. *Product Engineering* carried a report in mid-1960 of an industrial designer who related that in talking to prosperous people in San Salvador he found they were buying their typewriters, radios, and refrigerators from countries other than the United States. One plantation owner said that he now refused to buy American products because of the difficulties of getting them repaired. He felt that products from other countries were likely to be better engineered. A devastating comment on this foreign "invasion" appeared in the trade journal *Leather and Shoes*.[2]

Despite all the publicity given foreign "cheap labor," it said this factor can no longer be cited factually as the lone advantage that European producers have over American producers. It noted that the overseas producers were no longer confined to selling the United States such things as toys, novelties, and textiles but had expanded to technical and scientific fields which require a great deal of precision and knowhow. It pointed to the electronic equipment now "pouring into our country from Europe and Japan . . . transistors and radios . . . cameras, scientific instruments . . . and precision machinery." It argued, for example, that Japan could not sell cameras, transistor radios, etc., in the United States—regardless of price—if "their workmanship were not high grade."

The journal cited four reasons why the invaders were able to give the United States stiff competition on its own ground: rising productivity, careful marketing, "better choice of items to fit consumer wants and needs," and, finally, "better craftsmanship."

Perhaps the journal's most searching criticism of American producers was in this sentence: "We pride ourselves in our marketing alertness but it was Europe which first saw the promise of the smaller car, the economy sewing machine, the light-weight bicycle." It is possible that the Americans had not overlooked these possibilities but instead had actively tried to avoid them because of their lower unit profit.

In late 1959, *Home Furnishings Daily* carried a report on cornercutting in the electric-houseware field that was bringing a debasement of quality in several lines. Its investigator quoted one spokesman for independent housewares repair shops as declaring that "Japanese and German electric housewares would be known for their quality within a few years while American electrics would be 'famous for low price and low quality.' He claimed that this comparison already was true in some cases 'where only a year or two ago that would have been a ridiculous statement.'"

The growing reliance on promotion to sell goods is encouraging the rise of business oligarchies. In a market where heavy reliance is placed upon the skills of promotion, advertising, and display in order to command the consumers' interest, large producers have a clear advantage over the small ones because they can command greater image-building resources and can maneuver—as by issuing a profusion of brands—to gain greater display for the company's output. Writer John Ness discussed in *The Atlantic Monthly* the failure of most of the smaller automobile manufacturers during the fifties and stated: "Clearly the great edge of the great companies lies in the vast advertising budgets and marketing organizations—the standard brand, the slogan dinned into the subconscious."

The outpouring of goods and people which marketers are counting upon will change the style of life in the United States. Even though consumption continues to churn upward, it seems inevitable that the United States will see a real decline in the amenities of life.

If marketers have their way, American citizens will have at least forty million more vehicles on the roads by 1975. Millions of acres of land will be bulldozed for highway rights of way. More elevated highways will slash into the cores of American cities to try to loosen up the congestion. Such highways, by their size and divisive nature, seem to demean the cities they are designed to rescue. Despite the thruways, urban experts predict that congestion will grow faster than relief of congestion. When one magazine forecast that in a decade most American families would have two cars in every garage, a Boston reader wrote back that if the prediction came true then "we'll also need two hospitals in every block."

Many European cities likewise were finding that Europe's soaring output of motorcars was forming massive clots in their central areas during the hours of maximum traffic. Anyone trying to cross Geneva's main bridge or the Place de la Concorde in Paris in late afternoon knows that colossal traffic jams are not unique to America. Although a smaller percentage of European families own cars than do American families, there are as many motorcars per square mile in many European countries as in the United States.

And what will happen when, to the delight of marketers, a hundred million more customers are crowded into the United States by 1980? Most of this growth, whether Americans like it or not, will take place on the perimeters of present cities rather than in the inhospitable wilds of the Dakotas. (Those two states are among the nation's slowest growing.)

Already bulldozers, like droves of army ants, are chewing up the loveliest pastoral settings outside such cities as Boston, Philadelphia, and San Francisco. William H. Whyte, Jr., in the book, *The Exploding Metropolis*, estimates that bulldozers are flattening three thousand acres every day as "urban sprawl" spreads. Great metropolitan areas once widely separated are starting to bump up against each other. Metropolitan Dallas is bumping into metropolitan Fort Worth; Cleveland is on the verge of bumping into Akron; Hartford and Springfield have almost merged as areas; and even those two great colossi, metropolitan New York and metropolitan Philadelphia, are at the point of colliding—and swallowing up the breadth of the sovereign state of New Jersey between them.

Suburbs that were once semirural in character are being transformed as the population explosion produces subdivisions, gasoline stations by the hundreds, roadside stands, and light industries. W. L. C. Wheaton, director of the Institute for Urban Studies at the University of Pennsylvania, points up another important characteristic of this urban sprawl. It is low-density sprawl. In the suburbs each family expects to have its own little plot of ground, and so takes up more land space than a city dweller. Thus, he says: "Cities will spread out over vastly larger areas than ever before. Indeed, it is not unreasonable to expect that the next hundred million urban residents will occupy five or six times as much space as the first hundred million." Those suburbanites who formerly lived in working-class areas of cities at least are getting a little more air and elbow room. Residents on the outer edges of metropolitan areas will have to go thirty to fifty miles just to get "downtown," if their place of work is near the core of the metropolis. It is partly to ease this growing strain that many business plants and offices are moving into— or setting up branches in—the perimeters and in previously rural areas. As for homes, residential sites that still have a "view" in Los Angeles now cost up to $100,000 per acre. Metropolitan Los Angeles spreads over an area that would engulf the entire state of Connecticut.

Dr. Wheaton points out another hardly cheering characteristic of the suburbs that will appear by the late sixties. By then, nearly 40 per cent of the inhabitants will be teen-agers, who have a high degree of velocity, audibility, energy, and visibility.

At least one population expert (P. K. Whelpton) has estimated that ideally, from the standpoint of individual economic well-being, the United States population should have stopped growing at around 110,000,000. Others feel that figure is too low. What is optimum for a Henry David Thoreau who loves the grandeur of a lonely stretch of beach would be decidedly different from the optimum chosen by a hard-driving subdivider. At any rate, the quiet places of beauty where people can meditate and recuperate and exhilarate are disappearing at a very fast rate. Once lonely lakes are crawling with powerboats roaring out gasoline fumes. Ohio's beaches on Lake Erie are fast disappearing. At this writing it is unclear whether the tiny stretch of fine Indiana dunes can be saved from groups that want to establish industries there. Many of the beaches on Lake Ontario, in western New York State, are developing a stench because of the contamination of the water by chemical plants in the area.

Twice as many people already crowd into national parks as can be comfortably accommodated. One of the nation's loveliest remaining stretches of open ocean beach on Cape Cod, south of Provincetown, is showing subdivision signs. And on Cape Cod a newspaper sadly commented on the "spreading carnival atmosphere on the Cape" and said there is "less and less to hold the tourist seeking Cape atmosphere and scenery. Our historic places are hidden. Our populous beaches aren't what they're looking for."

Further crowding also promises to aggravate grievously the nation's already serious problems of water and air pollution. Even before Americans put those forty million additional motorcars on the road, many citizens are gasping for fresh air. Hundreds of billions of cubic feet of exhaust fumes are pushed out into urban air each day and are starting to put many cities in addition to Los Angeles under a pall. An official of the United States Public Health Service warns that "the amount of chemical junk in the air will grow astronomically as time goes by." The rivers of the nation from which dozens of down-river towns are dependent for drinking water have become dangerously polluted with industrial wastes, household detergents, and sewage-born microscopic worms called nematodes. The nematodes are proving to be able to survive chlorination and give tap water an earthy, musty odor. In one check by United States health officials, drinking water from thirteen out of fourteen rivers sampled had nematodes.

In many suburban areas where homes are dependent upon septic systems and private wells, so much detergent has been seeping into the wells that water drawn from the tap has a sudsy head. Commenting on the growing problem of such pollutants as nematodes and detergents, *U.S. News & World Report* observed: "As population rises and demands upon the nation's water supply grows . . . these problems will multiply." Several northern New Jersey cities had to find, hurriedly, new water sources when pollution of the Passaic River reached the point where thousands of fish were found dead.

Then there will be the spiraling costs of supporting the growing urbanized population with its demand for many services. As a metropolis grows, it costs more per person to operate the city.

And we should not forget those tens of millions of additional school-age youths that the marketers are happily viewing as their customers of the future and the present. They will need to be supported and educated. By 1970, a majority of the American population will be either under or over the breadwinner age.

Sharply increased population may bring momentary prosperity to producers and sellers of consumer goods, but it is likely to bring more grief than benefit in the long run to the general economy and the general public. Some businessmen are beginning to sense this. A vice-president of the Ford Motor Company surveyed all the complications that an upsurge in population promises to bring and stated: "There can be no doubt that the increase in population will reduce the rate of improvement in our standard of living."

A final price American citizens will almost certainly have to pay for increasing-sales-through-increasing-population will be curtailment of individual liberty. There is often a tendency to have less respect for individuals in densely populated areas or nations. And there is a greater demand for intervention by government to solve problems that have grown beyond the possibility of solution by individual intervention. Perhaps the most eloquent warning ever to appear on the hazards of seeking prosperity through population growth comes from an economist, Dr. Joseph Spengler of Duke University. He points out, in *The Harvard Business Review*, the common tendency in thickly populated countries to try to relieve intensified social and economic problems attending increased population by state intervention and adds:

"Should this come to pass the economy will become less flexible and the freedom of individuals to do as they please would tend to become highly circumscribed. In this event the stork would have managed to do what the followers of Marx have found themselves unable to do for all they tried—fasten fetters on mankind."

Now we come to three prices that American citizens are paying for a force-fed society which are so momentous in their implications that they deserve exploration in separate chapters.

18. THE VANISHING RESOURCES

"We Americans have used more of the world's resources in the past 40 years than all the people of the world had used in the 4,000 years of recorded history up to 1914.... Man is becoming aware of the limits of the earth."—Fairfield Osborn

THE AVERAGE AMERICAN FAMILY THROWS AWAY about 750 metal cans each year. In the Orient, a family lucky enough to gain possession of a metal can treasures it and puts it to work in some way, if only as a flower pot.

When the President's Materials Policy Commission surveyed United States consumption patterns in the early fifties, it concluded that "the United States' appetite for materials is Gargantuan—and so far insatiable." It found that each individual man, woman, and child was using up an average of eighteen tons of materials a year.

Other estimates have suggested that the average American requires, for his style of life, ten times as much raw materials—not counting food—as the average citizen of the rest of the free world. Only in America would a housewife hop into a two-ton vehicle and drive downtown to buy the thumbtacks that she forgot to buy on her regular shopping trip. And only in America do people in midwinter warm themselves almost entirely by the wasteful method of burning thousands of gallons of oil to heat up a house rather than by getting much of their warmth by wearing warm clothing.

The virgin continent that American settlers fell heir to a mere three centuries ago is being stripped of its material riches at an ever-accelerating rate. This wealth has made chronic optimists of the people of the United States. There has been so much wealth that they have come to assume there will always be more where that came from. As an American, Rowland Howard, observed in the last century, "You never miss the water till the well runs dry."

Today, however, the weight of the evidence does not support much optimism. Even by the early fifties, the Materials Policy Commission was observing: "The plain fact seems to be that we have skimmed the cream of our resources as we now understand them." Since then the skimming has cut down into the milk still further. Today, Americans are consuming considerably more materials than they produce. The United States must now depend on other lands for most of the "strategic and critical" materials essential to the nation's defense. The warnings and recommendations of the Materials Policy Commission were largely ignored.

Historians may say that the most fateful change occurring to the United States during the first six decades of the twentieth century is that during that period the nation changed from being a "have" nation to a "have-not" nation in terms of essential natural resources. On December 9, 1958, *The New York Times* carried this memorable front-page headline: "DANGEROUS DECLINE FOUND IN U.S. NATURAL RESOURCES."

In the four-part analysis that followed, *Times* writer Richard Rutter left his readers with little ground for optimism. He found "an enormous drain on supplies of vital raw materials" and added, "The survival of the nation is involved. An assured supply of iron ore, petroleum, natural gas, metals, coal, and a host of other materials is essential to the strength of the American economy. Without these, the greatest industrial machine would come to a halt." Later on he stated: "Run down the list of the twenty-six most important materials ranging from antimony to zinc. The 1975 outlook: The United States dependence on foreign sources will range from 100 percent to 25 percent."

As the United States became more dependent upon foreign sources for its supplies of vital materials, it of course became more vulnerable to a cutoff in case of war or in case a foreign government chose to hoard its resources or chose—or was induced—to sell its prized resources elsewhere.

The United States dependency on foreign sources is bound to grow with each passing decade at a violently increasing rate if the population and the individual consuming habits of its citizens grow as briskly as marketers hope they will.

It should not be long before even the most blissfully optimistic American will recognize the truth of Fairfield Osborn's comment in *The Limits of the Earth*, "It is evident that, year by year, the entire problem of adequacy of natural resources for the maintenance and development of our civilization is becoming more acute."

Let us, then, look briefly at the present and future prospects of a few of the main ingredients of the United States standard of living.

Metals. The high-grade ores of many metals found in the United States are running out; and United States mills are mostly geared to high-grade ores. The price trend of metals is upward. Steel, of course, is the main sinew of American industrial might—and way of life. Most of the United States steel mills require ore containing at least a 50 per cent concentration of natural iron. Such rich ore is almost exhausted from Minnesota's Mesabi Range, which was long considered to be "inexhaustible." The amount of such rich ore left in known deposits in the United States would not meet American needs for even a decade. And these known deposits are at deeper strip levels or must be got underground. Both make the ore expensive to get.

More and more, the United States is being forced to use thinner ores, which require special treatment to get them up to a concentration acceptable in the mills. The United States still has mountains of lowgrade ore (taconite), but such material must be ground down to a powder and then molded into pellets. This process adds several dollars a ton to the cost.

These expenses are driving the steelmakers into foreign lands in search of ores suitable for milling directly. They have found—and are vigorously drawing upon—such deposits in South America (principally Venezuela) and Canada (principally Labrador and eastern Quebec) and elsewhere. Already foreign sources are supplying a third of the iron-ore needs of the United States (the percentage of iron ore imported quadrupled within a decade), and the percentage will continue to mount. These foreign sources can meet the needs of even a profligate United States for many decades assuming that the United States is not cut off from them by warfare or the action of local governments or by mounting competition from other industrializing nations. One can reasonably inquire why United States residents should worry about their growing lack of self-sufficiency when they can get resources elsewhere in an increasingly interdependent world. Perhaps we should not worry, if all goes well. But this situation does leave the United States more vulnerable in case of war, revolution, or intensified competition for access to the planet's irreplaceable resources.

Of the seven metals most needed in making steel alloys, only two are in adequate supply from domestic sources.

The once-rich United States reserves of zinc and lead have become so low that they are rapidly approaching the point of being uneconomic to work. Domestic production of both has recently fallen to all-time lows. United States deposits of bauxite—the base of aluminum—have become of such poor quality that the United States hauls more than three quarters of its supply from overseas.

Probably the most ominous depletion of a vital ore is occurring with that lovely, versatile metal crucial to industrialization—copper. The United States has been forced to resort to mining leaner and leaner grades of the ore. Most copper ore mined today contains less than 1 per cent of the metal, and much of the ore used is approaching ½ of 1 per cent. Many mining companies are being forced to process six times as much ore to get a ton of copper as they did at the beginning of the century. Partly as a result copper costs have risen about 600 per cent in three decades. Meanwhile, the United States has changed from being the world's leading exporter of copper to being the world's leading importer of copper. And overseas sources are showing signs of depletion, and will be available in currently acceptable grades for only a few decades at most. Meanwhile, United States marketers have been promoting the use of copper as decorative gas lamps to hang outside homes. And American women each year are throwing away several hundred million brass lipstick holders. Brass is made primarily from copper.

This developing exhaustion of copper is likely to confront the many nations now starting to industrialize with a most disagreeable problem. Can they industrialize at all if copper becomes more and more of a rare and precious metal? Substitutes such as aluminum can be used in some situations at a loss in efficiency but in some crucial uses in the power industry adequate or acceptably priced substitutes are proving difficult to find. Conceivably, further progress can be made in mining extremely low-grade ores, but the gains here are likely to be relatively small.

Harrison Brown, the eminent Caltech geochemist who has taken a long, hard look at United States reserves for the future, summed up the copper situation in *The Challenge of Man's Future* in these words: "It is clear that vanishing copper reserves will constitute a formidable barrier to world development."

So much for the sinews needed by industry to expand to meet the goals of United States marketers. What about the energy needed—and the lubrication needed—to make the wheels turn and keep the homes warm and bright? In 1956, the president of General Electric proposed as a goal for the electric industry that it increase average home use of electricity by two and a half times in a decade. More recently, a vice-president of Georgia Power Company proposed that each customer be induced to use 7,000 kilowatt-hours a year by 1969. In 1959, customers were using barely half of that amount.

Fossil fuels. For energy the United States is dependent primarily upon the so-called fossil fuels derived from organic materials laid down millions of years ago: oil, coal, and natural gas.

United States consumption of oil, the chief source of the nation's energy, has tripled since the end of World War II. With only one seventh of the world's proved reserves of oil, the United States has been consuming considerably more than half of all the world's production.

Superficially the United States seems overblessed with oil today. Overeager or overgreedy producers have been probing the planet so intensively that they have glutted the world market. However, the rate of discovery of new fields in the United States has been declining in recent years. Those discovered tend to be at the bottom of deeper and deeper holes. In oil, the United States is clearly approaching depletion. At today's rate of consumption—not tomorrow's—the United States has proved reserves of oil sufficient to meet the nation's needs for thirteen years. There have been several authoritative predictions that United States oil production will "peak out" in the present decade. An official of Ford has asserted that the United States will be "peaking out" on oil within at least twenty years. It is known that deep in the rocks underlying the United States are billions of barrels of oil, but their location makes them presently unattainable at reasonable cost. Other billions, possibly attainable, are assumed to exist. But a study made for Resources for the Future, Inc., by Bruce C. Netschert, counted up the hundreds of billions of barrels of crude oil still conceivably present and noted that there had been a rather sharp decline in the oil discovered per exploratory well and also an increase in average depth. This didn't mean that ways could not be found to recover oil under the United States, but the study commented: "A declining success level in the search for oil may indicate that the limit of oil discoverable with current technology at current costs is being approached." And it added, "There is general agreement in the industry that spectacular innovations in discovery techniques are improbable. . . ." Mr. Rutter concluded from his investigation that the supremacy of the United States as an oil producer was "drawing to a close." In the future, the United States will be drawing more and more upon foreign oil fields, and this is putting the United States deep into the hands of Arabian and Latin-

American politicians.

The United States will still have access for many decades to liquid fuel that can be extracted from its reserves of shale and its still abundant reserves of coal, but both processes are expensive, especially the latter, and probably will remain so though some gains in producing efficiency undoubtedly will be achieved. The cost of obtaining oil by conventional drilling, at least in the United States, is likely to rise substantially in the coming decade. And it is only when the price of crude oil becomes sufficiently high that the wholesale mining of shale for oil will seem economic.

If oil producers seem complacent about the growing inadequacy of proved United States oil reserves, one reason may be that the growing domestic scarcity does not directly threaten them. To them, the important thing is the prospect of ever-greater demand for oil. They can supply it by processing coal or shale or digging ever-deeper holes, all at higher cost, of course. They will have the nation over a barrel. Dr. Brown summed up the long-range world-wide outlook for fossil fuels by observing:

"Within a period of time which is very short compared with the total span of history, supplies of fossil fuels will almost certainly be exhausted. This loss will make man completely dependent upon waterpower, atomic energy and solar energy." As I'll show in a few moments, this is not the altogether happy prospect that often is envisioned.

Now we come to those crucial resources that have long been considered among the outstanding symbols of United States abundance: food, timber, water.

Food. United States granaries are bulging with surplus grain, and per-acre yield of calories is still far lower than Europe's or Asia's. Therefore, food would seem to be no problem for many decades. It should be noted, however, that the exploding population of the United States will greatly increase food requirements, while the same expanding population will swallow up millions of areas of farmland by covering them with homes, shopping centers, and factories. Meanwhile, erosion is continuing. The United States has already lost a third of the rich top-soil—average nine inches—that it had when the Pilgrims landed.

Because of such foreseeable pressures, several authorities have suggested that within two decades the farm lobby can relax its pressure on the United States government and stop impelling the government to subsidize the growth of unwanted food. All food then, quite likely, will be wanted. *U.S. News & World Report*, for example, reported from Washington: "A population increase may also bring about a solution to today's troublesome farm problem. Some officials of the Department of Agriculture are inclined to regard the present surplus as a short-term problem." On the other hand the revolution on the farm due to chemicals and pesticides may assure even an exploding population with adequate food for quite a few decades.

Wood. As for timber, each man, woman, and child in the United States consumes nearly a ton of wood products a year in the form of pine-paneled playrooms, chairs, comic books, and so on. The nation's stand of saw timber has shrunk by nearly one half since Teddy Roosevelt's day. The chief of the United States Forest Service has warned that by the end of this century the nation's original stand of timber will have virtually disappeared and the wood industry will then have no choice but to cut only what it can grow. Industry spokesmen profess to be less worried about future supply of wood for lumber and paper.

However, some of the major timber companies such as Weyerhaeuser have finally taken action to work out a "perpetual yield" for their timberlands; but in general the United States has at least until very recently been taking down substantially more saw timber than it has been replacing with new growth. One result is that the real price of forest products—corrected for inflation—has doubled since the turn of the century, and wood has become too expensive to use in many situations where it has been traditionally used and where its qualities make it ideal for use.

Water. The task of maintaining an adequate water supply for a violently expanding population accustomed to heavy use of water presents an urgent and immediate problem. The water needs of the average American citizen have doubled in this century, partly because of the demand for showers, flush toilets, air conditioners, dishwashers, lawn sprinklers, and swimming pools. The really heavy users of water, however, are industry—it ordinarily takes 60,000 gallons of water to make a ton of paper or steel—and farmers, for irrigation. Farmers use half of all water consumed in the United States. Geographer Gilbert F. White of the University of Chicago asserts that the United States is running out of water and will face serious difficulties within fifteen years. He points out that many communities in western Texas and in Arizona, by their irrigating and sprinkling, are draining their underground water at a rate that far exceeds natural replenishment. Water tables are falling. In some communities water is being withdrawn twenty times as fast as it is being replaced. And in some areas of North Dakota and Long Island, underground water levels have fallen so low that further "mining" of the water is curbed by regulation. Most of the towns in western New York State have a chronic water problem and tens of thousands of residents regularly pay one dollar for a five-gallon jug of cooking and drinking water.

Some arid communities such as in Hudspeth County, Texas, have just about given up because of lack of water. Many cities in the West are foreseeing the day when they will have to turn away all industries that are large water consumers. Long Beach, California, recently sought permission to start reclaiming for certain uses purified sewage water which had been flowing into the ocean.

A select committee of the United States Senate has warned that many signs point to an "impending water crisis."

Perhaps the taps won't literally run dry, but still the United States resident will pay a price. The price was described by Harrison Brown in these terms: "As time goes on we will see an ever-expanding network of aqueducts, dams, reservoirs, sewage-treatment plants, and waterpurifying units. The penalties for the improvements will be greatly increased cost of water and, above all, increased per capita expenditures of energy."

United States residents tend to view all assertions about depleting resources with equanimity. As optimists they know—and are constantly reminded—that modern technology is building a golden future for them. The atom will solve all their problems. The chemists will create entirely new and magical resources to replace the vanishing old. And engineers will build machines that can economically mine leaner and leaner seams of copper, and substitutions can be made.

Some of this optimism undoubtedly is justified. Aluminum is being used instead of steel in some instances to make electric light poles. Pound for pound, aluminum is a much more expensive metal—largely because so much more energy is required to produce it—but the fact that it is light in weight and doesn't have to be painted still makes it desirable. Aluminum is also starting to be used to make motorcar bumpers and wheels. Again the pound cost is high, but the motorcar makers are anxious to reduce shipping costs by employing lightweight materials. There are abundant reserves of bauxite—from which aluminum is made—overseas.

And plastics—which, lest we forget, are based primarily on chemicals derived from petroleum—are proving to be acceptable and feasible substitutes for metals in a number of uses. United States Steel, for example, is now in the business of producing plastic pipe. Quite possibly by paying a price we will come to plastic motorcars and even plastic houses. E. I. du Pont reports that it has a new plastic called Delrin that is tough enough to serve for many uses where metals have traditionally been required, such as machine parts and fittings for appliances. For many uses, however, the plastics now available are clearly inadequate. There is presently slight possibility that they can make adequate substitutes for steel in structural functions. Also their vulnerability to temperature and their frequent tendency to shrink are limiting factors, and their energy cost is often high.

The supply of steel also can be stretched, it now appears, from new discoveries about the breaking point of steel. Engineers are finding that steels in some uses and designs can safely take 15 to 20 per cent more stress than was previously assumed to be true.

Yes. there will be many substitutions, including combinations of material still undiscovered; and there will be much greater efficiency achieved both in the use of materials and the operation of machines. Still, it is questionable whether these advances will enable the United States to maintain as pleasant an environment for the individual during the last third of the twentieth century as existed during the first two thirds of the century. The cornucopia of United States industry may still pour forth a host of consumer products. And it is quite probable that the United States can, by ingenious use of substitutes and new discoveries, avoid passing any real peril point. But in general there will be more straining, more expensive price tags on many of the amenities of life, more shortages, and more obstacles to personal dignity.

The expected rise in the cost of petroleum, as the United States is forced to turn more and more to shale and coal for oil and to oil shipped from abroad, will increase, among other things, the cost of food. Farmers will begin yearning for the good old days before they sold off their horses as dog food and bought gasoline-guzzling tractors.

But what about the wonders promised by harnessing the atom to produce cheap, inexhaustible energy? Subsidized atomic power plants have been built. There has been no rush, however, to duplicate them. The reactors are proving to be too expensive to build and operate to excite private investors. Lawrence Halfstad of the Atomic Energy Commission has explained, "Another widely held misconception is that atomic energy will provide cheap power for the next generation. Power from uranium is not going to be cheap soon."

As the advent of the Golden Sixties was being widely heralded in late 1959, the sixth annual conference of the Atomic Industrial Forum was held in Washington. The mood of the industrialists attending it was distinctly doleful. The head of Atomics International Division of North American Aviation, Inc., told the meeting, "Achievement of a true commercial atomic industry has been pushed off many years." And the financial weekly *Barrons* pronounced the whole program for developing commercial nuclear power "a gigantic fizzle."

In addition to the cost, another complication dimming the prospect of utilizing atomic energy in the long-term future is that the reactors largely depend upon uranium for fuel, and the United States has in known deposits only a decade's supply of uranium. If uranium becomes a major United States source of energy, the United States will find itself bidding on the world market for uranium within a short period. And many other industrializing nations—with no coal supply of their own— will be willing to pay a higher price than the United States should be willing to pay as long as it has coal available.

Some observers see atomic energy based on the hydrogen-bomb reaction of thermonuclear fusion as a possible way out. Hydrogen as a source of steady energy is becoming at least conceivable as a result of break-throughs in research; but here, too, there is considerable doubt that a thermonuclear reactor can ever produce power economically by today's standards.

A third complication that will arise if the United States turns primarily to the atom as a source of energy is that the disposal of the mounting radioactive wastes will become a monstrous problem. Many United States coastal cities already are alarmed by offshore dumping of the wastes.

Some modern soothsayers have been saying that ultimately the world will get most of its energy by harnessing the sun. Gathering solar energy by giant mirrors, etc., appeals to the artists illustrating wondersto-come, and we may come to it; but probably not happily. Solar energy won't be cheap. Harrison Brown finds that using solar energy to generate mechanical power and electricity will be more expensive than nuclear energy "by a considerable margin."

One of the great technological promises for the future is that the United States will find a cheap way to convert the water of its seas to fresh water. Industrial statesmen have painted appealing pictures of arid wastelands being converted into bountiful truck gardens, from Death Valley to the Sahara. While miracles of transformation should not be expected soon because of the cost factor, this is one of the more promising challenges, and we will examine it in more detail in Chapter 24.

Another phase of the Golden Future widely predicted is that in a few decades the world's food supply can be assured by taking algae or plankton from the sea. Here the cost problem may well be overcome. But the result will not be an improvement aesthetically on the diet of today. Persons who have sampled plankton say it is no diet for joy. And it is doubtful that algae will ever match as a taste treat the cherry pies Grandma used to make (before pies went on the assembly line).

It should be recognized that in a scientific sense very few United States resources will ever become really exhausted, if you are willing to go deep enough or are willing to extract from extremely low-grade ores. A hundred tons of ordinary igneous rock, Harrison Brown points out, contains among other things: about 8 per cent aluminum, about 5 per cent iron, about ½ per cent titanium, about 1/11 per cent manganese, and about 1/100 per cent copper.

The factories of the future are likely to be giant chemical plants that will gulp in rocks, sea water, and air and break them down into industrially usable components. But such operations will require fantastic amounts of energy and fantastically complex plants. Unit costs of metals produced would inevitably be considerably higher than their costs today.

Another uncomfortable thought that should be pondered is that most of the developments which are supposed to produce a golden era require fantastic amounts of fresh water. Nuclear power plants, plants for drawing oil from shale, and plants for preparing low-grade iron (taconite) for the steel mills are voracious gulpers of water. And if the nation's exploding population is to settle the nation's open arid areas, then air conditioners will be a required amenity of life. And air conditioners are substantial water users.

Still more disconcerting, the task of making the United States economy function will become so complex when resources are no longer readily available that the lives of the human participants will have to be more highly organized. Dr. Brown suggests that the complex society of the future will require such an all-pervasive social organization that the state will completely dominate the action of the individual.

There is, however, another significant possible source of raw materials which we should not overlook. That is the salvaging of existing materials. Theoretically this can greatly ease the material shortage since there are millions of tons of motorcars, refrigerators, alarm clocks, and metal play wagons cluttering attics and landscape. Much of it, however, is in town dumps or wayside gullies losing weight each year as rust devours it.

In the course of pondering the wastefulness of modern Americans, I visited a number of salvage yards from New Orleans to Connecticut. It gives one a macabre feeling to watch workmen gut a 1951 passenger car before it goes into the jaws of a giant crusher. The doomed car is pushed on its side just as a butcher pushes over a chicken. Men with torches deftly remove the front and rear ends and chrome. Then gasoline is poured onto the body, and in a flash the upholstery, floor mats, sky-blue paint, and other nonmetal parts are burned away. A crane then drops the body into the crusher, which within a minute reduces it to a solid metal bale the size of an orange crate.

This seemed like both a profitable and patriotic enterprise. But the salvage operators I chatted with were a gloomy bunch. They were being ruined, they said, and were glutted with "junker" motorcars and other steel scrap that seemed to hold little interest to the steel companies. Scrap prices by 1959 had fallen disastrously. Rubino Brothers in Stamford, Connecticut, was reduced to trying to buy cars for $7 or $8 and selling the scrap for about $19. This left the company, on lucky days, with a $2 profit on each motorcar crushed and shipped. In 1959, the salvaging of unwanted motorcars in the United States had fallen to the lowest point in recent years. Less than half as many motorcars were sold for scrap as were sold new. Motorcars still are being sold for scrap if the motorcar owner lives near an efficient scrapping plant, but hundreds of thousands of cars are simply piling up in junk yards and gullies.

What is behind this paradox of low scrap prices in the face of shrinking iron-ore resources in the United States? A spokesman for the Institute of Scrap Iron and Steel, Inc., told me that the recent drop in demand for scrap is due to "technical changes in steelmaking which serve to reduce steel mill use of iron and steel scrap. Under the circumstances, of course, much scrap today is not being collected, a great deal is being lost by being dumped, or through erosion."

One technical change occurring is the introduction of a much-discussed oxygen steelmaking process that uses much less scrap than former processes did. Tom Campbell, editor of *Iron Age*, told scrap men about the new development and pointed out still another factor working to shrink steelmen's interest in scrap. He said that several major steel companies now have hundreds of millions of dollars tied up in investments in ore deposits in Quebec and South America and need to get their investment back by using as much ore from those places as possible. He said that such factors as these have created "an absolute desire on the part of steel people to become less dependent on scrap and apparently they have succeeded."

He gave to the scrap men this straight-from-the-shoulder advice: "You are now facing some of the most difficult problems that any industry could face. . . . I think that if there are anyboys among you, you had better start looking for another job because the scrap industry is only an industry for men."

Any realistic appraisal of the United States' prospects on resources must also take note of the violently accelerated demand upon resources by the other nations of the world. The demand for petroleum, for example, is rising faster in the rest of the free world than it is in the United States. Italy's landscape is starting to show many great, gleaming gasoline stations. In Britain, the number of motorcars on the road has doubled within a decade. And there is the fantastic world population growth. Each year the world as a whole is adding the equivalent of the population of France to its numbers.

Further, many nations have desperately ambitious plans to industrialize; and their people have learned from American movies, tourists, and advertisements to desire such things as telephones, refrigerators, television, and motorcars. Joseph Spengler, Duke University economist specializing in world population trends, points out that shortages of materials available to the United States "will be greatly intensified by the progress of population and aggregate consumption in other parts of the world, since these other areas will be drawing increasingly on relatively limited sources of supply, major access to which has heretofore been enjoyed by Americans."

As industrialization spreads in Asia, Africa, and other areas where per capita consumption of materials has been extremely low by American standards, demand for raw materials and energy will expand swiftly and produce scarcities that will force rises in price. If the rest of the world—even with its present population—were to achieve the level of material wealth enjoyed by the people of the United States, there would be a sixfold increase in need for materials. Actually there is no longer enough copper, tin, and lead left in the world to permit such a duplication on the basis of today's technology.

As pressures mount for access to the available raw materials, nations will tend to protect their own interests by restricting export of materials that they know they will need for their own future development. India, for example, possesses very little in the way of fossil fuels. It obtains most of its inanimate energy by the burning of dung. India, looking to the future, has clamped down on the export of thorium. This element, like uranium, can be used in the production of atomic energy.

In the future we are likely to see such actions as India's become common. Brock Chisholm, former director general of the World

Health Organization, predicts that within a decade North Americans, who have been using up half of the world's production of irreplaceable natural resources, will be cut off from many resources now used in abundance because many of these resources have been coming to a very large extent "from heavily populated, over-populated countries." He asks: "How much longer will North America be able to have the lion's share of natural resources? Probably not ten years longer, because the other countries are beginning to recognize that from their own point of view the welfare of their own people and the world's welfare, perhaps, they would be wiser to keep their own natural resources even though this means somewhat slower development, to do their own manufacturing and sell finished products."

Furthermore, some of the countries that have in effect become colonies of United States corporations may quite possibly buy out or throw out those companies. Venezuela is as good an example as any to consider. It is now the largest supplier of iron ore to the United States and a major supplier of oil. A study of its turbulent past would indicate that the nation has probably not seen its last abrupt change in policy or governing personnel. In early 1960, the moderately leftish government of President Romulo Betancourt had to put down a small rebellion by force. Suppose that ten or twenty years from now an opposition leader on the order of Peron or Trujillo or Castro comes into power in Venezuela with a highly nationalistic and perhaps anti-United States orientation. Suppose also that the rest of the world is then bidding for Venezuela's oil and iron. If such a leader decided to take over the holdings of United States companies and sell most of the nation's iron ore and oil elsewhere, what would the United States do? I put this question to a number of American businessmen. None had a ready answer. All agreed that such a turn of events would present the United States with an extremely sticky problem and that the United States should strive by skillful diplomacy to prevent such a situation from developing.

It would seem inevitable that if the world's population and the resources are not soon brought into a more tolerable balance, some of the competition by nations for badly needed resources is likely to generate ugly frictions that could explode into warfare.

The widely accepted notion that more population brings prosperity is overdue for examination. It apparently is true that up until quite recently more babies meant more business for industrialized societies. The availability of resources and living space had not been a serious problem. But for the future, businessmen who extol the wondrous prosperity that a larger population—and more consumption per capita— can bring for more than a short term are encouraging the nation to flirt with serious trouble.

Sir Charles Darwin contends that in terms of population the United States has become "one of the most dangerously increasing countries in the world." Some, however, argue that while overpopulation is bad in underdeveloped countries, it is needed by highly industrialized societies in order to provide customers to keep the factories busy. Such a viewpoint leaves out of account, at least as far as America is concerned, the factor of diminishing resources. Professor Spengler, for one, has concluded: "Population growth does not guarantee endless prosperity. . . . It solves only temporarily certain problems whilst creating bigger ones. It resembles the dope a sick man takes, only in the end to become a dope addict, and hence sicker than ever."

More people and more per capita consumption will tend to force up the prices of resources in short supply and ultimately produce a drop in individual living standards.

Some businessmen are beginning to be apprehensive about the widespread faith that prosperity requires more people. The senior vice-president of the Mellon National Bank and Trust Company in Pittsburgh has observed that "our rising population is creating pressures on natural resources which in a number of respects tend to retard further increases in material well-being." He said that the strain of going deeper and farther for resources and using leaner and leaner veins all adds to unit costs and is creating a "drag on prosperity." And Columbia University economist Roy Blough points out that "undoubtedly one of the offsets to increased productivity will be the increasing difficulty and cost of supplying many kinds of raw material. . . . There can be no doubt that some materials important to our industrial growth are likely to become much more difficult and costly to get; and the country is becoming increasingly dependent for them on other countries just when these countries are industrializing their own economies."

When you add the further strain on resources that comes from the proposals of marketers to persuade each citizen in the rapidly growing United States population to increase his consumption, you are compounding the strain. A projection of current population trends suggests that the United States will have as many people within a century as China has today. This trend can—and probably will— change. But let us assume it does come to pass that the United States in a century will have a population of more than 600,000,000 people and that the United States is encountering intensified competition from the rest of the world for resources available outside the United States. If that occurs, what would happen to the high, wide, and handsome mode of living Americans are pursuing today? The nation would be sucked virtually dry of resources economically feasible by today's standards within a very few years. Actually, such a possibility is not likely to confront the nation. Something will have to give—either mode of living or population growth or both—long before a mere century has passed.

19. THE COMMERCIALIZATION OF AMERICAN LIFE

"How can the public absorb so much shrieking in the market-place?"—*Printer's Ink*

ALL THE EFFORTS TO KEEP CONSUMPTION RISING—when taken together—amount to an unprecedented saturation of American life with pleas, hints, and other inducements to buy. The sheer dimensions of the current and contemplated selling efforts are becoming a national problem. Commercialization is becoming so all-pervasive that at times it seems to be getting into the air the public breathes. The public is under a fairly constant siege of hard sells, soft sells, funny sells, sly sells.

More and more money is being set aside to create a demand for each unit of goods to be moved. Money spent for advertising in the United States has risen considerably faster than total sales have risen. The money spent to sell motorcars is a case in point. The amount spent per car more than doubled on almost every United States make of car during the fifties, and for most makes the amount more than tripled.

As United States citizens are coaxed to buy more and more quantities of goods that are not essential to their physical well-being, more and more reliance upon the skills of professional selling experts is required. It takes no persuasion whatever to induce people to buy enough daily food to sustain them, but it does take persuasion to sell them optional goods such as sixty-horsepower motorboats.

"Advertising must mass-produce customers just as factories

massproduce products in a growing economy," stated the publisher of *Printers' Ink*. He suggested that outlays for advertising might reach twenty-five billion dollars by 1965. That meant more than doubling the amount being spent to create want and discontent within a few years.

An official of General Foods reported that a typical American family is exposed to 1,518 selling messages in the course of an average day. And this does not include the material stuffed into the nation's mailboxes: a total of sixteen billion pieces a year, or four times the amount found in mailboxes a decade earlier. United States taxpayers are charged an extra $190,000,000 a year to make up the deficit incurred by the post office in delivering this "junk," or third-class, mail.

Members of this average family, he stated, are exposed to 117 television and radio commercials a day. Other studies have shown that on television alone programs heard in the average home by one or more members in a day carry nearly an hour of commercials. The growth of messages beamed at the public over the airways is worth special note because airborne messages are hard to ignore and because the public presumably controls the airways in its own interest.

On a nighttime television network show it has not been uncommon to find fifteen or more commercials packed into a half-hour segment. Broadcast Advertisers Reports made a survey of the number of nighttime shows packing six or more commercials into a fifteen-minute segment. Such a load of commercials, it agreed, represented "extreme" overcommercialization. During the week monitored, it found 389 instances of such extreme overcommercialization. It said the figure would have been far worse if it had included daytime shows.

Officially, members of the National Association of Broadcasters are pledged not to "triple spot" their commercials, or run three in a row, back to back. The Broadcast Advertisers Report survey found 1,287 such triple-spotting "irregularities" by the seventy-one stations monitored. It found 111 instances where four or more commercials were run back to back. Other investigators reported instances in which up to nine commercial messages of some sort were run in a row on television.

The increase in commercials has complicated the life of television writers, directors, and performers as they have tried to sustain their moods of gaiety, tragedy, or suspense. In the spring of 1959, Peter Lind Hayes gave up his ABC daytime show because of the "pressure-cooker existence" the network proposed to inaugurate by cutting his hour-long show to a half hour. He explained: "When you figure the number of commercials we have to give, it actually takes an hour to do a half-hour show. Can you imagine half a dozen commercial interruptions in thirty minutes? That is what it would amount to." Garry Moore revealed that he left daytime television "because, frankly, I couldn't cope with the number of commercials we had to accommodate." And, in 1960, he won a singular battle for his nighttime show by successfully demanding that commercial interruptions of his hour-long show be limited to four rather than the then-prevailing seven interruptions.

All this growing pressure of commercials has generally been attributed to increasing costs by the media accepting them. Some broadcasters, however, have resisted the trend and have seemed to prosper by being able to offer an advertiser a medium where competition for the listener's eye or ear is less frantic. New York's radio station WQXR is one of several that made such a move. It reduced by seventy-seven the average number of commercials it carried each day.

The tastefulness of television and radio commercials likewise has shown signs of deterioration as the pressure to sell has mounted. Selling messages for "intimately personal products" such as feminine-hygiene products and hemorrhoid treatments are beamed into many living rooms. At this writing, more than 140 television stations accept commercials for the hemorrhoid treatment Preparation H.

When the National Association of Broadcasters announced it would drop from membership stations carrying the hemorrhoid commercials, several of the offenders—many of them National Association of Broadcasters members—shrugged and went on using the commercials. Three dozen National Association of Broadcasters stations chose to lose their National Association of Broadcasters seal rather than lose the revenue that came from broadcasting the commercials that were banned. After the ban, in fact, the sponsor of the hemorrhoid preparation had little difficulty in booking more than a million dollars' worth of commercials on television. The National Association of Broadcasters also frowned on commercials for "feminine hygiene products," but a number of American stations reportedly went on using them.

Officials of the National Association of Broadcasters made a distinction between commercials for "intimately personal" products and those that were just "personal" such as laxatives, deodorants, depilatories, toilet tissues, corn and callus remedies, and corsets. The National Association of Broadcasters' Review Board announced that commercials featuring these latter "personal" products were, while "sensitive," perfectly all right but should be handled with "ingenuity" and taste. Abuse had become so widespread that it issued a "guide." Here are some of the suggestions:

Laxative commercials should avoid overdramatizing discomfort, avoid duplicating the "mechanics of elimination," avoid words such as "bloated" and "gassy." And the setting should be elsewhere than the family bathroom.

Deodorant commercials should use the word "perspiration" rather than "sweat" and should avoid photographic shots of armpits, at least those of live humans. The public continued to see the armpits of Greek statues.

Depilatory commercials also should keep out from under the armpit, and should avoid focusing the camera on "unsightly" body hair.

Toilet commercials should avoid using the blunt term "toilet paper," should not have settings "associated with actual use," and preferably should have an air of fantasy about them.

Commercials for remedies for athlete's foot, corns, and calluses should avoid the word "itching."

Still, television viewers have to sit and watch ladies shaving their legs to "protect their loveliness," watch pictures of toes throbbing for lack of Outgro for their ingrown toenails, and hear that the sponsor's girdle is never "clammy or sticky."

Great thrilling songs turn up with commercialized lyrics. That haunting melody from Italy, "Volare," was converted within six months of its introduction into the United States into a Camel cigarette jingle, "Fumare." One of the memorable tunes from *South Pacific* came pulsing over the airways with the words, "Wash that dandruff right out of your hair." And that sentimental old song, "I want a girl . . . just like the girl . . . that married dear old Dad" has been coming over the radio with the words "I want a girl . . . just like the girl . . . that's in the Rheingold ad."

The quiz-show frauds revealed, among other painful things, that in order to sell products sponsors have not hesitated to use or misuse people who are often symbols of respectability. Revlon's sales tripled while it was sponsoring two quiz shows that ultimately became involved in a national scandal.

Many television sponsors have insisted that the name of their product be featured on a sign conspicuously displayed as a billboard throughout the program. "I've Got a Secret" and the Lawrence Welk shows have carried such signs. On one daytime variety show sponsored by Nabisco, the master of ceremonies carries a large sign bearing the word "Nabisco" dangling on his forehead throughout much of the proceedings. During at least one day's program of "Keep Talking," the sponsor's billboard not only was conspicuously in evidence but jokes and "ad libs" were slanted to commercial benefit. And when television with much fanfare presented Ernest Hemingway's *The Killers*, Buick automobiles turned up in a number of the scenes of the show itself and in one sequence in particular the camera seemed to linger on a Buick. The sponsor of the program was Buick.

Despite all this increase in commercialization some—but not

all—advertising men have wanted still greater control of the total content of the shows they sponsor. One producer, John E. Hasty, who had madeshows for both Hollywood and television, was quoted as arguing that television could reach its full potential as an advertising medium only when advertising men produced the shows. "TV viewers cannot be regarded as an audience to be entertained," he said. "They are prospects . . . for what the sponsor has to sell. This fact constitutes the show's reason for being. . . . Thus in a TV production the selling motive stands as the dominant factor."

He granted that showmen from Broadway and Hollywood might possess certain important skills that affect scripts, talent, music, and choreography and that they might be generously endowed with skill and imagination. But, he asked, "Does this overbalance a seasoned adman's experience in mass selling?"

Many sponsors tend to view their television vehicles as total advertisements. The Institute for Advertising Research has begun offering a new measuring technique called Television Program Analysis which weighs the total value of a program as an ad for the company. And an advertising trade journal in 1960 observed, "From all indications, a better tailoring of program type to advertiser, and commercial to program, is in the making."

Taken together, commercials and program in many cases accentuate the values of a high-consumption economy.

Marketing consultant Victor Lebow summed up the powerful appeal television has as a selling medium when he pointed out: "It creates a new set of conditions, impelling toward a monopoly of the consumer's attention. For the first time, almost the entire American consuming public has become a captive audience. . . . Television actually sells the generalized idea of consumption." Cases in point to support this theory that television sells "the generalized idea of consumption" might be the squeals and ahs of television audiences on panel shows when prizes such as stoves, refrigerators, rotisseries, and matched luggage are unveiled amid fanfare.

One might speculate also on what it does to a people's sense of values—especially to children's—when discussions of significant events are followed on television by announcers who in often louder and more solemn voices announce a great new discovery for a hair bleach. Or, to consider another kind of juxtaposition, a broadcast appeal to aid hungry children in mid-1960 was followed immediately by a dogfood commercial.

Television, of course, has not been the only place where the stepped-up effort to exert selling leverage on the public can be noted. Some American newspapers, especially on Thursdays and Sundays, have become so bulky because of many dozens of solid pages of advertising that finding the editorial matter leaves the reader's arms weary from turning pages. The chairman of the McCann-Erickson advertising agency complained about the "advertising traffic jam" in all media and said some Sunday newspapers were "becoming so filled with advertisements that they can grow only so much more and still remain portable." It was not the portability as much as the frequent difficulty of finding any news amid all the ads that bothered the general reader. Some of the news one found in some periodicals, it should be added, upon inspection turned out to be advertisements. I have before me a page from the Montgomery, Alabama, Advertiser that at first glance seems to contain about half editorial matter and half advertising. But the apparent news stories carry such headlines as "WOMEN, DON'T BE OVERWEIGHT, LET DAHL TAKE YOU DOWN A BUTTONHOLE OR TWO."Still further inspection reveals that up in the upper right-hand corner is a small-type notice: "This Page All Advertising." In a Kansas town, florists threatened to withdraw their advertising from the local newspaper if it continued to accept funeral notices that contained the objectionable phrase, "Please don't send flowers."

Certain of the magazines, too, showed the impact of commercialism as their publishers sought to create an editorial climate attractive to advertisers. In some cases, articles appeared which while possibly appealing to readers were most certainly gratifying to advertisers and potential advertisers. One of the mass women's magazines with a primarily working-class audience carried an article called "What's the Big Attraction?" in early 1960. Its illustration showed an attractive girl surrounded by six handsome men. The article purported to show the secrets of the Feminine Girl who is irresistible with the Water Cooler Set. Before you were eight hundred words into this revealing article, you were aware that she relied upon "hand lotions," "moisture creams," "cleaning fluid," "scarves," "fresh glove supply," "bath salts," "bath oil," "special foot lotion," "creamy depilatory," "silky -body lotion," "antiperspirant," "cologne," "cosmetics," "shampoos," "astringent-saturated cotton balls," "nail enamels," "make-up shades," and "lipstick." Later on, it also mentioned she is "a great milk drinker" and gets eight hours of sleep a night.

Advertising messages have begun appearing in places where heretofore they have been banned, usually on grounds of taste or public policy. Entrepreneurs and public officials are proving to be willing to let down the bars in order to gain extra revenue. For the first time in half a century, thousands of buses in New York have been carrying advertising posters on their exteriors. Many railroad terminals are so crowded with billboards and commercial displays that it is difficult for a traveler to find the announcement of departures. A New York television station has begun beaming its programs into more than four hundred supermarkets and into three hundred self-service laundries. In the stores the housewife finds herself exposed to as many as eight television screens and to about twenty commercials in the course of her average shopping trip.

So pervasive have billboards become along many stretches of highway in the United States, that even an outdoor advertising expert publicly lamented that a journey he and his wife took to Florida had been "ruined" because "hundreds" of miles of what would have been beautiful highways had been lined with signboards. Lobbyists for the outdoor advertisers have been charged by a New York state legislator with keeping state legislators in their debt—to forestall restrictive legislation—by giving them free sign space, or space at reduced rates, at election time. An investigator for the Reader's Digest concluded that the new 41,000-mile federal highway system would become "a billboard slum" unless state legislators acted to prevent it.

In order to cope with situations that arise when states do outlaw billboards along highways, an enterprising signmaker developed a lightweight sign so gargantuan it can be seen from many hundreds of yards away.

A still more ingenious entrepreneur has begun offering admen the chance to plant their messages against clouds and mountaintops. Unexcelled Chemical Corporation has been inviting advertisers to use its giant magic lantern called Skyjector. It is capable of beaming an advertisement one-half-mile wide against a cloud five miles away. And the company expects that within a year it will be able to create its own clouds if there are none handy. Columnist Inez Robb commented: "It opens up the prospect of a horizon-to-horizon gray-flannel world with the sky . . . available to nature lovers only in rainy weather; with America's rocks and rills and wooded hills covered with gigantic exhortations."

People who wish to stroll along the few public beaches of Florida's Gold Coast are not able to let their fancies roam too far off the notion of consumption. Every hour or so old biplanes roar along just offshore, hauling hundred-foot-long sky billboards. And on the backs of hundreds of ocean-front benches are tacked small billboards. Advertising men offered to install benches in many downtown areas of Philadelphia— and pay the city in addition $15 a month for each bench—if they could merely plaster the backs with ads. The offer was rejected.

Some paperback book publishers have begun accepting paid advertisements in their books. One book on child care has been carrying more than a dozen full-page advertisements scattered through the book.

There has also been a notable upsurge in the introduction of advertisements onto the screens of motion-picture theaters. The number of national advertisers using this medium has doubled in three years. By 1960, more than four thousand drive-in theaters were exhibiting advertisements to their paying customers, along with the entertainment. Advertisers credited much of their new fascination with movie advertising to the ironic fact that cinema's worst competitor, television, has proved to be so effective in reaching the consumer. Furthermore, television has conditioned the public to expect commercials along with its entertainment so that public resentment toward advertising in motion-picture houses purportedly has been melting. The fact that the theatergoers are paying to be entertained—not seduced—seemingly does not loom as an important distinction in their minds! Meanwhile, advertisers using the movie screens have been finding they have an even more captive audience than on television. The theater seats are in rows so that there is less tendency for a person, when commercials come on, to use the break in entertainment to make a dash to the washroom or go for refreshment.

The growing difficulty in finding ways to break through what McCann-Erickson's Mr. Harper has called the "advertising -traffic jam in media" and reach the public's eye or ear has inspired him to suggest that the advertising industry might have to help create new media. He asks: "Won't we have to encourage the development of new publishing properties? . . . Isn't it possible in the '60s that we'll require a fourth network? Isn't it possible we'll need to invent an entirely new ad medium?"

The growing pressure to move goods by more aggressive promotion can best be seen, perhaps, in the changes taking place in the American pharmaceutical industry. It has traditionally been cautious, courteous, and restrained in bringing its drugs to the attention of the nation's doctors and druggists. All that changed when the producers of bulk chemicals moved into the field and initiated aggressive tactics which the old-line ethical houses felt forced to imitate. As a result, the major drug houses have begun pouring four times as much money into selling as they do into research. In fact, they are spending about $5,500 on sales and promotion for each doctor in the land. They inundate the doctors with brochures about the new and old drugs. They send a swarm of 27,000 detail men into doctors' offices and drugstores to induce doctors to prescribe their particular brands and to induce druggists to stock them.

One such detail man in West Virginia told me there was now a detail man for every twelve prospects, and he said that he personally called on 129 doctors in each two-week period, as did many of his rivals. A little arithmetic and projection produced a stunning thought. If the other detail men were as energetic as he was, then detail men were making many millions of calls on doctors each year. My informant blinked at that thought but didn't contest it. He said he goes and sits in the doctor's office with the patients to wait his turn—because patients resent doctors who seem to let someone into their office out of turn. Very often, he said, he may find another detail man already in the waiting room. In that case he will leave and come back later, because doctors don't like to have too many detail men in their waiting rooms at one time. It discourages the patients.

One result of all this selling pressure is that doctors hear so much about brand names that they usually prescribe by brand name rather than by the generic or scientific name, as they were usually taught to do in medical school. Brand-name drugs usually cost the patient a good deal more than a non-brand-name drug filling the same specifications. The average doctor influences the sale of about $20,000 worth of drugs a year.

The growing recklessness of businessmen in many lines as they have sought to keep sales rising is reflected in two extreme examples worth noting.

The Hat Council, Inc., employed the services of a public-relations expert famed for the success of his tactics, Russell Birdwell. Soon the Birdwell firm was circulating under its letterhead a startling statement on hat-wearing or rather non-hat-wearing by a psychologist whom the Birdwell firm had discovered in Dallas, Texas. According to this psychologist, "Men who go bareheaded . . . are betraying their feminine instincts." Such a man is announcing to the world that "he doesn't want to be a man."

Another sample of the extravagant devices used to catch public attention was the advertising theme used by the maker of a nationally advertised aerosol shaving cream. One advertisement pictured the side view of a smiling, voluptuously proportioned girl with her posterior thrust back conspicuously as she held a giant can of the cream. The headline of the ad read: "IF YOUR CAN'S TOO SMALL TRY MINE FOR SIZE." And another headline over the same sort of photograph had the lady saying: "I HAVE THE BIGGEST CAN . . . AND THE BEST CAN . . . AND IT COSTS THE LEAST. . . ."

As advertising men have found themselves with more and more billions of dollars at their command, they have moved into a role of considerable power in influencing the behavior of the entire populace. They have become to a very large extent masters of the nation's economic destiny, and perhaps the nation's most influential taste makers. They have become dictators of the content of many if not most radio and television programs, judges with life-and-death power over many periodicals, and at least co-designers of many products being offered to the public.

The rationale they have worked out to justify their new power is that advertising is the bulwark of the American way of life. A Cleveland billboard announced: "America is a Better America thanks to advertising!" Admen recently have responded to criticism by becoming quite aggressively defensive about their role. Charles H. Brower, president of Batten, Barton, Durstine & Osborn, acknowledged that perhaps admen had some housecleaning to do but he added: "The house of advertising is a mighty fortress in our economy. . . . Pull down advertising, and a frightening number of things will fall with it." The heroic role of advertising in providing a "bulwark" or fortress for the national way of life became somewhat hard or embarrassing to explain in detail. More than half of all advertising dollars went to promote cigarettes, alcoholic beverages, patent medicines, soap, and cosmetics. Other advertising men preferred to put the contribution to a better America in dollars and cents. They asserted that advertising brought down prices by providing the mass market for mass production. Undoubtedly this argument has a strong historical basis. And it was advanced as recently as 1959 by Mr. Harper, whose agency had just become the largest in the United States. But in the developing Age of Abundance this argument was less convincing when you got down to specifics. Why had the cost of automobiles, all intensively advertised, risen every year for twelve years? Why did brand-name products nationally advertised generally cost more than private brands of identical quality? When the magazine *Progressive Grocer* sought to explain the growing volume of private brands sold in American stores, it concluded that "the most convincing clue" was the fact that they generally cost the consumer less than the nationally advertised product. And the price differential was growing. It now ranged up to between 10 per cent and 20 per cent. In the field of drugs and cosmetics, the differential was even greater. A comparative study made in New York City showed that nationally advertised brands tended to cost about twice as much as "substantially identical" private brands of the same products. (It should be conceded that many private brands are bought with confidence only because the customers are buying the image of the store's name—which often is intensively advertised.)

Many producing companies have begun playing both fields. They promote heavily their own brand—say, a detergent—and quietly furnish the identical product to stores to be sold under the store's private label, at a lower price.

By 1960, even some advertising people were conceding that the argument that advertising brought lower prices was starting to pass into the hands of "cynics and disbelievers." Still, there is no disposition in or out of advertising to doubt that advertising does indeed stimulate consumption, especially in the case of products that are innovations or are optional, or unnecessary. In that sense advertising has indeed become the bulwark of the American way of life, and I certainly would not be among those that Mr. Brower feels are trying to "pull down advertising." Much of advertising is still simple announcement of product performance and availability. It is time, however, that the United States economy's growing reliance on advertising be carefully assessed and appraised for its impact on American life.

The cost of getting the consumer's attention—or a "share of the consumer mind," to use adman lingo—is getting higher every year simply because of the competitive din. In 1959, *Sales Management* made the point that for every dollar spent for advertising early in the fifties an additional half dollar should now be added just to offset the greater competition of messages. There were 551 different brands of coffee on the market, 177 brands of salad dressing, and 249 brands of powdered soap. A vice-president of the Batten, Barton, Durstine & Osborn agency complained that "the amount of advertising in existence today is staggering. It must at least have doubled in the last ten years. There is no escape from it; no place to hide any more." His point that consumers have "no place to hide any more" was made not out of compassion for the consumer but rather as the lament of an adman who is finding it harder and harder to get himself heard. Others complain of encountering a "fatigue of believability" among consumers and of a lowering of the customers' "credibility quotient." An editor of a trade journal offered one hopeful thought. He said that "methods of communication are perfecting themselves so fast that it's easier for people to learn now."

The selling pressure is being turned up not only at the image-building level of advertising but also at the over-the-counter level of retailing. Spokesmen of the marketing industry have called for the training of at least a million more "well-talented salesmen" by 1970. Otherwise the expanded economy predicted for that year will be "stifled by overproduction."

More and more stores are staying open nights and Sundays to keep goods moving in ever-greater volume. A few years ago, custom dictated that only stores dealing with necessities of life open their doors on Sunday. By the sixties, thousands of appliance stores, clothing stores, hardware stores, supermarkets, and automobile dealers were staying open on Sundays. This trend is particularly strong in the West. In California, 80 per cent of the supermarkets are open on Sunday. Many stores in the Los Angeles area are staying open around the clock, seven days a week. It is an eerie sight to arrive at the Los Angeles airport at two o'clock in the morning and drive to a hotel. En route one sees dozens of giant stores bustling with selling activities. Sunday has proved to be an excellent time to move goods because the spirit of the carnival prevails among the customers. Operators of shopping centers affirm that on Sundays the people show less concern about getting good values for their money than on other days. Another reason why night and Sunday shoppers are especially prized is that at those times husband and wife are more likely to shop together, and will buy 30 per cent more than the wife would buy if she were doing the family shopping alone.

Merchandising experts are learning many strategies to keep customers coming through the doors—and buying. The general philosophy of the anonymous appliance salesman who wrote the series for *Home Furnishings Daily* on selling techniques was summed up in this self-justifying remark: "After all, the shopper walked into the store looking to cut my throat. I just got to him first."

If a customer seems to be the polite, timid type, the salesman explained, you nail him after the spiel by whipping up a bill of sale "without a word from him." More often than not, this timid type assumes he has somehow committed himself and digs out a deposit to spare himself embarrassment." If the customer seems resistant, you use the warehouse trick. The item is selling so rapidly, you explain, that there is only one left. So you call the "warehouse" and ask that the last one be held for your prospect. He added: "My wife is quite used to receiving such calls for me."

Another trick he recommended was the "burn and switch." The salesman "burns" himself in order to excite the prospect's initial interest by quoting a price at cost. Once the prospect's interest is stirred, "you gently start to switch him to a make he hasn't even thought of buying." You do this by confidentially explaining the shortcomings of the make you had offered at such a bargain. The washer may have a filter that rusts, or it is reputed to tangle clothing.

If the customer seems confused about which brand actually offers the best value, the solution is easy. You strongly recommend the brand that has the highest "spiff" or "PM" riding on it. The spiff or PM is the "push money" offered as a reward for each item of the brand that is sold. The salesman-author commented: "I've never seen so much spiff money floating around as today with this tough competitive situation."

In many instances the PM or spiff is provided to the clerk by the manufacturer's representative who is striving to increase his volume. The sales manager of one major-appliance producer referred unhappily to the spiff as "the new law of the land." And an industry survey disclosed that spiffs were coming to play an important part in selling lamps. Home Furnishings Daily carried a report from Boston in early 1960 that "spiffs from manufacturers have been a part of the bedding business for so many years that they have become an institution." It cited one salesman as estimating that the average bedding salesman "adds $50 a month to his salary through spiffs. 'No salesman would ever want the practice discontinued,' he says." And the same journal reported from Detroit that appliance-television dealers in that area expressed "qualified" disapproval of spiffs. It seems that "leading merchants believe if push money is being offered it should be given to the retailer to dispense, preferably in the manner in which he sees fit."

That pretty well sums up the morality of one segment of entrepreneurs feeling the full force of consumerism.

20. THE CHANGING AMERICAN CHARACTER

"... whose God is their belly ..."—Paul, Philippians 3:19.

A FINAL PRICE THAT MUST BE CONSIDERED IN assessing the implications of the current drift of American society under the impact of an economy based on ever-mounting consumption is the change it may be producing in the character of the people involved.

What is the impact on the human spirit of all these pressures to consume? What results are already beginning to appear as a result of all the efforts to make Americans more hedonistic? What is the mere availability of ever-greater material abundance doing to American habit patterns?

Business Week made a report on the many subtle and adroit persuasion techniques being developed to encourage Americans to be more zestful consumers and commented: "... it looks as though all of our business forces are bent on getting everyone to ... Borrow. Spend. Buy. Waste. Want."

It is unrealistic to assume that all such pressures are not producing changes at a deeper level than mere consumption habits. For example, a person who finds himself induced to spend beyond his income habitually does not wish to feel guilty about his excesses and welcomes a system of morality that condones such habits. Much of the average American's consumption has been channeled into frivolous or playful or whimsical outlets, which also requires rationalizing. United States residents have been spending more on smoking, drinking, and gambling than they have on education. They have been spending more on admission tickets to pastimes than they have on foreign economic aid. They have been spending more on jewelry and watches than they have on either books or basic research.[1] Further, they spend more for greeting cards than they do for medical research.

The people of the United States have been thrust into making a more abrupt transformation in their system of values since World War II than in just about any comparable period of time in the nation's history. Some of the changes in values, attitudes, and outlooks might be considered most attractive or encouraging, such as the increase in world-mindedness and the more accepting attitudes toward people superficially unlike themselves. Some of the changes, however, are directly related to the pressures and stimulations that encourage Americans to increase their consumption, and those are what concern us here. Joseph Wood Krutch believes that the transvaluation of moral values required in adjusting to an economy of abundance is as drastic, in fact, as any posed to civilized man since Christianity proclaimed that humility not pride is the source of all virtue.[2]

These new pressures are causing ever more people to find their main life satisfactions in their consumption role rather than their productive role. And these pressures are bringing forward such traits as pleasure-mindedness, self-indulgence, materialism, and passivity as conspicuous elements of the American character. It is perhaps no coincidence that the areas of the United States where the spirit of hedonism is most rampant—Los Angeles, Miami, and Las Vegas—are also among the fastest-growing cities in the land.

Whether this trend to hedonism represents regress or progress may be arguable. It seems reasonable, however, that Americans should take stock of the changes taking place. Then they can decide whether they like them or not, and act accordingly.

If we try to visualize the future course of a society based so largely on an ever-expanding economy as the American model, we must conclude that it will require a more and more voluptuous mode of living until the process is slowed by growing depletion of the resources essential to support the voluptuousness. Another possibility is that resisting citizens may modify the model.

Aldous Huxley in his *Brave New World* of the twenty-sixth century appears to assume that the problem of diminishing resources can somehow be managed. Or perhaps he did not take the resource problem seriously into account, since the drain had not yet become critical when he wrote his book in 1932. In any case, he has Mustapha Mond, the controller of his highly regimented world state of the future, explain:

"But industrial civilization is only possible where there is no self-denial. Self-indulgence up to the very limits imposed by hygiene and economics. Otherwise the wheels stop turning."

In the current American model there is abundant evidence that rankand-file Americans are co-operating wholeheartedly in the task of taking up ever-greater consumption as a way of life. Those who thought that preoccupation with possessions—and consumption— might lessen with the easing of the prod-dings of poverty did not take into account the new proddings of the marketing persuaders. Preoccupation with possessions instead has increased.

This preoccupation with consumption so assiduously nurtured by the marketers is leaving its marks on the people involved. These marks show up in a variety of ways. They showed up, for example, in the study of "Interurbia" conducted by *Fortune* magazine, the J. Walter Thompson advertising agency, and consultants from Yale University. The particular interurbia—or massive metropolitan complex—studied was the urban sprawl that stretches almost continuously from Portland, Maine, to Washington, D.C. Because of its concentration of tens of millions of humans, this has been a prime target of marketers for years. The study reported that the typical consumer in this area is developing characteristics that make him a superb consumer. He tends to be restless, conforming, aggressive in his interpersonal relations, and chronically has a "hunger for hard goods," to use one marketing columnist's phrase. He may buy these hard goods—or consumer durables—even when he has no real need for them, perhaps because he has developed an inner need to keep buying things.

A perceptive writer on family life, Hannah Lees, has commented, too, on the many modern women who seem preoccupied with getting for themselves such things as wall-to-wall carpeting, completely automated kitchens, fur jackets, and their own convertibles. She noted that many such women—and they are in every income bracket—are "going around with the uneasy feeling that without all those possessions they would just disappear."

Some Americans have become so habituated to continuous impulsive consumption through shopping that they are distressed when the process is disrupted. During the 1958 recession, customers suddenly started robbing the supermarkets blind to the tune of a quarter billion dollars' worth of goods a year. In southern California, arrests for supermarket shoplifting soared 50 per cent within a few months. It was found that some mothers were training their children to slip parcels out through the guard rails. One explanation for the great increase apparently was that so many families had been committing so much of their paychecks to installment payments that they were strapped for food when the husband's overtime was cut back. *Time* magazine, however, in citing the upsurge, suggested that a new morality might be a major factor. It commented on "the easy conscience that assumes a high standard of living to be everybody's right, whether the money is around or not."

And some religious leaders have been speculating what is likely to happen to the sense of proportion in living in a people that are encouraged to become quickly dissatisfied with last year's models. There is also the thriftlessness that is being so widely encouraged. A syndicated columnist on family finance admonished readers to step up their spending of any income they had after the "necessities" of life were attended to. This counselor advised readers in early 1959: "If you decide to save, pay off debts, you help slow down business. If you decide to buy cars and appliances enthusiastically, you put a glow on the entire country."

The absorption with consumption also unquestionably is having some impact on family solidarity. Frequent purchase of such appliances as dishwashers and clothes driers and prepackaged meals with their "built-in maid service" has two noteworthy effects on family living; at least at the lower-white-collar and working-class level. It tends to keep the family strapped for money. And it tends to disenfranchise the wife by depriving her of many traditional, time-consuming homemaking functions. Both effects—the pinch for money and the growing lack of challenge to women in the home—tend to send the wife out looking for a job. A high-school official of a Chicago suburb told me that in that town of skilled workers and white-collar workers "most of the mothers of our students have jobs. Some students say they see their folks together only on Sundays." A teacher in San Francisco has offered the opinion that parents take less interest in their children's schoolwork. She explained: "It may be because so many mothers are working. Everybody has to have new cars, refrigerators, so they work. Often the children lose out." If the trend toward working mothers continues—and it seems likely— Americans might well consider adopting the Danish system of setting up high-grade facilities for child care manned by professionals.

All the preoccupation with consumption—and other forms of materialism—appears to be having an especially heavy impact on the attitudes of the young people of the United States being reared in the new environment. A number of investigators are reporting findings that hardly match our traditional concept of American youths as ambitious, dedicated, self-sufficient, individualistic idealists who hope to build a better world.

Two psychologists, James Gillespie of Colby College and Gordon Allport of Harvard University, made a survey of attitudes of college students around the world several years ago. It indicated that American youths were more self-centered and materialistic in their aspirations than were the youths of most of the countries surveyed. The investigators asked eighteen hundred youths in ten countries to visualize their future.

One rather conspicuous finding was the preoccupation of American youths with the material aspects of their existence to the exclusion of most other concerns. These young Americans knew pretty specifically the kind of rich, full life they wanted to build. They talked in terms of the hi-fi set they would have, the outdoor barbecue, the game room, where they would take their first vacation, the kind of car they aspired to, and so on. They showed little interest in making a career of public service and little apparent concern for their fellow man. Professor Gillespie commented on the intense "privitism"—or preoccupation with their own small world—that seemed to characterize the American students, who presumably were representative of the nation's leaders of tomorrow. You get the feeling, he said, that a cloud of opprobrium hung over participation in public affairs in the United States. (Possibly this is because in an age of abundance challenging public problems seem less apparent to youthful eyes.)

Mexicans, in contrast, were aglow with idealism and showed only casual concern about the material surroundings of their lives. Six times as many Mexicans as American students foresaw that their greatest sources of pride would be in service to their nation. And a majority said that helping others would be one of the goals of their life.

In the matter of teaching young children, the difference between the youths of the two nations was interesting because the young students from the United States tended to evaluate experiences on the basis of their "fun" potential. Thus American girls who said they hoped to have jobs working with little children explained in a number of cases that such work would be fun. Mexican girls, in contrast, saw working with small children as an opportunity to help mold future citizens.

Students in the various countries were asked, "If you should get a large sum of money five years from now, what would you do with it?" The American students had a different—bigger—idea of what was meant by "a large sum of money" than the others. But more significantly, only 2 per cent of the Americans thought of sharing such a windfall with anyone beyond their immediate family. The impulse to share the windfall with other people in need was higher in virtually every other national group.

In this connection, we might note the observation of Rabbi Philip S. Bernstein of Rochester, New York, who states that "materialism, the pursuit of wealth, deadens sensitivity to other human beings." Might such a deadening be a cause of the startlingly callous behavior of race fans at the Indianapolis Motor Speedway when an aluminum tower collapsed May 30, 1960? It occurred shortly before the big race was to begin. Two men in the tangled mass died of broken necks, and seventy persons—many of them screaming—were injured. Some people in the crowd tried to rescue moaning persons from under the collapsed tower. But, the Associated Press reported, "others on the ground and on other near-by towers went on drinking beer and munching fried chicken, concerned mainly with the start of the race."

Consider another study of the emerging character of American college students. This more recent study was sponsored by the American Council on Education. The provost of the University of New Hampshire, Edward F. Eddy, Jr., and two assistants made a study of attitudes on twenty American campuses by living with the students long enough to win their confidence. Commenting on today's student, Dr. Eddy said: "He is interested primarily in the maintenance of the status quo—a very comfortable status quo, which makes him the sought-after darling of business and industry." Dr. Eddy, too, commented on the conspicuous "privitism" of the American student, who seems absorbed in achieving "a rich, full life" for himself. (That phrase "rich, full life" could come out of a General Motors advertisement.) Dr. Eddy continued: "His strong interests are centered on the material benefits which he and his family may be able to enjoy. . . . The constant question is first: 'What's in it for me?'"

Brains, it might be added, appear to be no defense against the materialism of the age. The president of the National Merit Scholarship Corporation reported on the aspirations of the National Merit Scholarship finalists. He said that "to an astonishingly large extent [they] look forward to the easy, pleasant life in the suburbs with ample income for the material luxuries. Very few speak of a willingness to work for ideals or to pursue knowledge no matter what the cost."

So far we have talked mainly about the emerging attitudes and character of students in the United States. The Korean War, on the other hand, provided a testing ground of sorts for American youths of all ranks. For several years after that war, the Army conducted a painful study to try to account for the fact that so many of the American men who became prisoners became collaborators, or showed appalling selfishness, or just curled up and died. A third of all GI's captured engaged in some form of collaboration, and more than a third died in captivity. And most startling, twenty-one of the men captured—for the first time in history—did not choose to return home when first given a chance. In contrast, of the hundreds of Turkish soldiers who were captured, virtually all of them withstood all pressures to induce them to become collaborators. And although half of the Turks were wounded when captured, not a single one of them died in captivity. An Assistant Secretary of the Army has called the Army's findings about the behavior of American prisoners in Korea "distressing." Writer Eugene Kinkead talked with many Army officers involved in the post-mortem. One Army doctor involved in the analysis told Kinkead he could only conclude that "a new softness" had come into the character of many young Americans. He said they seemed to lack the old Yankee resourcefulness of their fathers.[3]

An official of the United States Department of Justice is still another who has been forced to ponder the impact of the materialistic culture of the United States upon its youths. He was trying to understand why youthful lawlessness was rising at such a "startling" pace. At the present rate, by 1962, one million American teen-agers will be arrested each year. He was forced to the conclusion that "we seem to have misplaced the sense of values which made this a great nation. Self-indulgence and the principle of pleasure before duty on a vast and growing scale have become a phenomenon of the adult world. These are warning symptoms of the decadence disease which has contributed to the decay of so many civilizations throughout history." Then he asked bluntly:

"When children, without discipline and without moral standards implanted in a stable home, are thrust into a culture in which pressures from every direction promote the principle of self-indulgence, what reaction can be expected?"

The juvenile delinquent in the United States, he concluded, "is a byproduct of our self-indulgent age."

A good many citizens in the United States, it should be emphasized, are beginning to feel vaguely uneasy about the impact of ever-greater consumption on their lives. Investigators for *The Chicago Tribune* reported—in *The New Consumer*—finding a good many people ridden with guilt feelings because of all their purchases. One housewife, cited as typical, said: "After I've been shopping, I often feel guilty about having spent too much." Such guilt feelings, however, seem to be more characteristic of women in the older settled areas of Chicago than of those in the new suburbs. Some of the comments by women in Golf, the more prosperous of the suburbs studied, indicate that even in the changing suburbs there is a good deal of uneasiness about the growing materialism. The investigators reported that most of the residents felt they were more adept at the art of making money than their own parents had been. Then the investigators added:

"Some of them, however, feel that, all questions of money aside, their parents had something that they admire but lack—the capacity to use their own inner resources. This is a capacity which will be even more strongly lacking among the Golf dweller's children, who may be expected to be extraordinarily thing-minded people."

At least some American businessmen, too, have been uneasy about this growing thing-mindedness created to a large extent by the pressure for ever-mounting consumption. *Business Week*, which certainly is on the side of the sellers, concedes that "many people are upset by what they see as an enormous emphasis on materialism and triviality and as a saturation of American life with the false standards of the market place."

In the late fifties, a marketing and economic consultant from Chicago, Theodore Levitt, kicked up a tremendous furor in business circles by urging businessmen to stop fretting about the social implications of what they were doing. His comments appeared in *The Harvard Business Review* ("The Dangers of Social Responsibility"), *Sales Management* ("Corrupting Tender Souls"), and *Advertising Age*. This last offered a presentation by Dr. Levitt entitled: "ARE ADVERTISING AND MARKETING CORRUPTING SOCIETY? IT'S NOT YOUR WORRY, LEVITT TELLS BUSINESS."

Dr. Levitt discussed "management's mission in the new society." He said it was quite possible for many businessmen to conclude that they were contributing "to decadence, self-indulgence, materialism, cynicism, irresponsibility, selfishness. . . ." He cited questions being raised by the prospects of achieving ever-higher consumption. What would this do to people's dignity, their culture, their spiritual values? Would their standard of living actually be higher simply because they were persuaded to throw away earlier models faster? And what are the effects of manipulation by persuaders? Dr. Levitt conceded that conceivably marketers could eventually become so successful in "loading people up with redundant goods, creating superficial and vulgar wants, and generating the kind of opulence that turns luxuries into necessities," etc., that perhaps "we will get soft and decadent and finally drift down into a quagmire of decay that was Rome's fate."

"But," he quickly added, "let's not go overboard in an orgy of moral self-flagellation. A lot of this viewing with alarm is an irrational Puritan reaction against the good life. . . . It is not at all a settled matter that luxury creates softness and decadence. . . ."

Therefore he urged marketers not to get "all excited about the human consequences of so-called successful marketing." Instead, he argued, the marketer should tend to his knitting. Society needs always to be asking itself where it is headed. And someone must think and act on the questions being raised by the prospect of ever-higher consumption; but that "someone" should not be the businessman. He concluded that "cultural, spiritual, social, moral, etc., consequences of his actions are none of his occupational concern." In truth, he said, "the businessman exists for only one purpose, to create and deliver value satisfactions at a profit to himself." He suggested that businessmen leave soul saving, preserving spiritual values, cultivating human dignity, and conserving self-respect to others.

Dr. Levitt's elaborate rationalization of nonresponsibility for marketers obviously touched a very raw nerve. Subsequent issues of *Advertising Age* carried pages filled with angry denunciations and rebuttals by marketers and other readers. An official of the advertising agency, MacManus, John and Adams, wrote: "The immense benefits of business to society are obvious. Dr. Levitt's uncalled-for defense is so weak it is, in effect, damnation, for which the advertising and business world should not soon forgive him." And the promotion art director of *Architectural Forum* wrote: "The businessman's responsibility, whether moral or material, will always be with him and he cannot be relieved of it—and neither Mr. Levitt's article nor wishing will make it so."

Now we approach the final—and most perplexing—phase of this exploration of the pressures toward, and implications of, ever-mounting consumption in the United States. What, if anything, should be done?

If a projection of present trends seems to confront United States citizens with an exceedingly unpretty picture for the future, is there any escape from these pressures that would not disrupt the economy? And if some disruption is unavoidable in any correction of current trends, would the disruption be acceptable as an alternative to the present headlong course? This course appears to be taking the people of the United States toward more and more force feeding, more and more manipulation, more and more fast-fading or deteriorating products, more and more self-indulgence, more and more depletion of irreplaceable resources.

In view of the sharp acceleration involved in the demand in the United States and abroad for resources and living space, it seems urgent that citizens of the United States begin taking a long view of the drift of their society. When we say that the nation may be feeing a real pinch for such resources as copper, lead, zinc, and oil within two decades, that may sound like a deadline that is still far off. After all, the year 1980 puts us close to the time of George Orwell's fictional Big Brother. But twenty years is no further ahead than Pearl Harbor is behind us. Or consider that far-distant date of A.D. 2000, when the country's present population will have doubled if present trends continue. That is no further ahead than the beginning of the Jazz Age is behind us. Or look a full century into the future when, if present trends continue, the world will be approaching exhaustion of most of its presently known vital raw materials and energy sources and probably will be largely dependent on ordinary rock, sunlight, air, sea water, and perhaps coal to develop its living standards. That is only as far ahead as the outbreak of the United States Civil War is behind us. A century represents less than 2 per cent of man's brief recorded history.

All this suggests that the people of the United States and elsewhere begin thinking of the long haul. Otherwise, they and their children face a rigorous, regimented, and teeming future.

Is it possible that the people of the United States can still work out for the long run a sane, intelligent, and satisfying way of life while preserving a reasonably thriving economy?

There is no absolute assurance that they can. But the possibilities should be explored before it is too late to start. If there are available any simple solutions to this challenge, the author is unaware of them.

A number of economic thinkers are increasingly aware that not just the United States economy but the drift of the United States civilization is involved. Some few economists are becoming oriented as much to the needs of the consumer as to the better-understood needs of the producer. An outstanding example of this latter breed of economist is Leland Gordon of Denison University, author of *Economics for Consumers*, who states: "Economic stability and high-level employment are desirable goals. But the well-being of consumers is a desirable goal, too."

Let us then look at some suggested courses for the future that seem to deserve the consideration of the American people. They deal with the twin challenges of developing more enlightened consumption patterns while evolving an economy that can thrive reasonably well without force feeding and, further, can have a reasonable chance of enduring for the long run.

PART IV

Some Suggested Courses

21. RESTORING PRIDE IN PRUDENCE

"The unorganized consumer must resist blind conformity to the group and to the commercial persuader. Education is central to his resistance."—Leland Gordon, Denison University.

IN EARLIER YEARS, ECONOMISTS PONDERING THE controls necessary to keep the seller-buyer relationship in fair balance concluded that ordinary human prudence would protect the buyer from being exploited or overwhelmed. Caveat emptor, they intoned.

Letting the buyer beware was thought to be no real problem because the buyer was assumed to hold the whip hand since the money was in his pocket. The consumer was assumed to be sovereign. And marketers and merchandisers still like to flatter the consuming public by referring to it as "king."

Today, there is less outright hoodwinking of the old-fashioned variety in the market place. Lately, "fraud" has been the whipping boy of the Federal Trade Commission and of marketers who want to "clean up" practices that have proved embarrassing when exposed. Actually, from the general public's viewpoint, fraud is not the major problem. Outright fraud has become too dangerous for all but fly-by-night operators. It is no longer considered to be even sporting. Ethics in the market place have risen at least in this respect. Further, it should be stressed that many producers and retailers persist in the old-fashioned habit of viewing the consumer with respect and strive to the very best of their ability to serve his best interests.

On the other hand, marketers in general have been subjecting the consumer to a barrage of selling strategies that has rarely heretofore been matched in variety, intensity, or ingenuity. Millions of consumers are manipulated, razzle-dazzled, indoctrinated, mood-conditioned, and flimflammed. They are conditioned to be discontented with last year's models, and they are conditioned to accept flimsily built products.

The attitude of all too many marketers was revealed in the January 29, 1960, issue of *Printers' Ink*—"The Weekly Magazine of Advertising and Marketing"—when it earnestly reported efforts being made by marketing researchers to understand how people acquire and retain information and attitudes. It stated: "Perhaps most important of all, [the researchers] are edging toward that ultimate question for advertising: How can the consumer, like Pavlov's dog, be taught the habit of buying a specific brand?"

If that truly is the "ultimate question" for advertising, then the industry had better search its soul. And consumers had better take to the barricades.

One measure of the difficulty that the lone consumer faces today is the warning made by three psychologists at the University of Michigan. They stated that "the indiscriminate and uncontrolled application of psychological principles is increasing at a fearsome rate" in marketing uses on an unwary public. They suggested that a "trusted scientific group" be set up to keep an eye on all these freewheeling applicators.Another measure of the challenge confronting the lone consumer is the statement of Colston Warne, president of Consumers Union. He states:

"The consumer is asked to choose wisely under circumstances which often baffle even the trained technician. He is faced with product differentiation, brand differentiation, model differentiation, price differentiation. He is offered bonuses of extraneous products for purchasing. He is faced with trading stamps, special discounts, and trade-ins. Products are sold in varying quantities and in containers often deceptive to the eye."

The consumer also is faced increasingly with buying products of such complexity in their electronic or chemical composition that an expert assessment is beyond his capacity. He finds himself choosing on a superficial basis such as color of the trim or the brand image that has been etched into his mind by the seller.

In the unequal relationship between marketer and buyer, it should be added, the federal government—which is supposed to "promote the general welfare"—has in recent years offered more comfort and aid to the marketer than to the consumer. It has spent billions of dollars to help producers with their problems and has a number of cabinet officers to promote the interests of producers. It has no cabinet officer specifically charged with protecting the interest of the public in its role as a consumer.

During the early days of the Eisenhower Administration, the modest product-testing and consumer activities of the Bureau of Home Economics (Department of Agriculture) were sharply curtailed. The Consumers Union protested at the time that compared to the oceans of aid to retailers, wholesalers, manufacturers, importers, exporters, bankers, etc., that was flooding from the Government Printing Office, the publications of the Bureau of Home Economics were a scant trickle indeed. Appropriations for the Food and Drug Administration were not permitted to keep pace with the growth in population and the flood of new products. In the mid-fifties, the Bureau of Standards was ordered to stop publication of *Care and Repair of the Home*, which had sold more than 175,000 copies at sixty cents a copy. The director explained: "We have no authority to run a consumer advisory service."

The story is much the same with other federal agencies purportedly dedicated to the public welfare. Members of the Federal Housing Administration, the Federal Trade Commission, the Federal Communications Commission, and the Federal Power Commission have come predominantly from the industry groups whose regulation was entrusted to them. And for the most part—and at least until very recently—the agencies have shown far more zeal in promoting the producers' welfare and refereeing producer quarrels than in protecting the consumers. Two Federal Communications Commission members were so deeply involved in fraternizing with the industry they were supposed to regulate that they were encouraged to resign. A doctor with the Food and Drug Administration told Senate investigators that when she sought to require the manufacturer of a new drug to warn against drug addiction on the label of the product, a high official of the Food and Drug Administration responded by saying that he did not wish to have his policy of friendliness with industry interfered with.

In the face of all these pressures, the lone consumer of ordinary intelligence and impulsiveness is usually no match for the subtle and massive onslaughts aimed at him. Today, the consumer is far from sovereign. To restore the consumer to any real sovereignty, there needs to be a return on a large scale to pride in prudent buying and informative support for that prudence.

What—if anything—can be done to restore today's consumer-citizen to this sovereignty he has lost?

There are a few things that each individual consumer can do—if he or she is so minded—to regain a posture of self-respect in the shopping situation. And in doing so, he may well serve as an example to others. For example: He can demand that he be approached on a rational basis, and protest when he is not. Usually, when Americans find themselves the owners of handsome but malfunctioning products, they complain to their friends rather than to the maker or distributor. A Carnegie Tech professor has expressed amazement that so few complaints go to a company that has marketed an indisputable lemon.

A lone consumer may feel helpless in facing up to a giant corporation with plants in 123 cities. Actually, this lone consumer should know that this monolith tends to over-react to criticism to its products. One strong letter, neatly typed, addressed to the president, can create concern in the executive suite (even though the president himself is probably spared from seeing the letter). Two letters of protest will create panic. Three letters of protest will create pandemonium.

Kiwanis International took a salutary step a few months ago when it established as one of its twenty criteria for good citizenship whether the member was doing his part in "rebelling against" false and misleading advertising.

A promising area for citizens to test their claws as self-respecting consumer-critics is in the area of drugs. As indicated, many doctors by and large have fallen into the habit—as a result of being cultivated by hordes of pharmaceutical detail men and by onslaughts of drug advertising—of using a brand name rather than the scientific name in writing a prescription. Both meet the government specifications as to purity and potency and are substantially identical. Drug firms argue that they individually strive to improve upon the government standards. (Some famous name brands have been found to be substandard.) Whether, however, a possible slight improvement is worth the frequent doubling of cost can be left to the consumer's judgment.

A family with heavy medical bills can save $50 or $100 a year if it asks its family doctor to use the scientific name in writing prescriptions except where he may have some strong preference among brands. In 1960, several states began urging doctors to use the scientific rather than the brand name in prescribing when state funds were involved, as with welfare patients.

As a longer-range goal the consumer-citizens might work for a more rational way for dispensing drugs than by hocus-pocus. It is a travesty of free enterprise when twenty-five companies are issuing essentially the identical drug under twenty-five different brand names at greatly varying prices. Word artists invent the brand names, and often try to make them sound like some other highly successful drug. All this represents not only economic waste but danger. Doctors are complaining that disasters can arise in the jungle of nomenclature that is developing, as a result of a doctor's confusion. In a rational society, I would think, the medical profession would arrange for a simple way to get pure, high-quality drugs to the public at a cost not inflated by rivalbrand promotional activities.

The individual consumer can insist that producers who wish to win his patronage start stressing function over fashion. One does not have to be a killjoy—such as the technocrat of the thirties—to see that the emphasis on styling in the United States consumer-goods mart has exceeded the bounds of rationality. It is one thing to have natural swings in style in design and quite another to have designers seeking ways to outmode all the bathroom scales or washing machines in American homes by mapping style changes.

Industrial designer Henry Dreyfuss points out that American automobile makers have been so preoccupied with styling in some recent years that they have forgotten that cars are supposed to be comfortable to sit in, convenient to operate, safe to take out on the road, and economical.

The prudent segment of the consuming public should favor those brave entrepreneurs who have braced themselves against the tide of styling and have tried to offer to the public products designed for function rather than style by giving special consideration to their offerings. American Motors is one producer that deserves special recognition in this regard because in both its automobiles such as the Rambler and in its Kelvinator appliances it has made a bold effort to swear off the annual style change. It is one of the few companies having heavy durables that have seriously sought to reduce planned obsolescence.

Another company deserving the consumer's gratitude because of its considerateness is Polaroid Corporation. A grateful camera owner first pointed out the Polaroid situation to me. She said that although Polaroid has produced a number of significant functional improvements over the years, it has designed virtually all of them so that they will fit on her original camera bought more than a decade ago. I find that this represents a deliberate policy on Polaroid's part. Its new wink-light was made to fit all the old cameras in existence. When Polaroid came up with a film fifteen times as fast as its then-current films—a film so fast it could take pictures indoors without a flash bulb—the company gave to owners of any old cameras desiring to use it free light seals which would enable the owner of an old camera to use the new improved film.

Polaroid keeps right on issuing its older models. Its very first camera—the 95—was a brown camera with a conspicuous shutter faceplate. After twelve years, the 95 is still sold. Furthermore, it looks no different from the original camera, although dozens of improvements have quietly been incorporated.

The prudent consumer can also make life more difficult for the style-obsolescence marketer—and more pleasant for himself—by buying his new products just before the restyled models are to be introduced for the "new" year. This is when the dealers are under great pressure from the manufacturers to unload remaining models of the current year. Substantial discounts are offered, and many excellent buys become available. If such prudent shopping becomes the general pattern, the manufacturers might very quickly lose much of their fascination with change-for-change sake.

The consumer who would be prudent will insist that manufacturers show greater responsibility for the satisfactory performance of their products. In view of the high rate of product breakdown in many lines, he will read the guarantee with particular interest while shopping, before making a purchase. Does it cover both parts *and* service? And for how long? A washing-machine producer who has enough confidence in his product to offer a five-year, no-strings-attached guarantee covering parts and service should quickly win a vast following of enthusiastic buyers.

This would-be prudent buyer might also give sympathetic attention to the wares of the producer who offers to help him be his own repairman, just as Henry Ford I issued his do-it-yourself kits. Many parts of modern appliances—such as timers—are, of course, too complicated for home repair. But the Norge Division of the BorgWarner Corporation has launched a campaign to help owners of its products to make simple repairs, and is designing its products to simplify such home repair. It might also help in restoring prudence if across the nation husbands and wives spent a few evenings a year in adult classes at local schools that are devoted to conveying an understanding of how to select and maintain various appliances.

The consumer who would be prudent in today's economy will buy the basic product rather than the one loaded down with accessories— whether it be a woman's dress, a refrigerator, a washing machine, or an automobile.

Finally, the consumer should be honest with himself and inquire whether an ailing product became that way because of his own carelessness.

In the task of recapturing sovereignty in the sales mart, the consumer is getting some organized backing, and more might well be encouraged. Concerted efforts to assist the consumer are still on a modest scale when compared with the massiveness of the selling effort—stoked with billions of dollars—on the producers' side. However, this force for the consumer is growing every month as the pressures on the consumer have grown, as if expanding to fill a vacuum in a field of forces.

There are now nonprofit associations of consumers such as the Council on Consumer Information, currently headquartered at Colorado State College, Greeley, Colorado. This has only about a thousand members, but the members are almost all college and high-school teachers in a position to teach prudence to young people. The council circulates newsletters and booklets and holds an annual conference. As the sixties were beginning, a number of annual conferences on consumer problems sprang up in the United States. They were sponsored by colleges, state governments, and consumer-testing organizations.

It is these consumer-testing organizations that undoubtedly have the greatest impact as countervailing forces. There are two principal ones in the United States. One is Consumers' Research, Inc., of Washington, New Jersey, which publishes monthly the nonprofit *Consumer Bulletin*, with a circulation of more than 100,000. More famous and influential is the fast-growing, nonprofit Consumers

Union with headquarters in an imposing complex of old red-brick buildings at 256 Washington Street in Mount Vernon, New York. It is the largest consumer-testing organization in the world. *Consumer Reports*, its principal publication, has grown from a circulation of less than 75,000 at the end of World War II to more than 800,000 today.

Consumers Union has a staff of more than 150 persons, including a number of engineers, chemists, physicists, and several dozen testing technicians. Its board of directors is composed primarily of scientists and educators. Consumers Union has shoppers in sixty-three cities who buy products to be tested on the regular market and pay the usual retail price. It never accepts free samples from manufacturers.

During a stroll through the rooms of Consumers Union's seven testing divisions (appliances, audio, automotive, chemistry, electronics, textiles, and special projects), you may see dozens of cake mixers whirring away, stirring bowls filled with a mixture of oil and sawdust. That makes a relatively heavy load. Or you will see dozens of women receiving home permanents. Each half of a woman's head gets a different preparation for comparative purposes. "Afterward," my guide Morris Kaplan, Consumer Union's technical director, explained, "we give them all a good permanent and rectify any damage done."

In another room you may see people soiling dishes with a standardized mixture of tomato paste, spaghetti, spinach, and eggs. After the soiling the dishes are aged for a set period before being placed in dishwashers to see how well the various machines rise to the challenge of removing the food.

You see refrigerators being tested in a controlled temperature room that cost $50,000 to build. And you hear record players being tested in a room so fully soundproof that you can hear a heart beating. Much of the automobile testing is done on a very rough, twisting course near New Haven, Connecticut, and on a sports-car racing track.

In the early days of Consumers Union, manufacturers and advertising agencies were distinctly hostile to its testing activities. Today, the hostility has virtually disappeared. Mr. Kaplan states: "Most manufacturers bend over backward to co-operate with us." They know from their dealers that a favorable or unfavorable report from Consumers Union can make their selling task easier or harder. There have been a number of instances in the past few years of manufacturers hastening to change a design when Consumers Union reported the product "Not Acceptable" because of shock hazard or other weakness. Often the manufacturers themselves inform Consumers Union that the objectionable feature has been corrected and ask for a retest. Consumers Union does so at the first opportunity.

This testing organization derives its financial support entirely from the sale of its publications. In order not to affect his impartiality, no employee may have any direct connection with any commercial firm. Consumers Union forbids the use of its product ratings in advertising or for any other commercial purpose. In its twenty-four years of existence, no suit has ever been successfully sustained against Consumers Union for publishing its often unflattering findings.

One of the major needs of consumers today is guidance on the durability of products. Consumers Union feels this is still an area where advances in testing must be made. For many products, durability is one of the most difficult characteristics to assess. How can you subject a new refrigerator to a "lifetime" test? It can be done on an accelerated basis—including the door slamming—but it is costly and, of course, the refrigerators tested are a dead loss at the end and cannot be resold. Recently, Consumers Union completed an accelerated life test on automobile tires at a cost of $50,000. As it gains in circulation and thus resources, it can increase its testing for durability.

In seeking to assess motorcars for their durability, Consumers Union has mostly used an indirect approach. It conducts an annual survey among thousands of subscribers who are owners of motorcars. Each owner states the make and year of his motorcar and then lists the major repairs that have been necessary during the year. The results show that two of the best cars produced in the years 1954 through 1959 in terms of trouble-free performance were the 1955 Oldsmobile and the 1958 Rambler. Among the most troublesome American motorcars reported for this period were the 1958 Mercury, the 1958 Lincoln, and the 1957 Buick.[1]

One aspect of its service that concerns Consumers Union as a shortcoming is that most of the readers of its *Consumer Reports* are the kind of people who need it least. It has appealed most to those people who were prudent to start with: males of relatively high intelligence in business or the professions. Currently, *Consumer Reports* is seeking to expand its readership among women—who make most of the family purchasing decisions—and among the lower-income groups who, though they need to stretch their dollars further, tend to be more flamboyant, impulsive, and unthinking in their buying habits than people with higher incomes. They are the ones most likely to be exploited, the most likely to have the expensive patent medicines in their bathroom, and the 36 per cent interest installment debts.

Another nonprofit advisory firm of considerable indirect interest to consumers is the Drug and Therapeutic Information, Inc., in New York City. It is staffed by distinguished physicians who became weary of trying to wade through—and make sense out of—the thousands of brochures from drug houses hailing their new brands. These doctors have begun publishing for doctors a newsletter called *Medical Letter on Drugs and Therapeutics*. It carries no advertising and endeavors to shed light on pharmaceutical claims. The letter already has more than ten thousand doctors on its subscription list. The chief of its advisory board is the director of Clinical Pharmacology at Johns Hopkins Medical School.

The anxiety that this *Medical Letter* created among the drug houses is indicated by the fact that one drug house published a full-page denunciation of the *Medical Letter* in its magazine for doctors and then refused to publish the *Medical Letter's* reply—even in paid advertising space. And the medical list house that had been addressing the *Medical Letter's* mail to doctors suddenly withdrew its list.

Belatedly some government groups are being mobilized to assist the bedazzled lone consumer.

A pioneering move was made by New York's former Governor Averell Harriman when he set up a Consumer Counsel attached to his office. The counsel, Dr. Persia Campbell, sought to advance and protect consumers' interests on every front and at every level of the state government. She was so successful that the idea of a special counsel or department of consumer protection has spread to California and Massachusetts, and at this writing is being proposed by the governors of Michigan and Minnesota. The California Office of Consumer Counsel has become a permanent part of the state government. In proposing this office to the legislature, Governor Brown said: "We consumers have little defense against highly organized special interests." Meanwhile, there was an overturn of the governorship in Albany. The new Governor Nelson Rockefeller disbanded the temporary office of Consumer Counsel, and remnants of the program went under the state's Department of Commerce. This move, Dr. Campbell told me, "was worse than abolishing the whole program, since it made the consumer interest captive to business policy."

In Washington, twenty-four senators headed by Estes Kefauver began promoting a bill to set up in the federal government a Department of Consumers headed by an officer with cabinet rank. It would promote the interests of consumers at all levels and in battles before federal regulatory agencies that are now largely fought out by lobbyists of the various organized commercial groups. This department would provide a more congenial consumer-oriented home for such agencies as the Federal Food and Drug Administration, the Bureau of Standards, and the Bureau of Home Economics. A wide variety of Administration spokesmen have opposed the creation of such a Department of Consumers on the ground that it is not necessary. They say the work is already being done.

Norway, incidentally, has such a cabinet post. The minister, a woman, has as much status as the minister of agriculture or commerce. As a member of parliament stated it, one function of the ministry is to encourage Norwegian consumers to return "to their rightful role—that of being appropriate hell-raisers concerning the prices and quality of goods."

Meanwhile, so many United States congressmen have been starting to promote measures affecting buyer-seller relations that marketers are apprehensive. One congressman, John Blatnik, has been pressing the United States Public Health Office and the United States Office of Education to offer to children educational materials on the health hazard of cigarette smoking to offset partially all the appeals reaching them in cigarette advertisements.

All in all, signs are appearing that the consumer may soon be started on a swing that will eventually return him to a position approaching equality in the buyer-seller relationship.

22. RESTORING PRIDE IN QUALITY

"I imagine the fabric mills are going to do a lot of squirming before they agree to anything resembling a set of rules about how good their products have to be."—Furniture manufacturer quoted in *Retailing Daily*.[1]

THE MANUFACTURER CITED ABOVE EXPLAINED that while the mills had been doing a fine job on "styling," they had not been paying "sufficient attention to durability and quality." It might be added as a postscript that the upholstery-fabric manufacturers succeeded in getting their product excluded from the provisions of the Textile Fabric Products Identification Act, which went into effect in 1960. They registered opposition that in some instances was vehement.

This manufacturer's indictment regarding quality could apply equally appropriately to a number of fields producing goods for consumers. Some producers still struggle stubbornly to produce the very highest-quality product possible. Many more, as noted, feel they can build a greater over-all volume if their goods don't last too long. Still others would like to strive for quality, but often feel they do not dare to because their corner-cutting competitors might push them to the wall by using the savings to throw more money into promotional display and advertising that would catch the public's attention.

From both the viewpoint of the consumer and the conscientious producer, it seems highly desirable that the United States move toward a return to a passion for quality on the part of each producer of goods. Ideally, he should develop this resolution as a part of his quest for life satisfaction and feel dissatisfied with himself until he achieves this quality.

We must concede that anyone with such resolution must expect to face discouragement as long as the market place remains as presently motivated and operated. In the jungle of today's market a host of products appear and disappear each year. In earlier decades product qualities were more widely known.

How can a modern consumer looking at an appliance judge factors he cannot see, such as insulation, durability of parts, electrical hazard, and rust resistance of finishes?

How can he know—as I discovered in a most exasperating way—that the handles of one brand of streamlined luggage nationally advertised for its ruggedness would come off within a week? In my case this happened with not one but two of the bags.

How can the modern consumer choose plywood furniture intelligently—in the absence of a wood-labeling law—when wood labeled "driftwood walnut" or "silver oak" contains neither walnut nor oak?

How can the consumer choose carpets intelligently when carpet dealers themselves have lamented that they are so confused by various exaggerated claims for fabrics that they would be grateful to have some honest appraisal of the performance that might be expected. They have admitted—among themselves—that they've often been selling "a blind item."

In such confusing situations it would help both the consumer and the conscientious producer if agreed standards—or yardsticks—of quality were available to assist the consumer in making a choice. Today, there would seem to be an urgent need for quality standards— and yet in the consumer field they are almost nonexistent. (Milk and bedsheets are two of the exceptions.) Morris Kaplan, technical director of Consumers Union, says: "There are almost no uniform standards on consumer goods." And a leading authority on standards, Jessie V. Coles, chairman of the Department of Home Economics at the University of California, has stated: "Efforts have been made from time to time to set up national standards for various kinds of consumer goods. . . . Except for those enforced by federal law, relatively few standards are in existence."[2]

Miss Coles blames this partly on the fact that consumers have not demanded or understood the need for standards. But also, she said, there was the factor of "resistance of producers."

Why do the producers resist? In theory they should be dedicated advocates of quality standards because they insist on using them every day in buying their materials. They buy on the basis of standards or specifications. No motorcar manufacturer, for example, would dream of buying its steel on the basis of a double-page advertising spread in a periodical. It buys steel on the basis of specification numbers established by the Society of Automotive Engineers. (But even the motorcar industry could have done a great deal more than it has to standardize basic components throughout the industry.) Large institutional buyers such as hotels, hospitals, universities, and railroads buy their textile supplies on the basis of established performance criteria.

Yet producers have tended to react as if faced with ruin when suggestions have been advanced that comparable quality standards be set up to guide them and their consumer-customers.

Consider the frozen-food makers. At their own trade meetings they have heard charges that they "were getting away with murder" in the matter of quality of product. Frozen orange juice has declined in quality since first introduced. A dozen years ago, frozen orange juice tasted very much like freshly squeezed orange juice. But over the years the producers have been squeezing the fruit harder and harder, and getting more and more pectin into the product. Yet Eastern frozen-food producers registered almost unanimous opposition to a proposal for compulsory grading.

Or consider the shoe manufacturers. In the past decade, there has been a growth in the use of paper fiber as a substitute for leather in making parts of children's shoes. The paper fiber can be a mean deception because it is likely to reveal itself only when the child wearing such shoes gets his feet wet. Yet when Congressman Charles Porter (D., Ore.) proposed a shoe-labeling act, thousands of people in the shoe industry opposed it.

What is behind the hostility of most producers to publicized quality standards for their particular products? For the record, they usually claim that quality standards would be expensive to establish, or bothersome, or somehow interfere with their present flexibility in shifting designs or merchandising appeals. In addition, however, there seem to be at least five other reasons—difficult to discuss in public—why talk of quality standards scares many producers:

Many producers are privately convinced that they can sell more products on the basis of gimmicks, special features, impulse, and innovation than on the basis of quality. Thus they are likely to feel that posted standards of quality might bring an intelligence and selectivity to the purchasing counter that would undermine a less rational approach.

Producers generally prefer to let the public make its choice on the basis of brand image and, to a less extent, price rather than posted quality. In this way each brand may be presented as possessing uniquely mysterious or magical powers or a unique "personality" that helps establish "differentiation" from competing products. And most assuredly—in the absence of quality standards—each brand can be presented to the public as the acme of quality and trustworthiness. Some brands may be close to the acme of quality, but the likelihood is just as great that they are not.

A posting of quality standards makes it more difficult, obviously, for a retailer to sell merchandise that deserves no higher than a mediocre quality rating, unless it is modestly priced.

In many cases the quality involved does not warrant the high prices charged. Products sold for their snob appeal often seem overpriced on the basis of any reasonable, objective quality analysis. And occasionally the producer may vary the quality of a particular brand in different geographical areas depending on the severity of his competition. Home economist Jessie V. Coles tells of a case in which a meat packer put his brand image on a lower quality of beef in the downstate Illinois market than on the meat sold in Chicago because he faced less rugged competition downstate.

And, finally, the big producers tend to be cool to any kind of grade labeling because such certifying of quality reduces their advantages over the small producer. When competition must be conducted primarily on the basis of the brand image, as it is conducted today, the small producer is at an enormous disadvantage even if his product is as good as the large producer's—or better. Today, just building a better mousetrap is not enough. You have got to launch it. It often costs tens of millions of dollars to launch a new product successfully on a national basis, etch an image of it in the public's mind, and commandeer good exposure space on the nation's store shelves. A former chairman of General Electric's finance committee was quoted as criticizing the high prices that the major companies were charging for their appliances. He charged that General Electric, Westinghouse, and RCA Whirlpool eventually could kill off competitors through the use of advertising unless the competitors merged into larger units.[3]

In contrast, if you have some form of grade labeling, the consumer can choose on the basis of assured quality rather than on brand image. This permits the small producer to compete with the large one on the more equal grounds of quality offered per dollar. Mildred Brady of Consumers Union pointed out the opportunities that open up to the small producer when quality standards are posted by citing the recent experience of meat packers on the West Coast. Government grade labeling of meat was started there after World War II. Within a decade the small packers had captured three quarters of the market. Recently, several of the big national meat packers have been campaigning to eliminate this grade labeling of meat.

Some very small steps have been made in establishing quality indicators to help guide the bewildered consumer. Congress has now passed laws requiring producers of wool, fur, and some textile products to specify contents on the labels. A mere listing of ingredients, however, is no assurance of high quality. How the ingredients are put together may be just as crucial to quality. Furthermore, a listing of the generic (chemical) names of fibers used in the new "miracle" fabrics is not particularly illuminating to a beleaguered consumer.

There are also a number of organizations that issue "seals" indicating that the products carrying the seal meet at least certain minimum specifications. There is the "UL" seal for much of the electrical equipment sold in the United States to indicate that the National Board of Fire Underwriters considers the equipment nonhazardous. And a similar "AGA" label exists for gas appliances. A few general magazines have testing centers and issue seals on products that have been approved after testing or use. These seals sometimes serve a second purpose of helping promote their magazine in the business world; but the seals do offer assurance that the testers found the products meet an acceptable quality.

Another possible approach is grade labeling, and this would be extremely helpful to consumers. Ideally, the grade labeling should be done by a universally recognized certifying agency. The grades—say A, B, and C or X, Y, and Z—would be based not on ingredients alone as in usual labeling but rather on an over-all rating of quality. This could be arrived at as a total score based on a number of characteristics most crucial to establishing quality in the performance of that kind of product. Mail-order houses, although they do their own certifying, attempt such a grading. Sears, Roebuck, for example, offers in its catalogue three grades of a certain line of stoves: "Good," "Better," and "Our Best." Further, it itemizes under the picture each of the features that helped establish its grade.

In theory an ideal certifying agency is already at hand to certify products for at least a minimum quality seal. That is the American Standards Association, set up forty years ago. It helped establish safety glass for motorcars and protective clothing during World War II. However, it offers little hope of being able to do a labeling or certifying job on any large scale. Its weakness from the consumer's standpoint is that it is made up primarily of industry members and it approves standards only when they have been unanimously accepted by the leading groups involved. No matter how minimal are the standards proposed, almost always there is some manufacturer who holds out and prevents its adoption. Furthermore, the American Standards Association has little power to enforce even those standards for an American Standards Association mark that its members can agree upon.

The British have progressed much further than we in setting up and enforcing meaningful standards for consumer products. They have their nonprofit British Standards Institution supported in part by industry contributions, in part by government funds, and in part from the sale of its publications. It might serve as a model for the United States.

British Standards Institution standards are hammered out by representatives of industry, government, and the consuming public, represented by an advisory council of consumers. Furthermore, for several dozen types of consumer goods it now authorizes producers of "sound" consumer goods to display the British Standards Institution's "Kitemark" on each article offered for sale. The Kitemark—a heart with an S inside it—now appears on such products as bedding, electric blankets, pressure cookers, bedsprings, and some furniture, if the products come up to British Standards Institution standards.

The use of this Kitemark is rigorously policed. And the British Standards Institution is experimenting with the idea of establishing grades of quality within the "sound" products approved for a Kitemark to meet the needs of those who want more than basic quality. Apparently this would be along the line of Sears, Roebuck's "Good," "Better," "Our Best." The British Standards Institution also issues a detailed guide on product quality, *The Shopper's Guide*, a small publication comparable to the *Consumer Reports* printed in the United States.

An example of the British Standards Institution approach is the test it conducted on "fireside chairs" before it would issue a Kitemark. More than one hundred firms have earned the mark. For fireside chairs, what does the Kitemark offer in the way of assurance? Here is an indication, from a British Standards Institution publication:

"In a word it means that the chair is sturdy. That the frame is made of properly dried timber, free of bad knots and splits, and of wormwood. That any veneers are properly applied and exterior surfaces well finished. Springs, fillings, and fabrics are also vetted. Kite-marked chairs have to go through endurance tests without flagging. For example, a 16-stone weight [more than 200 pounds] is thrust 20 times a minute—600 times in all—on back, seat, and arms. Joints must stay rigid, upholstery firm and shapely, springs as resilient as at the beginning."

It would be interesting to speculate how some of the flimsy furniture produced and widely sold in the United States would stand up under such a pounding.

At a time when United States trade papers were lamenting the decline in quality of many American-made products, an official of the British Standards Institution told me matter-of-factly, "The British are upgrading quality all the time." He added that in Britain companies selling raw materials now often sell their products only to manufacturers who have earned the Kitemark.

Canada, too, has gone considerably further than the United States in establishing and enforcing quality standards. It has grade labeling of canned fruits, vegetables, eggs, poultry, and other products. When nationally advertised brands of canned fruits and vegetables produced in the United States are marketed in Canada, they carry grade labels on them. It might also be noted that the standards set by the Canadian Standards Association for acceptable electric light fixtures are so high that some products widely sold in the United States are turned back at the border as inferior.

Is it unreasonable for citizens of the United States of America—the world's most productive society—to expect that as an ideal its products be designed from the consumer's point of view rather than the seller's? Is it unreasonable for its citizens to want to be able to choose products on the basis of posted assurances of quality rather than on the basis of a brand image learned by word of mouth or by assurances from television announcers?

Industry itself, it should be noted, is showing new interest in quality standards. When laments about the lack of standards in the rug field were reaching the scandalous stage, many of the large companies making "miracle" fiber rugs such as du Pont, Chemstrand, Celanese, Allied Chemical, and American Viscose instituted—or had already instituted—quality-standard programs on an individual basis. This was heartening, but did little to reduce the confusion of the consumer. Their various standards would have to be accepted on faith. The consumer needs uniform and readily comprehensible standards that will be respected and policed.

Letters from individual consumers to their congressmen might well hasten the day when an agency—official or unofficial—is somehow established along British Standards Institution lines, competent to establish and enforce quality standards when requested in the United States. Today, congressmen are becoming more aware of the problems of consumers than at any time in recent decades. *Sales Management* expressed anxiety about this new interest in helping the consumer. It said, "the general attitude of today's law-makers is seriously disturbing to many Washington representatives of big-company marketing executives. . . . The trend is alarming." A few thousand letters to congressmen probably would not produce any laws establishing machinery to set quality standards, but they would quite probably worry industry groups to the point where they would flock to the flag of an unofficial standards-setting agency in order to head off federal action.

And while the word "standards" still makes many manufacturers uneasy, there is a distinct trend toward winning good will of consumers by getting to a higher level of quality than has recently prevailed.

The editor of *Printers' Ink* admonished marketers that they probably ought to start giving more attention to product quality "since it is the basis of repeat sales."

It was during 1960 that a number of appliance companies announced they were stepping up the "torture testing" of their products. Maytag, which for years had given durability a higher priority than stylishness, began doubling the number of days it subjected prototype washer-driers to constant operation. Under the new schedule the washer-drier was expected to run 250 days—or the equivalent of ten years' use in the average home. Maytag also reduced the number of parts in its automatic washer and increased the warranty on washer transmissions up to five years. Only a few years ago, the warranty had been one year.

Motorola began guaranteeing parts on its television and radio sets for a year. Earlier, the warranty period had been the usual ninety days. Hotpoint, which had so much grief with defective laundry equipment in the 1955-57 models, by 1960 had quadrupled its investment in torture testing, and was subjecting its prototypes to a one-thousand-hour run with unusually heavy ten-pound loads.

All this was a trend to be encouraged.

In these past two chapters we have explored the possibility of restoring a larger element of sanity and mutual respect to the market place. But can the United States with its ever-expanding productivity and output afford the luxury of sanity and mutual respect? Certainly it is worth a try. Sooner or later the nation must learn to live within its means and pace itself for the long run. And the later that fact is learned, the fewer and more unattractive will be the remaining options.

23. RESPECTING THE ETERNAL BALANCE

"The Western wilds, from the Alleghenies to the Pacific, constituted the richest free gift that was ever spread out before civilized man. . . . Never again can such an opportunity come to the sons of men."— Frederick Jackson Turner

TWO RIVAL FORMULAS—BOTH SUPPOSEDLY magical— are being pointed out as the roads to a prosperous future. Together, they pretty much dominate speculation about the economic future of the United States of America.

On the one hand, the leading thinkers of business-Republican-conservative coloration argue that "population growth" will provide the golden pathway that will keep the economy humming for years to come by providing ever-more customers. And on the other, many people including the leading thinkers of liberal-Democratic-labor coloration have been insistently calling for faster "economic growth" to keep things humming. More money should be poured into the economy in the form of either private or public spending to double the annual rate of growth. This is seen as the only way to eliminate the danger of widespread unemployment created by the relentless rise in man-hour output in the nation's automated offices and factories.

Both of these paths to sustained prosperity might work for a few years. And some form of one of them may be inevitable. But both can be dangerously shortsighted, and should be very carefully explored before they are embraced. Both promise to increase the drain on the nation's already overstrained resources. Both are expedients at best. Both should be assessed in terms of at least the medium-long haul of the nation.

All enduring societies—human or animal—have had to achieve a tolerable balance between their population and their supporting environment, including resources. As indicated, a serious imbalance in the resources-population picture has been developing in the United States, while its people gaily step up their consumption.

In 1959, a design engineer from Sunland, California, expressed dismay at the waste of resources produced by American motorcar design. He charged in Product Engineering:

"I think the current auto design trend indicates a moral decay in America that is most alarming. When such a large share of the national income is squandered on useless glass, fins, overhang, etc., which require excess horsepower and attendant wasted fuels, then it is about time the federal government stepped in and placed a tax on auto body weight and horsepower." Later he added, "If an automobile requires over 100 horsepower, it is too damned big and wasteful." At this writing, about three quarters of all motorcars being made in Detroit are still "too damned big and wasteful" by the engineer's estimate.

It seems urgent that someone in authority in the nation begin looking a half century ahead in appraising the nation's available material resources and energy and start channeling the use of both accordingly. Far more can be done than is being done to reclaim scrap, to develop substitutes (especially substitutes that do not require an enormous energy output to produce), to reduce waste in both the mining and use of resources, and in finding outlets for the nation's need for economic activity that are sparing of the resources in short domestic supply. The industry making paper and cardboard products is one of the industrial groups starting to make extensive reuse of waste. According to one industry official, half of all paper products can now be made—and often are made—with reclaimed paper products that have been discarded. More than a fourth of all paper produced in 1959 was made from nine million tons of waste paper reused.

The last over-all look at the United States resource position occurred nearly a decade ago. And that one—by President Truman's Materials Resources Commission—was mainly preoccupied with defense requirements. Certain specific aspects of the United States position have recently been examined by an organization called Resources for the Future (Washington, D.C.), financed by the Ford Foundation. In 1960, after a year of delay, President Eisenhower named a Commission on National Goals that is to begin looking five to ten years ahead. It is still too early to report whether it will satisfy itself by calling for "growth," or will seriously seek to face up to the threat posed by shrinking resources and swelling population. Thirteen months were consumed in organizing the commission. Difficulty was encountered in obtaining private financing because, according to one news report, Mr. Eisenhower's aide "was unable to supply a prospectus that satisfied the foundations on what the commission was expected to do." In calling for his five-to-ten-year goals, President Eisenhower said the goals must "inspire every citizen to climb always toward mounting levels of moral, intellectual, and material strength."

Perhaps it is only natural that a people who have been so long overblessed with an abundance of materials and energy continue to squander them and think in terms of ever-mounting "strength" until a traumatic event abruptly forces them to realize that conditions now call for a more prudent and ingenious use of muscles and energy.

This point was eloquently made in early 1959 in *The New Yorker* magazine in a description of the philosophy of a cunning old-time Boston boxer identified as Eddie Shevlin. Shevlin's Law was that "you can't learn anything until you're tired." This law was explained to the editors in these terms: "A young fella bursting with energy he thinks is surplus won't bother to learn economy of motion; he won't learn not to make a move without possibilities, and not to take extra steps." Then the informant made this parallel: "Take a country hopped up with what it thinks is surplus productive capacity, or resources. It jumps around, bounding off the ropes when it doesn't have to . . . until the going is hard—a depression say or a war that begins badly. Then it starts to want to learn how to take care of itself."

It may well be that a majority of the citizens of the United States will become convinced of the need or wisdom of reducing their wastefulness of resources before a majority of producers preoccupied with sales figures reach the same conviction. In that case, the citizen consumers might wish to prod the producers by modifying their spending patterns.

They might, for example, embrace enthusiastically the new idea being tried in several cities of renting their cars, appliances, and home furnishings—with trouble-free service guaranteed as a part of the deal. This would be somewhat more expensive than buying the products and would remove whatever possibility still existed to feel pride in ownership of a product. But it would strike a solid blow against the whole concept of planned obsolescence. If a producer knew he was making products for a rental market rather than for retail sale, he would instantly become deeply concerned about increasing the product's durability, especially if he was doing the renting or his dealers were. He would become obsessed with the idea of simple design to cut down his servicing costs. And he would seek and use his influence in the trade to promote a design that would still seem appropriate over a period of years.

By 1960, many business executives and engineers were feeling uneasy about their role in encouraging or tolerating wasteful practices, including the making of shoddy products. The chairman of one of the nation's largest organizations of advertisers asserted: "The Great American Ailment is manifest on all sides by a deepening shade in our ethics . . . a sloppiness in our services, a mediocrity in our manufacturer, and a growing distrust and even anger in the public mind."

Many executives and engineers specifically felt uneasy about their role in promoting planned obsolescence. In fact, this uneasiness became so widespread that other executives urged them not to be hasty in trying to shift away from some form of obsolescence planning. On March 24, 1960, the board chairman of Whirlpool Corporation, Elisha Gray, II, delivered a speech to the engineers of the American Home Laundry Manufacturers' Association technical conference that was most forthright. In it he stated:

"An engineer's principal purpose as an engineer is to create obsolescence. Any attempts by various people to toady up to the public by saying they are against planned obsolescence is so much commercial demagogy. To pose as a protector of the public has become a fashionable pastime." He continued that if engineers and other professional people had not created "obsolescence at a tremendous rate," Americans would not be as prosperous, well fed, and long-living as they are. In his talk he appeared to be referring to both planned obsolescence of desirability and planned obsolescence of function (or basic product improvement). He said the first—style change—can be used to dramatize the second. Also he referred to the need of planned obsolescence "to meet the marketing moves of your competitors" and to the chronic need for fresh merchandise to stimulate sales. It is expecting a great deal of a salesman, he said, "to greet each new customer with a high sense of eagerness and excitement about his product if you don't give it a face lift occasionally." He added that advertising men and sales-promotion men need something new and fresh because such "creative people feed upon change."

Business writers at about the same time were pointing out that the controversy over planned obsolescence was important because the issue affects the very basis of private capitalism and free enterprise, since the American system is geared so importantly to consumer desires.

But still there was widespread uneasiness among businessmen about the philosophy behind much of the planned obsolescence going on. They might not feel guilty enough to forswear using the strategy themselves, but they felt that others should use it sparingly. They began wishing there were a less worrisome way to accomplish the same result in sales.

The Harvard Business Review asked several thousand business executives how they felt about planned obsolescence.[1] More than three thousand responded. The editors of the review concluded from the responses that "the subject was very touchy indeed." The survey disclosed a vast amount of uneasiness about the techniques being used nowadays to move goods. In fact, "the majority of American business executives feel that for the long-run benefit of the United States too large a part of our present economy is based on superficial product obsolescence: the ratio was two to one."

One third of the executives agreed that their own companies were making "periodic" model or style changes. The head of Westinghouse Electric Corporation was reported feeling that both styling and functionalism were needed to do a good selling job. As for appliances, he explained: "For appliances in which women play a large part in the purchasing decision, if you took the styling element out, sales would dry up."

Others were disturbed by even being asked to comment on planned obsolescence. They "seemed to feel obsolescence was such a fundamental part of our economy that it should not be tampered with."

The editors concluded that "there is general concern and interest in looking for and considering alternative means for maintaining consumer expenditures." Uneasy feelings had evidently still not pushed the executives to the point where they were certain they would be willing to stop using such techniques if that meant they had to be satisfied with a lower level of sales.

In June, 1960, *Advertising Age* editorially took note of the "increasing attack" on the "obsolescence factor," which it called "one of the great developments of American marketing." (It seemed to be referring, primarily at least, to the annual model change.) At any rate, it said: "We doubt that it will be abandoned, in the automotive field or elsewhere, but it is interesting to see it being questioned more and more frequently."

The consuming public had considerable grounds for uneasiness because of its own habit of throwing away functioning products or easily repairable products when new models were desired. Community officials might profitably backstop the citizens by starting salvage campaigns at the town dumps.

So much for the waste of the nation's resources. We might look now at the other side of the resources-population balance. To set the mood, we might note the warning of Dr. John Rock, Harvard's professor emeritus of gynecology, that unless the world curbs its proliferation of human beings within the next few decades, "hungry and crowded people will rise in bestial strife." This is perhaps too Malthusian a view to win much contemporary support, but certainly the current population explosion in the United States and abroad does raise disagreeable prospects for the future even of Americans, at least in terms of probable impact on style of life and individual dignity and freedom.

While this problem of the population explosion is characteristically seen in the United States as a foreign problem, a few businessmen are showing signs of uneasiness about their own growing reliance upon an exploding population in the United States. One of the regular adman-columnists for *Advertising Age*, E. B. Weiss, who is something of a maverick, commented a few years ago, when the golden opportunities of population growth were first being discovered:

"Ever since I've been regaled with the current multitude of wonderful forecasts of a prosperous future sparked by a remarkable growth of our population I have wondered about the magical powers of a large population automatically to assure eternal prosperity—at successively higher peaks. . . . The most populous regions of this mortal coil tend to be the most poverty-stricken."

And as the sixties were about to begin, a writer for *The Wall Street Journal* conceded: "This increase in the number of Americans . . . holds the prospect' of an expanding economy. But it also may bring new strains on roads, schools, and water supplies, to mention just a few items."

If the United States is to attain a tolerable balance for the long run between resources and population, it must stop glorifying a prosperous future based on bouncing babies, which has the effect of encouraging propagation. Curbing a people's procreation habits admittedly is an enormously complex matter. Joseph Wood Krutch offers the opinion that the impulse to multiply as rapidly and as profusely as possible is built into the living organism. Still, with the spectacular advances being made to prolong life, some curbing of the initiation of life seems imperative. Arnold Toynbee's view in this connection seems unassailable. He argues: "To let nature take her extravagant course in the reproduction of the human race may have made sense in an age in which we were also letting her take her course in decimating mankind by the casualties of war, pestilence and famine. Being human, we have at last revolted against that senseless waste. . . . But when once man has begun to interfere with nature, he cannot afford to stop halfway. We cannot, with impunity, cut down the death rate and at the same time allow the birthrate to go on taking nature's course."

Japan is one nation that has in recent years taken drastic and spectacular action to strike an equilibrium between its births and deaths. And in this action, according to the Population Reference Bureau, it has been the people themselves who have led the way in implementing the government policy of legalized abortion and birth control. Japanese males do not react favorably to the idea of using contraceptives, so that there is a heavy reliance on abortion whenever a wife finds herself pregnant against the wishes of herself and her husband.

In modern-day Japan there are more abortions than births. One man who has exhaustively investigated the Japanese situation finds that abortion there has become simple, inexpensive, and safe. He explained to me: "The doctor scrapes the wife's uterus, gives her a shot of penicillin, sends her home. It costs about five dollars. Largely as a result, the Japanese people have absolutely pulled it off. They have cut their birth rate in half within a decade. In a few more years their population should stabilize."

Advances being made in the development of pills that inhibit fertility can make birth control far more easily achievable than by the Japanese method, but the pills are still fairly expensive (ten dollars a month). Even when the cost comes down, however, will the American people be in a mood to start reducing the growing gap between their birth rate and their death rate? Possibly they will, as the discomforts of crowding become more oppressive. At least the moral objections are being softened. A succession of Protestant church bodies—including United Presbyterians, Methodist, Congregational Christian, United and Augustana Lutheran, and Unitarian—have sanctioned birth control. The Roman Catholic Church officially opposes artificial means of birth control by individuals. And Pope John XXIII made a plea for large families as recently as the spring of 1960. But the church does not oppose "population control." And there is some indication that Catholic leaders may not find some kinds of pill-taking as objectionable as the use of physical means of intervention. Some Catholic leaders make a distinction between pills that would prevent ovulation and those that help regulate ovulation. The latter, they indicate, might well be acceptable and would help control the size of the family by making the rhythm more exact. As for Catholic laymen, a survey of wives by the Survey Research Center of the University of Michigan indicates that most individual Catholics favor individual family limitation under certain circumstances, and a third of them approve family limitation without any qualification. The National Catholic Family Life Conference meeting in San Antonio in 1960 heard an "alarming" report of some studies showing that Catholic "married couples are using contraceptive birth control in about the same measure as nonCatholics."

A Fordham University (Catholic) professor of philosophy, Dr. Dietrich von Hildebrand, agreed in early 1960 that overpopulation might someday force on Roman Catholics a moral duty to limit their families. Further, he stated that the sexual act has values for the family beyond procreation. He still felt—as the Catholic Church does—that any individual interference with procreation should be by the natural or rhythm method of continence during the wife's fertility cycle. (The World Council of Churches sees no moral distinction between artificial contraception and the rhythm method.) Under a rhythm approach the most "safe" period usually is approximately the last week of the menstrual cycle. One shortcoming from the point of view of population control is the possibility of error in computing this period. The menstrual cycle is not regular in at least one out of five women. Perhaps another is that it leaves much of the month "unsafe" for the husband and wife to express physically and unstintingly their love for each other.

There is, however, more than technique involved in bringing a population into equilibrium. Inclination of the citizens is perhaps more important. Ireland, which is overwhelmingly Catholic, is outstanding among the nations of the world that have got their birth rate under control. The Irish did it—to combat the grinding poverty that is now only a distant memory—largely by postponing marriage.

The United States Congress could by a slight modification of the income-tax laws provide a powerful incentive to most Americans to get their nation's population into equilibrium somewhere short of 250,000,000. It could drop the present provision of allowing a $600 deduction for each dependent child. In its place it might provide an $800 deduction for the first child, $600 for the second, $400 for the third, and $200 for any additional children.

Even assuming that the people of the United States can achieve a tolerable balance between resources and population, two challenging facts already in existence remain to be contended with.

One is the generation of youths born in the postwar baby boom that is about to flood the labor market. These young people are already in the pipelines, to use the businessman's phrase. No amount of population control is going to change the fact that the labor force is expected to rise by 13,500,000 in this present decade.

The other challenging fact is the relentless rise every year in manhour productivity, thanks largely to the labor-saving brought by automation.

How to cope with these stubborn facts without resorting to profligacy poses the central economic enigma of our decade. Any efforts to come to grips with them will put the nation on largely uncharted trails. Solutions will not be easy. It does appear possible, however, to point to what seem to be the five most likely trails for breaking out of the dilemma that these facts present. As the dilemma deepens in the coming decade, they should be explored and subjected to trial.

Trail Number One leads in the direction of cutting down the hours a year that the average person works as the machines become more efficient. This takes us into the controversial area of the four-day week or some variation thereof. Steelworkers in their 1959 contract discussion seriously broached the novel notion of a three-month paid vacation every five years for each worker. It was estimated that this would create 30,000 additional jobs. And their president in 1960 began pressing the idea of a 32-hour week. Other suggestions have centered on reducing the number of teen-agers in the labor market by raising educational requirements.

John Kenneth Galbraith, Harvard economist, proposes that the United States remove any necessary connection between a person's income and his productivity. In *The Affluent Society* he argued: "If unemployment is a disaster for individuals, we have no choice but always to produce at or near the capacity of the labor force" and pour out increasingly unimportant goods. How do you remove the element of personal disaster? He proposed that "unemployment compensation should be increased as unemployment increases— and should be diminished as full employment is approached." This method would assure people of security in times of high unemployment, when they would have scant chance of finding work anyhow; and would prod them into hustling to find a job when unemployment was relatively low. He felt such a system would "enable us to take a more relaxed and rational view of output without subjecting individual members of the society to hardship."

Mr. Galbraith's theorizing led him to the possibility of the emergence of a large body of citizens who would be blessed with a great deal of leisure time. He viewed this with more cheerfulness than many of us—perhaps because of our baggage of vestigial puritanism— can still muster.

It is questionable whether American citizens are prepared yet to cope even with the semileisure of a four-day week. They hate to be idle even more than most people. Their three-week vacations are generally periods of frenzied activity. When they find themselves favored with a short work week, many get themselves a second job. More than four million of them have joined the ranks of the "moonlighters," or doublejob holders.

And then there is another hazard that growing leisure poses. It tends to stimulate the desire to consume. Paul Mazur pointed out that the growth in leisure time produced by the shorter work week "represents a huge increase in the time available for consumption." And *Business Week* has noted that "the more time people have outside their working day, the more marked is their propensity to consume goods and services of all kinds." This tendency to increase consumption as leisure increases may be exciting to the goods producers but offers little cheer to the conservationists concerned about the nation's shrinking resources.

Furthermore, in terms of life satisfaction, acts of consumption are no adequate substitute for acts of individual productivity. What will happen to the dignity of man if he finds that his main contribution is to be as a consumer rather than as a creator?

The Massachusetts Institute of Technology mathematician Norbert Wiener, one of the theoretical pioneers of automation, worries that he may have helped create a monster. He has expressed concern about what will become of man's dignity and freedom if we achieve a fully mechanized society where jobless, debased workers roam the streets and even receive their unemployment checks from a machine.

All this would seem to indicate that while Trail Number One

should undoubtedly be thoroughly explored, and does offer a major opportunity for easing the developing dilemma, it will need to be explored with care.

The second major possibility—or Trail Number Two—would involve an attempt to tune down the economy somewhat, even if it means settling for a more modest level of living.

This would focus on the challenge of removing the goad of everrising technological efficiency. The relentless pressure coming from the present annual increase in man-hour productivity—and its seemingly constant companion, ever-rising wage costs—may be the American Way, but it is also becoming a wolf nipping everlastingly at the nation's heels. It demands that the nation keep upping its consumption or face the consequences in sharply increased unemployment.

Obviously, chasing away this wolf will be a very tricky business. Even assuming it can be accomplished without disaster, what will happen to the restless, expansive American character in the process?

But just as obviously an attempt will have to be made sooner or later if the nation is to be saved from exhaustion due to hyperactivity. Somehow, sometime, American citizens will start modifying their value system by placing a lower value on the social usefulness of their machines. When that time comes, they will start viewing more skeptically the fairly constant current steam of exhortations for more growth, more product innovations, more sales.

As things stand, these clarion calls are accepted—at least by most businessmen—as mandates. Mr. Mazur exhorts: "Our economic system requires incessant growth." Mr. Mortimer, chairman of the board of General Foods, asserts matter-of-factly that "business must continue to grow or it will slip back swiftly. There is no standing still." And Ray Eppert, president of Burroughs Corporation, told a meeting of the National Association of Manufacturers:

"Top management's nightmare is the horrible thought 'What would happen to us if in the next quarter we suddenly saw our revenue, our sales, decrease ten, fifteen, or twenty percent?' In most instances this would not merely decrease profits correspondingly—it would wipe them out. Business must grow or die. . . . Now is the time to install costcutting equipment. . . . Now is the time to research and develop those products we are going to need in future years and to increase our selling impact. The dynamism of the American economy is not built in. It must be continually generated."

Bankers have been encouraging this straining for new products and new models by asking businessmen seeking credit what innovations they have up their sleeve. Many bankers are wary of applicants who have only "old" products.

Occasionally there have been protests from retailers charged with moving ever-higher mountains of goods. They have begged for relief. An appliance buyer complained: "Beating annual production records in electrical housewares has become a fetish that seems to serve no constructive purpose. . . . Why not accept the fact that the market is saturated on some items?" And a New Jersey automobile dealer protested what he felt was flagrant overproduction of automobiles and proposed that some sort of maximum yearly production figure be set for new cars each year by a committee representing the public, the dealers, and the manufacturers.

There is evidence, too, that some producers are learning to turn a profit while operating at substantially less than capacity or below generally accepted break-even points. The chairman of Republic Steel observed during the 1958 recession, "We intend to make money at whatever capacity." And Mr. Romney, the head of American Motors, has observed, happily, that his company has learned how to operate profitably on a break-even point in output of a specific make that is far under that of the Big Three motorcar makers.

It is conceivable that the United States may reach a point where it will even consider it advisable to turn down its machinery of desire stimulation somewhat, especially if the sellers keep stoking that machinery with more and more billions of dollars each year to stimulate desire. This is not an unprecedented suggestion. When consumer goods were scarce in Great Britain after World War II, a tax on advertising was being considered in order to keep down desire stimulation. The advertisers, under this pressure, came up with a Voluntary Limitation on Advertising. It was accepted by the Chancellor of the Exchequer. Major advertisers of rationed goods and luxuries agreed to cut back their advertising outlays 15 per cent.

They also agreed to "conduct their advertising" so as not to "increase inflationary pressure of demand." The agreement with modifications lasted for two years. And for a much longer period British advertising was curbed by a variety of controls. The use of electricity for advertising, for example, was forbidden altogether.

It is also quite conceivable that Americans might ultimately learn to lead stimulating lives at a somewhat lower level of consumption without feeling deprived or oppressed. My elderly friend running the supermarket in Indianapolis offers the opinion that any homemaker can cut family food bills by a quarter without noticeably affecting quality just by exercising prudence and frugality. Consider President Eisenhower's expressed fear that the young people of the United States are growing soft. While he was voicing this fear, school boards in many towns were each spending hundreds of thousands of dollars of taxpayer money to build parking lots capable of accommodating the hundreds of motorcars owned by students who might better walk to school or come by bus.

And then there is the question of how much real gain in the United States standard of living is involved when women are persuaded to own five bathing suits instead of one. And how much is involved when people are persuaded to cast aside their new car when it is twenty-seven months old instead of keeping it until it is fifty or one hundred months old?

A woman in Berkeley, California, wrote a magazine that she was starting to feel smug about the poor gadget-ridden Americans who were having so much trouble getting their motorcars and appliances serviced. She described herself as a free soul because she had no appliances or television in her home.

Samuel Butler in his *Erewhon* depicted a society of Erewhonians who concluded they were being enslaved by their machines. Politically they divided into two parties, the machinists and the anti-machinists. The leading philosophers of each faction argued the growing role that machines were playing in their lives.

The anti-machinists conceded that the machines were benevolent masters and would treat them decently just as the Erewhonians treated their own domesticated horses and dogs decently. Still they argued, "Is it not plain that the machines are gaining ground upon us . . . ? They serve that they may rule."

The anti-machinists won the day; and the Erewhonians proceeded to smash every machine and "mechanized appliance" invented in the preceding 271 years. The Erewhonians then returned to an idyllic pastoral way of life in which simplicity, kindly genial manners, and the quest of beauty were cherished above material possessions. Behind their mountains they shunned the bustling materialistic world thereafter, and without regret.

It undoubtedly is a little late for Americans to consider putting sledge hammers to their robot machines. But quite possibly in coming decades the rewards these robots can bring may be less highly prized. Such a shift in attitude would help ease the problem of coping with the nation's fabulous production machine.

A third possibility—or Trail Number Three—would be to devote more energy and more money to searching for brand-new kinds of innovations for the consumer that would fill a genuine need and represent a real break-through for technology.

I'm thinking of innovations on the order of the motorcar, the radio, the refrigerator, the jet airplane. Each upon its appearance has given the United States economy an enormous boost and, directly or indirectly, has created thousands or even millions of new jobs.

If United States industry would divert into the quest of such revolutionary innovations a fraction of the billions of dollars now being poured into devising flossier packaging, improving product mix to command greater shelf space, developing patentable imitations of existing products, and creating obsolescence of quality or desirability, then epoch-making breakthroughs might well occur. George Romney of American Motors seemed to allude to this challenge when in mid-1960 he observed, "The attempt annually to create products that are merely camouflaged to seem better is a colossal misdirection of effort away from useful innovation."

One example of an innovation that would represent a real and useful break-through if reasonably priced would be the use of ultrasonic devices to clean fabrics and cooking and eating utensils. Another that could be enormously useful in many situations would be the picture telephone.

Some of the most obviously needed innovations are in the area of travel because of the present traffic-clotted highways, the widespread deterioration of railroad service, the growing depletion of known United States reserves of oil, and the growing pollution of the urban air with gasoline fumes. Vehicles are needed to cut through the congestion of urban sprawl. The small, safe one- or two-seater helicopter for family use is still a most attractive dream. The motorcar with a gas-turbine engine—and beyond that the electric-powered car—represents a highly desirable goal. A quiet electric car would reduce greatly the drain on both metal and petroleum supplies. It originally failed largely because no adequate power supply could be developed. Now, however, with advanced technology, including the development (and evident early suppression) of the nickel-cadmium battery which costs about $100 but outlasts the average motorcar, the dream of the electric car seems less remote. Quite possibly, service stations now devoted primarily to pumping gasoline products could become devoted primarily to battery recharging. A car owner on a long trip could simply turn in his depleted battery for recharging and for a fee take in its place a now-charged battery left there by an earlier motorist. If batteries can be made commercially that will power a car for, say, one hundred miles, then the electric runabout will come close to reality.

And then there is the levacar, a very attractive dream for mass transportation for short-haul trips to the suburbs or to nearby metropolitan centers. The levacar is much like a train except that a stream of compressed air lifts it a fraction of an inch above the track to reduce friction. The Ford Motor Company has already built experimental levacars. The advantage of the levacar over the train, bus, or motorcar is that it has the potentiality of going like a streak, 200 to 500 miles per hour. And its advantage over the airplane for short-haul trips is that its terminals or stations could be readily accessible inside cities and not out on the edge of the cities. As it is, if you wish to hop from Cleveland to Columbus by airplane, you may waste nearly two hours in getting to and from airports.

A fourth possibility—or Trail Number Four—would involve systematically encouraging the already apparent shift from the producing industries to the service industries (excluding those devoted to repair). Producing activities—or those devoted to fabricating such things as appliances, mining such things as iron ore, or growing such things as wheat—have for quite a few years been shrinking as sources of employment as a result of the impact of automation and other mechanized duplication of jobs once done by people. On the other hand, opportunities continue to open up in such service fields as travel, insurance, restaurants, hotel and motel operation, recreation, cultural activities, health-improvement activities, and education for both children and adults.

The service fields are particularly promising as areas for attacking the problem of maintaining reasonably full employment at annual incomes fairly close to present levels. (And any solution must meet these requirements in order for it to have any real prospect of success.) For one thing, the service industries generally make only modest use of the nation's natural, irreplaceable resources. And for another, they are capable of far greater reasonable expansion than the producing industries. Even by straining with such strategies as planned obsolescence, it is doubtful that the refrigerator industry can hope to do more than double the average family's consumption of refrigerators in the next several decades. On the other hand, the average family's involvement in travel, cultural, or educational activities can be expanded five, ten, or conceivably even twenty times. Toll television, it might be added, offers the potentiality for an explosion in demand for creative theatrical talent.

And now we come to possible Trail Number Five, which seems to deserve treatment in a separate chapter because of its importance, its ramifications, and the national controversy it is already creating.

24. FACING THE UNMET CHALLENGES

*"Bright new cars in sordid streets, ranch-type or split-level homes beside gar-
bage-filled gutters, the family picnic basket in chromium beside the polluted
stream—these are symbols of a national pattern of expenditure in desperate
need of redress."* —Barbara Ward

POSSIBLE TRAIL NUMBER FIVE WOULD LEAD TO
finding new outlets for the nation's creative energy.

The conservative-Republican-businessman school tends to the
belief that filling the desires of American consumers, exploring outer space, and maintaining whatever military posture is necessary to
keep the Russians in line are challenges adequate to drain off these
energies for years to come.

And pretty clearly the desires of customer-consumers come
first. Raymond J. Saulnier, chairman of the President's Council of
Economic Advisors, stated: "As I understand the economy, its ultimate purpose is to produce more consumer goods. This is the object
of everything we are working at: to produce things for consumers."

The liberal Democratic Senator Joseph S. Clark, Jr., of Pennsylvania, however, took sharp issue with this concept of "the object of
everything." He stated: "The goal of our economy is not the production of more consumer goods at all. The goal of our economy is to
provide an environment in which every American family can have a
good house for living and shelter, a good school to which to send the
children, good transportation facilities, and good opportunities for
cultural and spiritual advancement."

Not goods but environment! A number of liberal voices—and some moderately conservative ones, too—have been suggesting the need for a re-examination of priorities. And most of the proposals have centered on the need to start focusing on environment rather than goods.

One early voice was that of Harvard economist Alvin Hansen, who in the mid-fifties pointed out to Congress that the attainment of material abundance in the United States should be producing a change in major challenges. In relatively poor societies, he said, it was understandable that the acquisition of material goods should be the chief cause of concern. "But," he added, "have we not by now reached in the United States a degree of plenty with respect to the physical necessities which would permit greater attention to education, health, recreation, and the rich, varied range of cultural activities in general?"

When the Russians outachieved the United States in launching earth satellites, a host of protests were heard that the United States had got itself too preoccupied with the consumption of goods. The Russians themselves had gloated that they had been building satellites while Americans were busy building fancy tail fins for their motorcars. Whether preoccupation with satellites would impress historians as being more socially significant than preoccupation with tail fins might be arguable; but the tail fins did symbolize the American preoccupation with self-indulgence via goods consumption.

Walter Lippmann protested that "our people have been led to believe the enormous fallacy that the highest purpose of the American social order is to multiply the enjoyment of consumer goods. As a result, our public institutions, particularly those having to do with education and research, have been . . . scandalously starved." He felt that the country was waiting to be led by "another innovator" with the imagination of a Teddy Roosevelt or a Woodrow Wilson or a Franklin D. Roosevelt.

Economic writer Barbara Ward put this "starvation" of basic social needs in the United States at $9,000,000,000 a year. (Your author made his own first tentative observations on the need for a shift in challenges—and the need to give more attention to several badly neglected areas of national life such as urban blight—in the May 11, 19S8, issue of *The New York Times Magazine*.)

There were a number of references to the fact that the people of the United States were enjoying private opulence amid public poverty. City planner Victor Gruen offered the opinion that "although we are the richest nation with the highest individual living standard, we have one of the lowest 'public living standards' of Western nations. Our cities are littered with ugliness and choked with automobiles." Harvard historian Arthur Schlesinger, Jr., asserted, "It is not that our capabilities are inadequate, it is that our priorities—which mean our values—are wrong." On the other hand, *Fortune* magazine dismissed the talks of those who attack the public poverty amid private opulence as "New Mask for Big Government." Conservative economists challenged at least the alleged "public poverty" by pointing to the highways, schools, and hospitals built in the past decade. But was what had been done enough—especially when compared with the hundreds of billions of dollars spent each year in satisfying private wants through purchase of consumer goods?

Edwin L. Dale, Jr., writer on economic trends for *The New York Times*, reported in 1960 a widespread conviction in Washington that this issue of private vs. public spending would be the Great American Debate of the Sixties.

United States businessmen enjoy rising to challenges and like to say that they are glad to make an honest dollar wherever they can. The calls to tackle the American environment, however, left them wary. A person can't go down to the store and order a new park. A park requires unified effort, and that gets you into voting and public spending and maybe soak-the-rich taxes. As a result of the wariness of many powerful businessmen over the years, a heavy cloud of opprobrium had been hung over any proposals to do anything more than decency required about improving environment.

That appears to be the major reason why most Americans have

come to view any private spending—whether for deodorants, hula hoops, juke boxes, padded bras, dual mufflers, horror comics, or electric rotisseries—as good for the nation and any public spending as a necessary burden to be suffered.

The result has been a clear social imbalance. Professor John Galbraith has pointed up some of the odd results of this imbalance by noting the handicap of public endeavors when it comes to organized desire stimulation. "Every corner of the public psyche is canvassed," he states, "to see if the desire for some merchantable product can be cultivated." Yet, he adds, he would be immeasurably shocked to see the deliberate cultivation of wants applied to public services. He suggests that businessmen have sought to scorn public spending not only because they are large taxpayers but also for the more human reason that they see any expansion of concern with public wants as a threat to their own prestige. The result is "a vehement insistence that the government does not produce anything, that it is a barren whore," he observed in T*he Affluent Society*.

Actually, economists make no distinction between public and private goods and services when they tote up the over-all output of the economy, or gross national product. Even businessmen exult, as we've seen, when the gross national product rises for whatever cause. They see it as a portent of prosperity. An increase in teachers' salaries has the same standing in totaling the gross national product as an increase in the output of power lawn mowers. Still, according to the American business creed, which finds general acceptance in the popular mind, any spending for public wants is a barely tolerable burden. Galbraith points to some resulting contradictions: "Automobiles have an importance greater than the roads on which they are driven ... education [becomes] unproductive and the manufacturer of the school toilet seats productive. . . . Vacuum cleaners to insure clean houses are praiseworthy and essential to our standard of living. Street cleaners to insure clean streets are an unfortunate expense. Partly as a result, our houses are generally clean and our streets generally filthy."

There are some indications that even marketers are beginning to recognize that in coming years, for better or worse, more and more of the nation's productive energy may be channeled into trying to improve environment by filling public needs. *Printers' Ink* has published with seeming approval an analysis by Cornell University's Ernest Dale, which pointed to the advantages that might come to the economy from assigning "a higher value to public services." Dale in his analysis spoke matter-of-factly of reports that public services had been "neglected and starved for years." He added that, incredible as it might seem, the proportion of the gross national product going to public services— exclusive of defense—is "about the same as in President Hoover's day." And he suggested that marketers start pondering what products they could produce that "will fit in the government's increasing share of national output. . . . The expansion of the public market might do more good than harm to marketing men. It will mean better education, better recreation, more pleasant living conditions, and less waste through juvenile delinquency, crime, slums, and mental illness. . . . It may even raise the purchasing power of the private market."

Quite possibly one reason for the growth in resigned acceptance by business of the idea that public wants should be more fully met was its awareness that enchanting Americans purely with private consumer goods was becoming more and more difficult. *Fortune* magazine intimated this when it calmly predicted that during the sixties Americans "may show an increasing desire for technological advances other than the kind that can be bought at retail."

Although some public needs might be more obviously urgent than some of the private wants and needs being met, the nation would still lose if in satisfying them it brought a serious drain on its natural resources. Care would still need to be taken to see that the nation's raw materials and energy were not squandered. Fortunately, many of the more urgent public needs—such as for more street cleaners, hospital personnel, teachers, and technicians for building good will overseas—are in the area of the production of services rather than of goods.

What, then, are some of the important unmet challenges that might bear examining as possibilities for attracting a larger share of the creative energy of Americans?

One major challenge is to do something dramatic about the growing sleaziness, dirtiness, and chaos of the nation's great exploding metropolitan areas. The postwar trek of city dwellers to find a little patch in the country is becoming more and more irrational if the breadwinner must still work in the city. An exhausting daily journey is being added to his day's work, which leaves him time for only glimpses of his children. And to what end? The "country" place in the suburbs loses its "semirural" character as soon as a subdivision goes up beyond it, if not sooner (even though a subdivision house with its patch of grass in the suburbs may be preferable to an old row house in the city).

I overheard a shoestore owner in Montgomery, Alabama, voice a common lament. He said: "My wife and I wanted to get out in the country, so we bought a little place out on the edge of the city four years ago. Today, we're only halfway out."

Most of the developers, with their eye on total dollar return, have been skimping on parks and playgrounds. And their "community" centers usually turn out to be shopping centers from which they derive a large part of their profit on the total project. They sell captive audiences to the merchandisers.

The United States through most of its history has been an inviting target for spoilers who made their killing and moved on. Many spoilers have been at work among those who are expanding the perimeters of America's metropolitan areas. Vast smoke-blanketed wastelands of slums, junk yards, used-car lots, and row houses have been left behind as Americans have kept fleeing to the outer edges. It appears to be time for American city dwellers, and entrepreneurs, too, to begin looking inward rather than outward for their opportunities. Richardson Dilworth, the crusading mayor of Philadelphia, eloquently supported this point when he said: "The real frontiers of

America today are inside the big cities."

A survey reported by United States public-health officials shows that the air of cities across the land is getting dirtier. The dozen worst: Charleston, West Virginia; East Chicago, Indiana; Phoenix, Arizona; Los Angeles and San Bernardino, California; Chicago, Illinois; Philadelphia, Pennsylvania; Buffalo, New York; Detroit, Michigan; St. Louis, Missouri; El Paso, Texas; and Anchorage, Alaska.

Other investigations show that the slum problem in the great cities is worsening. William L. C. Wheaton, the director of urban studies at the University of Pennsylvania, summed up the over-all challenge by stating that Americans should "frankly recognize that older central cities are crowded and dirty. They lack open space; they lack playgrounds; they lack good schools; in fact they are deplorably short on the amenities that we might expect of the richest civilization in man's history."

These are challenges that require unified effort. A single property owner would justifiably feel discouraged. The national organization for civic improvement, ACTION, estimates that it would cost about one hundred billion dollars to wipe out United States slums. Billions more could justifiably be spent in general urban renewal each year and in cutting through the choking congestion brought by the automobile by developing swift public transit systems. This could help reunify the sprawling metropolitan areas.

A number of cities have started on long-range plans to rejuvenate and scrub up at least the cores of their metropolitan areas. Kalamazoo and Pittsburgh are outstanding examples. In some cases, however, all the overhauling and building of malls is aimed simply at making downtown more attractive for consumers to spend money and for other commercial purposes. In Toledo, Ohio, which built a fine downtown mall, the value of it was so largely judged by whether it helped the sales volume of downtown stores that the *Toledo Blade* felt it necessary to remind the city that malls should be regarded as city parks and not simply as aids for merchants. In much the same way, many cities have been scrambling to build big, new downtown auditoriums. The primary purpose usually is to attract business conventions that will bring freespenders to downtown areas. Little thought is given to the larger problem of civilizing these downtown jungles for noncommercial purposes.

One of the notable exceptions is the Lincoln Center, taking form on twelve acres in Manhattan, where libraries, museums, music schools, and concert halls will rise.

The thing that the traveler in the United States misses most in cities outside New England is a heart, a focal point. It can be a green, or a fountain, or a monument as in Indianapolis. Most European cities have their lovely Arc de Triomphe or Piazza San Marco, which give a sense of delight and majesty to their entire city. In most American cities the heart of the city is simply the street intersection where the biggest department store and bank face each other. And walk five blocks in any direction, and you are deep in slums, warehouses, or used-car lots.

The challenge of tackling urban blight in the United States does not necessarily mean tearing down miles of buildings and replacing them with thirty-story concrete slabs jutting up from fenced-off grassland. Inhabitants would be happier if they could simply have their old neighborhood homes and streets spruced up, with some pleasant open spaces added.

The authors of *The Exploding Metropolis*[1] repeatedly make the point that the grouped towers going up in many redevelopment projects already under way are pretty uninviting places. They are all very much alike. They lack intimacy or individuality or surprise. They are too orderly and cold. One architect is quoted as saying that most of the architects designing these grouped towers wouldn't be caught dead living in these dull Utopias themselves. Instead, they "look for a beat-up old house that they can fix up into something more amiable than a logical set of cells on the fourteenth floor."

Most urban areas are desperately short of the kinds of places where people can relax comfortably without spending much money: picnic groves, museums, libraries, public beaches, parks, ball parks for amateurs, golf courses, tennis courts, and gardens. Nothing seems to bring warmth and graciousness to brick and concrete surroundings more than splashes of flowers and rows of trees, as the managers of New York's Radio City have learned. A number of cities such as New Orleans, Seattle, Cincinnati, and Norfolk are seeking to add new vitality and beauty to their cities, and one way they are doing it is by large-scale planting of trees and flowers.

In an age when so many college students are cynics absorbed in "privitism," it is perhaps not surprising that at a school devoted to urban planning a professor told me of his delighted amazement at the passionate idealism of his students.

Another major challenge that invites the creative energy of Americans is that of remaking the great arid areas of the country, and helping to remake the arid areas of friendly lands overseas. This can be done by massive redirection, harnessing, and transformation of water. Water so redirected, transformed, stored, or harnessed in river-valley developments is likely to be relatively expensive water. But with the United States and world population growth already at hand and with water tables in many areas falling, the changes are needed even at high cost.

The United States government might greatly step up its investigations into ways to produce fresh water economically from salt water or brackish water. Until recently, it has been spending less per year than it spends on one bomber. Many scientists have long felt that salt-water conversion offers the most sensible way to make use of the slumbering genie of atomic power. In fact, the development of an economical way to convert salt water, with atomic energy or not, could do more to transform the world than atomic energy is currently doing.

Conversion of salt water or brackish into fresh water on a millions-of-gallons-a-day basis already is taking place in such water-short places as Aruba in the West Indies and Al Kuwait on the Persian Gulf. The Office of Saline Water of the United States Department of the Interior has pilot plants operating and is building five demonstration plants to try out on a fairly large-scale basis five of the most promising methods. All involve either taking the water out of the salt, by either distillation or freezing, or screening the salt out of the water, as with a membrane process. The plants will be located at such places as Freeport, Texas, and San Diego, California.

The cost is still a problem but is within sight of becoming attractive in many situations where water is short. Today, it costs only one fifth as much to obtain one thousand gallons of fresh water from the sea as it did in 1950. The director of the Office of Saline Water is now confident that the office can produce one thousand gallons of water for one dollar. That is still too high to appeal to most water users. However, in a few years he hopes to get the price down to forty cents per thousand gallons, which would make it appealing to many water-short cities.

It is doubtful whether in our lifetime the price can ever be reduced low enough to be economical for American farmers in arid areas many miles away from a coast. The cost would have to get down to about a nickel for one thousand gallons. But it is conceivable that within the coming decade costs can be brought down to close to twenty cents per thousand gallons, which would make it attractive for irrigation in some water-desperate countries.

As for redirecting water, the United States has a number of gushing little rivers that pour wastefully into the ocean—especially in the Northwest. By rechanneling or tunneling, these can be sent hundreds of miles overland to aid tired, shallow rivers. The Bureau of Reclamation is learning how to make rivers go uphill under their own power in a bootstrap-lifting operation. Its officials believe that the bureau can help transform millions of acres of desert into garden land if given the funds.

This is the bold kind of challenge that should appeal to Americans looking for new outlets for their energy. And in this connection we should not forget rainmaking and other weather modification techniques. Although rainmaking has largely dropped from the news, it is receiving very close study from such organizations as the National Science Foundation. One basic fact the investigators grapple with is that the great moist air masses that come in over the Pacific and cross the North American continent still have three quarters of their original moisture with them when they move on out over the Atlantic. And seeding the clouds with silver iodide will definitely bring down some of that moisture. A second basic fact is that ordinary snowfall and rainfall are most inefficient in bringing down the moisture that is up there. Even a very heavy snow brings down only a fraction of 1 per cent of the moisture overhead. One of the lessons learned is that cloud seeding works best near mountainous areas and seems to offer the most worthwhile results in the eleven most western states, particularly Idaho, Colorado, Washington, Oregon, and California. The Advisory Committee on Weather Control set up by Congress concluded that in western states cloud seeding produced an average increase in rainfall of more than 10 per cent. Such an annual increase in favorable areas could bring down an extra fifteen million acre feet of water onto the eleven western states. This could represent an enormous boon to local municipalities, farmers, and industries. But before weather modification can be attempted on any large-scale basis, a federal authority on the order of the Civil Aeronautics Board should be established to set—and enforce—the ground rules. Otherwise the program will bog down in wrangling—if not legal action.

The challenge of providing a good modern education for the tens of millions of youngsters born since Pearl Harbor could also quite reasonably command far more of the nation's energy than it does. In a number of cities, at least a fourth of the students are being instructed in substandard buildings. And in some California towns students have been going to class in tents. In many hundreds of schools, the teachers average more than thirty-five students to a class; or the schools are on double or triple session.

With the shrinking of natural resources, the nation's human talent is becoming more crucial to the nation's safety and well-being. In recent years, the nation has been spending less than 4 per cent of its national income a year on education. That is about the same amount that Americans pay each year to reduce their installment debts on their multitudes of motorcars. The President's Science Advisory Committee has proposed that by 1966 Americans, at the very least, double their spending on education. A spokesman for the United States Office of Education likewise has expressed conviction that spending for education should double. But it was made clear that this view did not necessarily reflect the thinking of the President. Such a program would channel more than fifteen billion additional dollars' worth of the nation's energy into education each year.

In 1960, the United States had a shortage of a quarter-million classrooms, and faced a minimum need of at least an additional quarter-million rooms within five years because of increased enrollments. It also faced the need of a full half-million additional teachers. And if the schools are to attract talented and ambitious young people into teaching careers, then average teaching salaries must be raised at least 50 per cent. In the past year I have visited more than a dozen American teachers' colleges. A few have been most impressive, but I must confess that I have left many of them feeling depressed about the caliber of students being attracted into teaching careers.

The federal government's role in promoting education needs reexamination. Over the past decade it has been contributing less and less of the total cost of education despite its far greater access to money resources than the local and state governments. Recently the United States government has been spending about one penny for education for every dollar it is spending for defense. Certainly at the college level the federal government's stake in assuring the nation of a body of scientists and responsible leaders for the future is obvious and urgent. Today, more than a hundred thousand talented high-school graduates—certified to be college material—fail to go on to college specifically because of lack of money. The cost of college is rising much faster than family incomes. Here seems to be an opportunity for the federal government to make a contribution. If it offered 48,000 scholarships—as Senator Humphrey proposed—it would still mean a scholarship for only one student in two hundred.

Even more imperative is the need to help the colleges themselves. It is hard to see how the usual arguments about hands-off-the-minds-of-our-children can conceivably be invoked in direct programs to help institutions of higher education meet their staggering increases in costs. With enrollments likely to triple in the next dozen years, the colleges face the appalling task of raising perhaps thirty billion dollars if they are to meet the challenge adequately.

The nation's critical and persistent shortage of health facilities and health personnel constitutes still another of the major unmet challenges facing Americans. Nurses, doctors, therapists, and technicians are in such short supply that the situation is becoming alarming. The nation's medical schools would need to grow by at least 40 per cent just to turn out enough doctors to cope with the population growth of the next decade or so. And that would not reduce the existing shortage of trained physicians. Even more alarming—in view of the population explosion—is the shortage of hospital beds: nearly a million. (And this is while a steel company is launching a million-dollar campaign to persuade Americans to throw away their old beds and get wider ones!) The challenge of eliminating the shortage of medical personnel and facilities would absorb more than twenty billion dollars in extra effort in the next five years.

And then there is the collateral challenge of easing the terror of the growing millions of people past sixty-five whom the nation insists upon retiring at ever-earlier ages even though their prime of life is continually being extended. Most of these people are being forced to subsist on incomes of less than $1,000 a year in an era of overabundance when average family income has passed $6,500 a year. These people should be assured they won't become a drag on their children or become wards of society in ill health or old age. Earlier societies took care of their old. But in hyper-mobile United States, families become scattered over thousands of miles, and distance helps offspring feel nonresponsible.

We should not overlook, either, the now poorly met challenges of reversing the shrinkage of forest lands, of conservation of the shrinking arable land, and combating the spread of pollution in both air and water.

A final challenge worth careful examination is that of helping the people of friendly nations enjoy a little more of the fabulous abundance attained in the United States. One way would be to help nations critically short on energy sources—such as Italy and Pakistan—set up atomic-power stations. Nuclear power is likely to be economically attractive to many other countries before it is to coal-rich United States. Another way would be by selling or sending overseas goods that the United States still excels at making.

Labor leader Walter Reuther tells of watching a dam being rushed in northern India to harness the monsoon rains. A few giant earthmoving machines made by members of his union back in Peoria, Illinois, were at work. But most of the earth moving was being done by thousands of men, women, and children working with little straw baskets and wooden shovels, and they progressed slowly. An Indian official of the project expressed regret that they didn't have a few more earth-moving machines. He said it would have enabled them to complete the dam a whole monsoon season earlier, build new roads and irrigation projects, and bring at least a trickling of prosperity and wellbeing to the valley. But he said his group lacked the cash to pay for more earth movers. Reuther went on to make the point that at that very moment there were "acres and acres of these machines parked" back in Peoria, sitting idle. And five thousand of his union members in Peoria were idle for lack of orders, and other thousands were working only part time. A more active policy of economic co-operation on the part of the United States government might have assured the Indians the credit they needed to buy the needed earth movers.

Senator J. W. Fulbright, chairman of the Senate Foreign Relations Committee, has been urging Americans to realize that a worldwide revolution is going on "in the will for improved living conditions." He feels that the position of the United States "demands that we export more capital to underdeveloped countries so that they can increase their own industrial production, to our mutual advantage." The senator adds that it would be dangerous for the United States to ignore this revolution or to try to discourage it for selfish reasons. He explains:

"We are in for serious trouble if we think that we are at liberty to get richer while most of the rest of the world gets poorer." That would appear to be particularly true since the United States must now depend upon the rest of the world for an ever-larger share of the raw materials it needs to prosper, or even to survive. At this writing the United States government seems rather desperately embarrassed by its lack of friends among the rank and file of Asiatics, Africans, and South Americans.

This does not complete the list of unmet challenges for building up the nation's social capital, but even these listed could readily absorb more than 10 per cent of the nation's total creative energy—or more than is now going to defense.

One formidable obstacle that arises when any enlargement of the public sector of the economy is considered—by meeting such challenges as here described—is the mechanics for paying for them. Few reasonable people, I suspect, would care to argue that the world's richest nation cannot afford to devote more than 4 per cent of its output to educate its swiftly growing population (and educate the millions of adults interested in self-improvement in their growing amount of spare time). Yet one gets the impression from listening to comments that school taxes have become an intolerable burden.

Perhaps the main problem centers in the fact that the word "tax" has become overburdened with ugly, negative connotations. A tax is imposed on people even though they may not recall being consulted about the project in question. Perhaps they didn't read the ballot carefully, or perhaps they gave their agreement a long time ago. Worse, taxes are plucked from money we thought we already owned, money we thought we could dispose of as we pleased. We prefer to forget about taxes until they are upon us. Also, there is the memory that in the past taxes have often been used to sock the well-off to help those not welloff. Finally, few Americans seem aware that taxes spent to improve their schools help the prosperity of their community just as much as money spent in the community's stores.

Taxes are seen as bad, as money down the drain. Business has successfully sought to picture them as destroying business incentive or as "creeping socialism."

Interestingly, the opprobrium generally attached to taxes does not apply to taxes spent to build military barracks in North Carolina or to maintain garrisons in Morocco. Rarely does the word "boondoggle" arise; and this perhaps is not entirely because of the businessman's concern that the United States maintain an impressive military posture. Businessmen are of several minds about this spending. Economist Robert Heilbroner points out that military spending has come to perform an interesting as well as a critical function in the economy.[2] It provides "channels through which large amounts of public funds can be spent without trespassing on the traditional areas of private activity." He explains that in many respects defense spending is an "ideal" source of economic stimulation. "Not only does much of its procurement reach down into the very heart of the nation's capital-goods industries such as aircraft, shipbuilding, steel, construction, etc., but the goods that the defense effort brings forth in no way compete or intrude upon the normal economy."

Thus businessmen can view without too much show of choler the fact that every tenth dollar in the American pocketbook must go to pay defense taxes and that within this decade it may well become every seventh dollar.

But let us get back to the anguish caused by the lesser civilian taxes. As the sixties were about to begin, the Scripps-Howard newspapers carried the report of a nationwide survey on attitudes toward taxes. *The New York World Telegram* and *The Sun* gave it this page-one banner headline:

DISCORD IN THE MIDST OF PLENTY
U.S. SICK OF TAX YOKE, SURVEY SHOWS

It reported a "new rise of nationwide tax resentment" and quoted the mayor of Bloomington, Illinois, as saying: "It's the first thing people talk about—the new penny on the federal gasoline tax, the Illinois sales tax increase. And money is being sent overseas when people here at home need help."

Thus it was that at the height of American prosperity twenty-nine state governments were in deep financial trouble. Michigan, where constitutional limitations complicated matters, was even unable to pay many of its bills for a while. Citizens had been indoctrinated that all taxes were a burden, and so were in no mood to pay for the new highways, schools, and hospitals that accompanied their carefree proliferation of babies.

The foreman of an auto-body shop in Pennsylvania sourly explained to *U.S. News & World Report* the standardized ritual that has developed in the United States for getting necessary things done. "Every politician who wants a job promises lower taxes; and every politician who gets a job increases taxes." A girl working for a radio station in Cedar Rapids, Iowa, offered this explanation for all the groaning about taxes: "It's because everybody is on such a long credit rope that they yell so loud about taxes. If any item in their budget goes up, they're in trouble. They can't afford heavier taxes."

Clearly the nation needs either a more mature citizenry or a more painless way of extracting taxes if there is to be any large-scale facing of unmet challenges in the public sector. Perhaps local, state, and the federal government should imitate private industry and offer projects requiring public consent to the public with such appeals as "ONLY 3% (a month)" or "ONLY $20 (down)."

More seriously, it seems apparent that resentment against taxes can be reduced only if they are collected before the taxpayer ever gets his hands on the money. Some suggest that the sales tax is the most logical way to pay for such public benefits in an era of abundance despite the theoretical inequity of the sales tax. It at least might soften the resistance of business groups. The big trouble with a sales tax, however, is its extreme visibility and nuisance characteristic. Sales taxes may be logical but not practical solutions. Ideally, the money needed for expanding public services should be collected wherever possible at a pay roll or other source, or should be paid on a straight commercial basis as tolls by those benefiting.

Another serious question arises in any move to shift more of the nation's energy to the challenges of improving the American environment. Since such a move involves more emphasis on the public sector, it raises the question of the possible impact on individual freedom. Would growth in public endeavors reduce the freedom of the individual?

Most Americans have been experiencing growing difficulty in being clearly defined individuals. There are so many pressures and so many things beyond their control. This growing difficulty constitutes a central challenge of the twentieth century.

At the same time it appears clear that the underlying cause of this growing impingement on the individual is not any shift to publicly organized activities from privately organized ones. The underlying causes, instead, seem to be the impact of the wondrous efficiency of modern technology on our lives plus the accompanying density of population. This efficiency of technology has led to the growth of giantism in organizations—big companies, big government, big unions, big subdivision developers—as the need has grown to cope with these changes effectively. Mr. Heilbroner makes this melancholy point in *The Future as History*: "Much of this progressive socialization of our lives will continue no matter what."

He goes on to explain that "we must . . . anticipate a further rise of the impotence and incompetence of the individual vis-a-vis the social environment which modern technology creates. . . . the individual will find himself forced to adapt to technological changes whose advent he did not order but must nonetheless accept, whose operation is beyond him, and whose ultimate impact he does not understand. This in turn implies a further growth of the private and public bureaucracies which control the complex whole and which support the dependent human beings."

Any differences between private and public bureaucracies today are relative—and quite possibly less important than their similarities.

In this connection we have the assurance, for what it is worth, of historian Henry Steele Commager that the lessening emphasis on private enterprise in Western Europe and the somewhat greater emphasis on public endeavor have not produced any notable "drying up of individualism" in such countries as England or Denmark or Holland. My own observations during brief visits to those countries do not inspire me to contradict that assertion. It should be stressed, however, that all three have systems deeply rooted in political democracy.

At any rate, the United States, as it plunges into the Soaring Sixties, seems desperately in need of knowing where it is going, what are its national aims. This need has become so clear that *The New York Times* and *Life* magazine organized an in-print debate on the general theme of "The National Purpose."

Which brings us to our final thought about suggested courses for the people of the United States of America.

25. ACHIEVING AN ENDURING STYLE OF LIFE

"Americans are suffering from a surplus of happiness."—Casual comment by a lovely, white-haired lady in Wichita Falls, Texas, whose name but not remark I have forgotten.

THE SUPERABUNDANCE IN QUANTITY OF THE GOOD things of life in the United States may quite possibly be producing a deterioration in the quality of life—or even the real enjoyment of life—being achieved by most of its citizens.

Ardent materialism as a guiding philosophy seemed more appropriate in an earlier day. Early in the last century, the French critic Alexis de Tocqueville observed that "America is a land of wonders, in which everything is in constant motion and every change seems an improvement." John Stuart Mill, observing much the same hustling and aggrandizement, put it in less flattering terms. He said the United States was a land where material progress was such a preoccupation that "the life of the whole of one sex is devoted to dollar-hunting, and the other to breeding dollar-hunters."

All this hustle and optimism and dollar-hunting produced a society whose material triumphs became the wonder of the world and whose style of life was picturesque, if not charming.

Today, however, with materialism pretty clearly in an overdeveloped stage in the United States, the nature of the challenge the society confronts appears to be changing. The absorption with—and pressure toward—acquisition that once had social value appears to be becoming a hazard of major proportions. Theologian Reinhold

Niebuhr put the hazard in these terms:

"The productive power of our industry threatens to make our culture subordinate to our economy. . . . More goods and services may lead to a tremendous pressure upon the consumer to adopt more and more luxurious living standards for the sake of keeping the economy healthy." He suggested that such straining to keep up with ever-higher living standards, especially if for the sake of mere novelty, can "become a threat to the serenity of life."

A further problem is that the lives of most Americans have become so intermeshed with acts of consumption that they tend to gain their feelings of significance in life from these acts of consumption rather than from their meditations, achievements, inquiries, personal worth, and service to others.

It is appropriate to wonder, in fact, if a society can have too much of a good thing and can begin suffering from a surplus of happiness. Consider a few items of evidence.

The Radio Advertising Bureau reports—with a note of triumph— that 40 per cent of all American groups going on outings to beaches, parks, and picnic areas now take along a portable radio. The figure would have been even higher, I suspect, if the study had been confined to young people.

Many young Americans have been conditioned to need the noise of radio pouring steadily into their ears, whether they are on a train, watching a ball game, or studying. Officials of an Eastern college told me that pandemonium broke out on their campus when the electric power went off one afternoon for two hours. Students complained that they couldn't study without the music of their radios to support them.

Many parents complain of their children's constant need for amusement via consumption. The children often spend their free hours moving between movie screen and television screen, with stopovers at the frappé fountain or at the play room where they play with their $5.95 model kits in which all the parts are stamped out for them. *The New Consumer* reported that parents in the town of

Golf protested to the investigators: "We spend more on the children [than our parents did]. The children can't entertain themselves—they need expensive equipment and toys. Very expensive amusements."

The children are not the only Americans who need fairly constant and expensive amusements. One of my informants informed me, from eyewitness experience, that in the gambling center of Las Vegas some of the toilet booths contain slot machines. (Some of the gambling areas, it might be added, have installed special slot machines that are childsized.)

Another problem is that the environment for a satisfying style of life is being undermined by all the emphasis on ever-greater productivity and consumption. As a result, the nation faces the hazard of developing a healthy economy within the confines of a psychologically sick and psychologically impoverished society.

All the current preoccupation of influential Americans with preserving a healthy economy through growth has drawn an eloquent retort from one of the nation's great editors, Henry Beetle Hough of *The Vineyard Gazette*, Edgartown, Massachusetts. He took as his text for an editorial a rosy report on the New England economy by the Federal Reserve Bank of Boston. The report spoke of the economic growth destined to come from greater investment, greater automation, higher productivity. Hough commented: "One hears the busy sound of machinery grinding past on the streets, headed for 1970." He granted that the prophecy was reassuring as far as it went, but he added:

"Would it not be well to hear from a poet, an artist, a naturalist, a humanist, based on considerations of the broadest and least tangible sort? More investment, greater automation, higher productivity—but will the geese still fly north and south in season, will there be white sand for the surf to roll upon, will trees and wildflowers beckon from beyond the door-yard, will pinkletinks sound their peeping from the marshes in April? Will the world be as livable as we know it today, and will new generations be as free?"

Those, indeed, are becoming desperately pertinent questions.

It is easy to recall, of course, that a number of past civilizations have collapsed because their elite classes became caught up in a preoccupation with pleasures, possessions, and trivialities. Then, it was not conceivable that there would be enough surplus of goods to permit the hedonism to extend to the masses. Adlai Stevenson, pointing to past societies that had collapsed because of the hedonism of their ruling classes, said: "All these facts of history do not lose their point because the pleasures of today are mass pleasures and no longer enjoyments of an elite. If we become a nation of Bourbons, numbers won't save us."

Two massive obstacles appear to stand in the way of any notable change from the current drift of the American style of life.

One is the widespread faith of Americans that their technology can solve all their problems. This faith persists even though this technology is pushing them relentlessly toward ever-greater giantism and evergreater productivity based on automation, which requires ever-greater consumption.

If Americans are to become masters of their destiny in terms of style of life, they must come to terms with their machines. A first step would be to recognize that the nation's exploding technology is not an unalloyed boon. A number of leading technologists are themselves now recognizing this.

Detlev W. Bronk, president of the National Academy of Sciences, now stresses that "the applications of science are creating problems as well as opportunities. . . . One thing that disturbs me is the idea that science can solve everything"—including the rapid disappearance of natural resources. Actually, he said, "what man chooses to do with the discoveries of science and their applications is beyond science."

Others have urged that Americans have no illusions about the capacity of technology to solve essentially human problems. One of the great heroes of modern technology, Charles A. Lindbergh, voiced his own disillusionment in one of his few public comments in recent decades when he stated:[1]

"I grew up as a disciple of science. I know its fascination. I have felt the godlike power man derives from his machines. . . . Now I have lived to experience the early results of scientific materialism. I have watched men turn into human cogs in the factories they believed would enrich their lives. I have watched pride in workmanship leave and human character decline as efficiency of production lines increased. . . . We still have the possibility, here in America, of building a civilization based on Man, where the importance of an enterprise is judged less by its financial profits than by the kind of community it creates; where the measure of a man is his own character, not his power or his wealth."

Americans need not stand by helplessly and let their technology carry them willy-nilly in a direction that raises their apprehension. They can refuse to let technology dominate their lives. They can deliberately decentralize its organized manifestations. They can insist that noneconomic factors as well as economic ones be weighed in setting their society's course.

One of the challenges they face is that of working out a tolerable relationship with their machines, a relationship that leaves the possibility for the human spirit to soar. It can be done. But, as Charles Lindbergh points out, the time is short.

The second massive obstacle standing in the way of any significant shift in the American style of life is the all-pervading commercialism of the environment in which they live and breathe. Americans consequently are under fairly constant pressure to appraise their life satisfaction on the basis of material possessions.

Before this can change, Americans need to develop a discontent with those among the admen who proudly call themselves merchants of discontent. Perhaps the average American will develop a resistance that will force a change, as a result of the mounting barrage of selling messages. It is even possible that the sellers, for the sake of their own self-esteem, will voluntarily seek to become more universally scrupulous, conscientious, discreet, and courteous.

Advertising men are more inclined now to self-examination

than any other group in the American society. They wince at the image of huckster that has become rather permanently hung on them and they seem willing to go to some lengths to remove it. This may be a happy omen for the future.

Advertising in the past three decades has grown into one of the great instruments of social control operating in the United States. It has joined the church, the school, and industry as a major influence on people's lives. David M. Potter, Yale University historian, points out, however, that the traditional institutions have tried to improve man and to develop in him qualities of social value.[2]

The church appeals to the spirit and conscience of man and tries to implement the golden rule. The school appeals to the reason of man and offers the hope of a perfected society through wisdom and stimulated ability. And even industry appeals to the ambition of man and offers the reward of fulfillment through one's creation. If advertising is to grow up to its power as an instrument of social control, it must develop ideals of social value for the improvement of man, ideas that go beyond keeping him discontented.

In fairness it should be noted that advertising does, by stimulating wants, promote a high-output economy, which in turn generates jobs and investment and raises the level of material consumption, whether that level particularly needs raising or not. But Professor Potter is correct in stating that advertising does little to develop qualities of social value in man himself. In early 1960, billboards were making perhaps the best claim currently possible: "ADVERTISING HELPS YOU ENJOY THE GOOD LIFE."

"The Good Life" here presumably means the abundant life.

Perhaps we will see a change. Perhaps this infant institution, as it matures, will develop an idealism, a deeper sense of responsibility, and a mission to improve man in ways that will have enduring value. Let us hope that this evolution will come in decades rather than the millenniums which it took the other institutions to develop.

Advertising leaders have recently been drawing up manifestoes that have a revolutionary ring. They talk about the need for a new ethical course and for helping the nation achieve a new sense of purpose and dedication to the right and good. The president of the Advertising Council asserted: "A good many people are getting fed up with dishonesty and phoniness and the extreme success worship."

The public can encourage the trend of advertisers to grope for a new and higher course by rewarding—by their purchases and comments— those advertisers who make their appeals in a responsible, respectful, and dignified manner, and who show awareness that there can be important nonmaterial values in life.

As we have seen, one area where excessive commercialization has in recent years particularly impinged upon the public is television, since the average family keeps its set turned on 38½ hours a week. It offers a good place for the public to demand a change because television stations are presumed by law to be serving the general welfare in their use of the airways.

Despite that legal assumption, the United States stands alone among the Western democracies in being bereft of any working philosophy about the use of the public airways in the best interests of the public.(Countries such as Holland and France have been barring television commercials entirely.)

Fortunately, a search has begun to try to find ways to reduce the high element of commercialization in television broadcasting—in both the programing and the commercials themselves. We should bear in mind that television—unlike the institution of the newspaper, which has had centuries to develop a tradition of editorial independence—is a new institution that came into being when the pressures of commercialization were most massive. Despite occasional brilliant performances and brave stands by individual broadcasters, television still has much to learn about establishing a philosophy of operation that will be a credit to the nation and that will endure.

One minimum objective, it seems to me, would be for the networks to take away from the advertiser all control over program content. Great Britain's commercial television broadcasting company, I.T.A., might serve as a model. It sells the advertiser spots for his messages but does not permit the advertiser to have any control over the program that comes before or after the message. Even *Advertising Age* editorially supported such divorcement—and was denounced by a great many admen for doing so.

A second minimum objective should be to require licensing of television networks, and on terms that require them to strive for a better balance of public-service programing. One of the most preposterous aspects of broadcasting is that individual television stations are licensed, but the networks which now handle the programing for most of the shows that appear over most of the stations are not licensed. C.B.S. and N.B.C. have sought to raise the level of public-service programing but have been largely checkmated by A.B.C., which pours out mass entertainment stuff most of the day and night. Television critic Jack Gould summed up the results in these words: "Three networks soliciting the same aggressive customers are functioning in a jungle of their own devising. Let one network aspire to nobler performance, and there will be others wooing its clients with the temptations of gangster shows and higher ratings." To license networks, legislation would have to be passed that would call for affirmative votes from congressmen who need exposure on television to get elected and who often need contributions from companies that are major television sponsors. However, congressmen have in the past enacted legislation in the public interest over the strenuous opposition of directly affected groups, and the number of bills congressmen have been proposing recently that are being opposed by advertising spokesmen in Washington suggests that many congressmen may be in a mood to take hold of the horns of the bull.

A third possibility—and now we are becoming more drastic—would be to establish a counterbalance to the existing networks by setting up a public corporation comparable to Britain's B.B.C., which would broadcast purely in the public interest.

John Fischer, editor of *Harper's* magazine, has advanced an interesting variation. He suggests that the government charge existing broadcasters a rental for their use of the public airways and use the money to endow a public-service broadcasting agency that would seek to improve the quality of broadcasting by buying time on the regular networks to present programs of excellence.

One of the best hopes for improving television content and reducing commercialism on the air is "pay-TV," which has proved highly successful in tests in Toronto, and trials are planned for the near future in a number of American cities, including Hartford, Connecticut. In pay-TV the cost of financing the broadcast of programs of high interest is paid by the owners of television sets. They may do this, for example, by dropping coins in a meter attached to their sets.

The potential of pay-TV is perhaps best demonstrated by the fact that many advertising and network television officials and motionpicture theater owners have been viewing it with unrelieved horror. The "free"-television people express concern about the great financial burden to the family that would have to spend a dollar in order for all its members to see a great current Broadway play on their set or a first-run movie.

Before we become too horrified ourselves at this burden, we might recall that the family listening to the "free," sponsored television programs typically spends about six solid hours a week listening to commercials on television. That comes to more than three hundred hours of listening to commercials a year. If a person were hired to sit through three hundred hours of commercials, what would he charge? The usual rate for human guinea pigs is about $2 an hour, which means that this person should want at least $600 a year for the time spent listening to the commercials that the average family hears in a year.

One hazard for pay-TV is that if it does become successfully established and draws a great audience, advertisers are likely to try to move in and offer to help the producers underwrite their costs in exchange for selling time. Advertising journals already are speculating that if pay-TV becomes too successful advertisers may have to "break down the gates" to "get their message across to viewers."

All this indicates, I think, that the problem of lifting the all pervading smog of commercialism in American life is going to be no easy task. But it must be done if the nation's citizens are to achieve an environment conducive to self-respect, serenity, and individual fulfillment.

Sir Herbert Read has suggested that "mankind will perhaps grow tired of its playthings and cast them aside; universal boredom will lead to universal despair, and art will be renewed when life itself has to be renewed."

Boredom and despair quite possibly are already starting to produce a cultural renaissance in America. A number of cities are planning cultural centers. We should, however, withhold judgment on the depth of this suspected renaissance until we know more about it. The mass marketers and status promoters have moved into culture in a large way. Thus we have tens of thousands of Americans taking art lessons by correspondence from organizations that often resemble factories.

We should perhaps be most heartened by signs of cultural pursuit that individuals undertake spontaneously by themselves and which require them to be more than passive listeners or spectators. Such forms of communication can give dignity and grandeur to man. Thus I think it exciting to come across a group of neighbors in Racine, Wisconsin, who have taken up madrigal singing on Saturday nights. Some families, turning inward, have been forming string quartets and voice quartets. And small neighborhood groups in many parts of the nation have been meeting once a month, often on Saturday nights, to discuss books that they have found to be particularly provocative or enthralling.

Serious reading requires an exercise of concentration, private imagination, and applied intelligence that takes it out of the category of spectator recreations. This is perhaps why it has far fewer devotees than television watching. A Gallup Poll has found that most Americans questioned could not recall reading any kind of book in the past year. This finding came at a time when American homes were reported to be almost fully saturated with television sets. Adult Americans still read only one third as many books per year as adult Britons. Only one American adult in about three hundred reads serious books on his own initiative with any regularity. Think of any important, serious book in the past year. You will not find a single copy of it *anywhere* in most of the counties of the United States, according to an estimate by the American Book Publishers Council.

Many million Americans are showing a new interest in expressing themselves through painting, sculpture, and handicraft, without the benefit of do-it-yourself kits. Such Americans might well emulate the Japanese in developing a private world of creativity for themselves. Most Japanese homes have a *tokonoma*, or honored alcove, for displaying the family's work of art. John Keats reports that no Japanese family is too poor to boast such an alcove, "for that work of art is nearly always handmade. It may be a flower arrangement, an illuminated scroll, a poem, a painting. But whatever the work, it represents in every way the spirit of the family."

Such reflective, private pursuits as I have briefly indicated may help Americans gain a new perspective on their possessions in relation to other life satisfactions. More of them may see that cherished values and integrity of the soul have more to do with a well-spent life than selfindulgence. As Reinhold Niebuhr has observed, the dimensions of human existence "which give dignity to man are easily obscured and vulgarized in a culture which places undue emphasis upon living standards."

Many Americans with a fine home and fine possessions lead civilized, modest, deeply meaningful lives. But they are not absorbed with their possessions, and they recognize that there is only a modest connection between possessions and life satisfaction, except as possessions are able to corrupt.

A sociologist in Endicott, New York, told me that the happiest, most satisfying days of his married life were spent living in a trailer camp outside Atlanta soon after marriage. All the couple's neighbors were as poor as they were. They all shared toilet and washing facilities. And they shared a can of beer, he said, as if it were champagne. After sixteen years, he related, four of this couple's closest permanent friends are people they met in that camp many hundreds of miles away.

Actress Siobhan McKenna makes a trip every summer to the bleak Aran Islands of Ireland to live a while with the fishermen and sheep clippers there. They are a joyful, hospitable people who always have a welcome pot of tea ready for a visitor. She says that she makes this annual trip in order to renew her faith in the essential pride and nobility of human beings who still come to grips with the cosmos instead of with artificial problems that people invent for themselves.

I find myself often seeking out the older New England villages that have changed relatively little—except for a gas station or two—in recent decades. I, too, feel a freshening of the spirit when I stroll about the tree-shaded village green, peer into the lovely old spired, clean-lined churches, visit the still picturesque stores, chat with the natives, and walk among their two-century-old homes.

It often occurs to me as I stroll that the mass merchandisers of the sixties—with all their huffing and puffing to sell their packaged dream communities—have not been able even to approach creating as fine an environment for life as was created in these old villages in what are now the backwaters of the United States. And by environment I mean not only physical but spiritual and political.

In my strolls I am reminded, too, that one of the wisest, gayest, most inspiring, and most courageous persons my family has encountered in the past decade is a woman in her seventies who lives alone by the sea in a lonely New England cottage. In her cottage she has no electricity, running water, or telephone. She chops her own wood, which she drags from the sea. This woman earns a very modest income floating sea mosses onto paper by a secret process she devised and selling the results as greeting cards. They are exquisite. Each one is different.

Encounters with such memorable individuals suggest to me that most of us might feel better about our lives if we gave a higher priority to striving for:

Greater humility and idealism.

At least occasional dedication to the problems of people beyond the walls of our home.

Deeply cherished personal goals.

A judicious attitude toward the values receivable from personal possessions.

Strongly held personal standards on what is good and evil.

Strongly held personal standards on what constitutes success and failure for ourselves.

If adversity must be the prod for us to take a larger interest in such matters, it might still represent a gain.

A people as ingenious and enterprising as Americans, however, should be able to solve the new problems posed by their fabulously productive machines without undue adversity and without being forced to make a virtue of wastefulness.

The central challenge seems to be this: Americans must learn to live with their abundance without being forced to impoverish their spirit by being damned fools about it.

NOTES

3. "Growthmanship"

1. John Keats, *The Insolent Chariots* (Philadelphia: J. B. Lippincott Co., 1958), p. 230.
2. Victor Lebow, *The Journal of Retailing*, Spring 1955, p. 7; Winter 1955-56, p. 166.
3. Vance Packard, *The Status Seekers*, 1959; *The Hidden Persuaders*, 1957 (New York: David Mckay Company, Inc. London: Longmans, Green & Co Ltd.).

5. Progress Through the Throwaway Spirit

1. *Sales Management*, August 21, 1959, p. 86.
2. *Time*, January 5, 1959, Business section.
3. *Sales Management*, September 19, 1958, p. 33.
4. Federal Trade Commission Order #6203, issued August 7, 1958.

6. Progress Through Planned Obsolescence

1. US. vs. G.E. Civil Action #1364. A detailed analysis of the case appears in a volume published by the Twentieth Century Fund entitled *Cartels in Action*. Its authors were research directors for the Fund's study, George W. Stocking and Myron W. Watkins.

7. Planned Obsolescence of Desirability

1. *Journal of Commerce*, February 26, 1959, p. 9.
2. *Women's Wear Daily*, May 7, 1958, p. 12.

8. How to Outmode a $4,000 Vehicle in Two Years

1. *Automotive News*, December 29, 1858, p. 13.
2. Report of the US. Senate Antitrust and Monopoly Subcommittee of the Committee on the Judiciary, 85th Congress, 2nd Session. November 1, 195S. "A Study of Administered Prices in Automotive Industry," p. 85.
3. *The Wall Street Journal*, March 23, 1960, p. 1.
4. *Business Review* of the Federal Reserve Bank of Philadelphia, April 1959, p. 2.

10. The Short, Sweet Life of Home Products
1. Reported in *Consumer Reports*, October 1955, p. 483.
2. *The New York Times*, September 21, 1958, p. 1, Business section.
3. *The New York Herald Tribune*, July 30, 1959, p. 5, sect. 3.
4. *The Appliance Manufacturer*, August 1959, p. 45.
5. *Retailing Daily*, March 7, 1957, p. 4.

11. Fashion Lines for the Kitchen
1. *Business Week*, November 10, 1956, p. 123.
2. *Home Furnishings Daily*, March 18, 1959, p. 24.
3. *Retailing Daily*, January 23, 1956, p. 130.
4. *Home Furnishings Daily*, December 31, 1957, pp. 3, 19.
5. *Retailing Daily*, June 7, 19S6, pp. 1, 32.

12. The Repairman's Paradise
1. From *The Machinist*, quoted by Sidney Margolius, April 28, 1958.
2. *Retailing Daily*, January 16, 1957.

13. Progress Through Planned Chaos
1. *Home Furnishings Daily*, July 24, 1958.
2. Louis Cheskin, *Why People Buy* (New York: Liveright Publishing Corporation, 1959), p. 65.
3. Pierre Martineau, *Motivation in Advertising* (New York: McGraw-Hill Book Co., 1957).

14.Selling on the Never-Never

1. William Attwood, *Still The Most Exciting Country* (New York: Alfred A. Knopf, Inc.), p. 39.
2. Joseph Wechsberg, *The New Yorker*, October 17, 1959, p. 166.

17.Ever-Mounting Consumption?

1. *Look*, October 28, 1958.
2. *Leather and Shoes*, September 19, 1959, p. 4.

20. The Changing American Character

1. *The New York Times Magazine*, December 1, 1957, p. 21.
2. Joseph Wood Krutch, *Human Nature and The Human Condition* (New York: Random House, 1959), p. 36.
3. Eugene Kinkead, "The Study of Something New in History," *The New Yorker,* October 26, 1957, p. 138.

21. Restoring Pride in Prudence

1. *Consumer Reports*, May 1960, p. 263.

22. Restoring Pride in Quality

1. *Retailing Daily*, January 23, 1956, p. 20, quoting president of the Quality Furniture Manufacturing Company.
2. *National Standards in a Modern Economy*, edited by Dickson Reck (New York: Harper & Brothers, 1956), p. 315.
3. *Home Furnishings Daily*, March 13, 1959, p. 1.

23. Respecting the Eternal Balance

1. "Problems in Review: Planned Obsolescence," *Harvard Business Review,* September-October 1959.

24. Facing the Unmet Challenges

1. *The Exploding Metropolis*, by the Editors of Fortune (New York: Doubleday Anchor Books, 1957).
2. Robert Heilbroner, "The Price of Growth," *The Reporter,* January

7, 1960, p. 32.

25. Achieving an Enduring Style of Life

1. Charles Lindbergh, *Of Flight and Life* (New York: Charles Scribner's Sons, 1948).
2. David M. Potter, *People of Plenty* (Chicago: The University of Chicago Press, 1954), p. 176.